Every day when we are confronted with problems and challenges, we draw on our experience. We learn from experience and so face new circumstances with fresh insights. Learning through experience is the normal, commonplace approach to learning, and we take it for granted.

Much is known about teaching and being taught. Far less is known about how we learn, and, in particular, how we learn outside the classroom. Yet this is in fact where most learning takes place. One especially neglected area is the role that people other than the learner play in facilitating learning. This role is undertaken not only by teachers, trainers, parents and counsellors, but also by managers, supervisors, care-givers and friends.

This book brings together the experiences of a number of practitioners, who write from often strongly contrasting perspectives; these include feminism, critical pedagogy and post-modernism and different psychological perspectives – Gestalt, humanistic, clinical and transpersonal. The authors come from a wide range of backgrounds, including adult, higher and teacher education, community work, organisational development and psychotherapy.

Each chapter is grounded not only in professional practice and theory, but also in personal experience. The book provides fascinating insights into what some good practitioners do to promote learning, and how they make sense of this.

David Boud is Professor of Adult Education at the University of Technology, Sydney. **Nod Miller** is Principal Lecturer in the Department of Innovation Studies, University of East London.

Working with experience
Animating learning

Edited by
David Boud
and Nod Miller

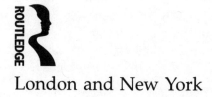

London and New York

First published 1996
by Routledge
11 New Fetter Lane, London EC4P 4EE

Simultaneously published in the USA and Canada
by Routledge
29 West 35th Street, New York, NY 10001

The lines from 'An Atlas of the Difficult World', from *An Atlas of the Difficult World: Poems 1988–1991* by Adrienne Rich; © 1991 by Adrienne Rich. Reprinted by permission of the author and W. W. Norton & Company, Inc.

Typeset in Palatino by Routledge
Printed and bound in Great Britain by T.J. Press (Padstow) Ltd,
Padstow, Cornwall

British Library Cataloguing in Publication Data
A catalogue record for this book is available from the British Library

Library of Congress Cataloguing in Publication Data
Working with experience: animating learning/edited by David
    Boud and Nod Miller.
    p. cm.
    Includes bibliographical references and index.
    1. Active learning. 2. Experiential learning. 3. Learning, psy-
    chology of. 4. Adult learning. I. Boud, David. II. Miller, Nod.
    LB1027.23.W67 1996
    370.15'23—dc20   96–21558
                                                                    CIP

ISBN 0–415–14245–8 (hbk)
ISBN 0–415–14246–6 (pbk)

Contents

Part 3

Part 4

Part 5

Epilogue

List of figures

List of contributors

David Boud is Professor of Adult Education at the University of Technology, Sydney, Australia.

Stephen Brookfield is Distinguished Professor of Adult Education at the University of St Thomas, St Paul, Minnesota, USA.

Jim Brown is a freelance consultant working mainly on community-based local economic development projects, who lives in Bristol, UK.

John Bernard Harris is an independent therapist, trainer and consultant, who lives in Diggle (near Manchester, UK).

John Heron was formerly Assistant Director of the British Postgraduate Medical Federation. He is now an independent consultant based in Italy.

Timothy Ireland is Senior Lecturer in Adult Education and Director of the International Office at the Federal University of Paraíba, João Pessoa, Brazil.

Bob Johnson was formerly Consultant Psychiatrist to the Special Unit, C Wing, Parkhurst Prison, Isle of Wight. He is now a Consultant Psychiatrist at Charing Cross Hospital, London, UK.

Jane Mace is Senior Lecturer in Community Education at Goldsmiths' College, University of London, UK.

Nod Miller is Principal Lecturer in Media and Communication Studies in the Department of Innovation Studies, University of East London, UK.

Jan Jindy Pettman is Senior Lecturer in Political Science, Australian National University, Canberra, Australia.

John Smyth is Professor of Teacher Education and Director, Flinders Institute for the Study of Teaching, Flinders University of South Australia.

Joyce Stalker is Senior Lecturer in the Department of Education Studies, University of Waikato, Hamilton, New Zealand.

Elizabeth Tisdell is on the Core Faculty in the Department of Graduate Programs in Education at Antioch University, Seattle, Washington, USA.

Acknowledgements

Gratitude is due to Rod Allen for computer consultancy and the electronic decoding of texts from all over the world, which he performed with endless patience, and for applying the seasoned eye of an experienced editor; and to Angela Brew for her continuing encouragement, skilled animation and many helpful comments.

We should also like to thank the many other friends and colleagues who have helped us in their different ways to learn from our experience, including: Lee Andresen, Paul Armstrong, Gerry Bernbaum, Nick Boreham, Ian Bryant, Ron Cervero, Ruth Cohen, Gina Conti-Ramsden, Margaret Crawford, Alv de Miranda, Chris Duke, Richard Edwards, Colin Fletcher, Griff Foley, John Garrick, Peter Golding, Virginia Griffin, Budd Hall, Graham Hart, Jeff Hearn, John Heron, Ken Hills, Annie Hudson, Tyrone Huggins, Pat Hurst, Melanie Johnston, David Jones, Nell Keddie, Miranda Kenny, James Kilty, Allan Kitson, Sue Knights, Jerry Kuehl, Michael Law, Rob Mears, Pam Mills, David Milton, David Morgan, Graham Murdock, Alex Nelson, Brian Nichol, Pete Nutman, Teresa O'Brien, John Pascoe, Steve Potter, Mike Prosser, Philip Radcliffe, Linda Raffell, Frances Rees, Eva Ross, Boyd Rossing, Ralph Ruddock, Duncan Scott, Liz Stanley, Arthur Stock, Rajesh Tandon, Teddy Thomas, Al Thomson, Mike Toye, Alan Tuckett, Robin Usher, Tom Valentine, David Walker, Malcolm Walley, Guy Wareing, Linden West, Tom Whiteside, Jane Williamson, Peter Willis, Sue Wise and Miriam Zukas.

David Boud, Sydney
Nod Miller, London

March 1996

Introduction

1 Animating learning from experience

Nod Miller and David Boud

Every day, we are confronted with problems and challenges which we address by drawing on our experience and by using this experience to find ways of learning what to do in new circumstances. The knowledge and skills we need to make our way through the world may include those in buying a car, administering an office filing system or getting on with a partner. We rarely enrol in a course or take a class or consult a teacher as part of these learning projects. Learning through experience is the normal, commonplace approach to learning, and we take it for granted.

When we learn, we engage in a complex process which draws on the behaviour, knowledge and skills of people around us as well as on the material and informational resources of the world we live in, such as bus timetables, library books, television programmes and the Internet. But we also use and build upon our own personal foundation of experience. Our learning is grounded in prior experience. It is profoundly influenced by this experience as well as the context in which we operate. The decision to engage in a learning project is governed by a mix of demands and expectations – from colleagues, from family, from customers, from other learners, from those who can influence us – and by our own needs and desires, which stem from our experience and what we believe to be possible in the situation in which we find ourselves.

A great deal is known about teaching and being taught. These processes have been the subject of numerous research studies in many contexts and countries. There is a substantial literature presenting findings derived from this research and from the wisdom distilled from the professional experience of teachers. However, much less attention has been given to learning in context, and in particular little is known about learning in settings outside the classroom. Yet the larger part of the learning undertaken in the world takes place under these circumstances.

Some important work focusing on this wider view of learning has emerged in recent years, although unfortunately much of it is not widely appreciated outside the particular tradition in which it was undertaken. Different approaches are represented, for example, by Paulo Freire (1972) who explored popular education and the vital role of learning in social change; Victoria Marsick and Karen Watkins (1990) who have drawn attention to the importance of informal and incidental learning in the workplace; Ference Marton and his followers (Marton, Hounsell and Entwistle 1984) who have emphasised learners' conceptions and approaches to learning; Jean Lave and her colleagues (see, for example, Lave and Wenger 1991) who have promoted an interest in situated learning and the way in which adults learn through participation in real world tasks; and work by Jane Thompson (1983), Mechthild Hart (1992) and Joyce Stalker (1994) which illustrates a tradition of feminist scholarship which focuses on oppression and deals with the darker side of learning. There is also now a growing literature on experiential learning (Kolb 1984, Weil and McGill 1989, Mulligan and Griffin 1992) and learning from experience in a variety of settings (Boud, Keogh and Walker 1985, Boud, Cohen and Walker 1993).

Other writers have been concerned with how learning from experience can be promoted and with the work undertaken by teachers when they are not instructing. For example, Carl Rogers (1983) focused attention on the facilitation of learning and the intrinsic limits on what a teacher can do; Allen Tough (1979) examined the characteristics of an 'ideal helper' as part of his studies of common learning projects; and John Heron (1989, 1993) analysed in detail the interventions of facilitators and their decision-making processes. Nevertheless, much remains to be understood about the role of others in learning from experience – what they can do and what perspectives they need to bring to the task.

Since much learning is mediated through and influenced by others, the issues surrounding this mediating role are of great importance. The promotion of learning is a fundamental part of many people's lives. This is clear enough in relation to the activities of teachers, trainers, parents, counsellors and therapists. But the facilitation of learning is also undertaken by managers, supervisors, care-givers, professionals of all types and, indeed, friends. Of course, the nature of the learning relationship varies greatly depending on the kind of explicit or implicit contract which exists between the learner and the other. In some cases the function of promoting learning is strong, as in the case of work supervisors, while in others, like friendships, it can be relatively weak.

There are difficulties associated with finding suitable words to describe the role of helping others learn from experience, with which we shall deal below; but the key issue is that of defining the explicit function in such a way that it can be clearly understood. In this book we are focusing on activities that create circumstances in which others can learn. Features of the process with which we are concerned include the following:

- the intentions of the learner and the extent to which they are revealed (or even capable of being revealed) to the other;

- the relationship between the learner and the helper, including issues concerning the power balance between the individuals concerned, and their respective expectations;
- the total context of learning, bearing in mind that learning and its promotion are highly situation-specific.

A focus on working with experience requires the crossing of boundaries. The ideas on which we draw do not sit neatly within the realms of education and training, the psychology of learning or the sociology of knowledge, although the concepts we employ come from these and other areas .

THE CENTRAL FOCUS OF THE BOOK AND ITS ORIGINS IN OUR EXPERIENCE

This book aims to provide insights into the activities of those people who contribute to others' learning from experience. It provides case studies and discussion about issues in promoting such learning. We selected contributors on the basis of their established expertise in this field and sought to include authors who employ strongly contrasting perspectives. They come from a wide range of backgrounds, including adult, higher and teacher education, community work, organisational development, group relations training and psychotherapy, and are based in many different countries – Australia, Brazil, Italy, New Zealand, the United States and the United Kingdom. They bring a wide range of theoretical perspectives to bear on their work, including feminism, Marxism, critical pedagogy, post-modernism, and Gestalt, humanistic, clinical and transpersonal psychology.

Contributors were asked to describe their own practice in as rich a way as possible and to write themselves into their chapters so that their accounts would be grounded in personal experience as well as in professional practice and social scientific theory. The accounts also contain reflections on the learning the writers themselves underwent as they engaged in the process of promoting the learning of others. An important element in the construction of the book was the process of asking the author of each chapter to comment on several other chapters. Our aim was to encourage contributors to engage in a conversation with other writers, some of whom offer widely differing perspectives on working with experience or operate in contrasting fields of practice. Although the settings from which contributors have been drawn and their range of perspectives is diverse, the book is not intended to be a work of comparative education. Rather, this book offers a variety of insights, taken from perceptive practitioners about what they do and how they make sense of it.

This book is the product of many face-to-face meetings and conversations as well as communications by post, telephone, fax and electronic mail. In the process of soliciting, selecting, assembling and editing the material which follows, we have built up substantial experience from which we have learned a great deal. What we have learned has taken us some way beyond our original conception of working with experience. Our emphasis on relating ideas about learning to the personal history of the contributors has led us to confront the origins of this book in our individual and collective experience and to explore how we arrived at our current conceptions. Ideas and theoretical constructs do not of course arise in an experiential vacuum; they develop from experience and context.

The two editors share an interest in experiential learning and in the use of autobiography in research. David Boud has developed models of the process of learning from experience to focus attention on the key factors which can enable learners and other parties to examine their own practices and to assess whether they are paying attention to the central learning goals in any given situation (Boud and Walker 1990). This book extends the examination of the experiential learning process and explores the wider context in which learners and others operate. It draws attention to the importance of context and culture and the ways in which they influence and shape learning. In particular, it focuses attention on the role which other parties play in helping learners to identify and use the opportunities which their environment offers them.

Some of Nod Miller's earlier work has been concerned with the exploration and use of sociological autobiography as a research methodology (Miller 1993). There is currently evidence of a growing interest in autobiographical methods among social scientists and adult educators, and several collections of papers (Stanley and Morgan 1993, Miller and Jones 1993, Swindells 1995) demonstrate the number of scholars who share this interest.

The focus on the researcher's personal experience can be seen as a return to long-standing concerns in sociology with self-reflexivity and to established definitions of social scientific activity. C. Wright Mills, for example, argues that 'as a social scientist, you have to...capture what you experience and sort it out' (Mills 1970: 216), and asserts that 'the sociological imagination enables us to grasp history and biography and the relations between the two within society' (p. 12). Autobiographical research and writing, in enabling researchers to link the personal and the structural, individual life-histories and collective social movements, and public and private worlds, can be seen as central and fundamental to the social scientific enterprise. The autobiographical influence in this book is a theme which is explored further in the final chapter.

ANIMATION AND LEARNING

One of the greatest difficulties in exploring the activity of facilitating or promoting learning is the lack of appropriate terminology for naming and describing it. It is difficult to work with a concept unless it can be named. Many people describe the role of helping people learn without formal teaching as facilitation, but the word facilitator comes with much conceptual baggage. For example, it has resonances of the practices of humanistic psychology and work with individualistic concerns. It does not readily connote the contextually aware and critical role that we are seeking to describe.

The alternatives are even more problematic. Words like teacher, trainer and coach emphasise the presentational and explanatory role; supervisor, manager or consultant emphasise the role of authority; mediator suggests the resolution of conflict; mentor now encompasses too many meanings; and catalyst is too technical and implies that the role leaves the person who adopts it unchanged. We tried experience worker, or worker with experience, for a while and although these terms gave some of the emphasis we were looking for, they felt clumsy and awkward to use.

We propose to refer to the function of working with the experience of others as 'animation', and to refer to the person who works to promote others' learning as an 'animator'. We do this in awareness of the fact that we are borrowing a term which has another set of meanings external to the learning context. We have chosen animation and animator to describe the activities to which we are drawing attention because of their connotations, which include to give life to, to quicken, to vivify, to enliven, to inspire, to encourage, to activate or to put in motion. These are notions which fit well with our conception of the function of an animator. We reached our view through a consideration of the French word *animateur*. Unfortunately, this word is associated too much with organising and acting on behalf of others as well as prompting and provoking activity. And it is, as a French word, gendered.

Any new use of a word will seem awkward at first and it may take on connotations which were not intended. We adopted animation while the rest of the book was being written and, rather than ask contributors to rewrite the chapters in the light of this decision, the variety of words used by authors to describe their roles in their own contexts remains. Readers are thus invited to test the applicability of animation as a useful term to encompass this variety throughout the book.

We see the function of animators to be that of acting with learners, or with others, in situations where learning is an aspect of what is occurring, to assist them to work with their experience. While teaching or instruction may be an aspect of animation, it is a secondary one which is subordinate to that of fostering learning through experience. One reading of the term animator implies that learners are rather lethargic and need gingering up.

The taking of responsibility for enlivening learning away from the learner is a trap which must be avoided.

Animation is a highly contextualised activity which cannot be properly reduced to a set of prescriptions. It must take account of the wider context of learning and the ways in which learners (and animators) interact with, are influenced by, and in turn influence that context. While some aspects of animation may appear to have the character of generic skills and may be discussed as such, it would be prudent to assume that they always relate to a particular context or set of circumstances. Transferability of animation skills is a complex and problematic notion.

In the sections that follow, we develop a framework for the analysis of animation in learning by identifying what we believe to be some important features of animation, and some elements in the contexts in which animation takes place, with illustrations drawn from work described in later chapters of this book.

The animator may not be someone with a teaching or training role. He or she may be a co-learner or someone in a relationship which is not normally thought of as one which focuses on learning (for example, a friend or a supervisor). Indeed, it is important to note that learning may well take place under circumstances where the people involved do not see themselves to be learners. In Chapter 10, for example, Jim Brown demonstrates that community development activities can be conceptualised as the promotion of learning, even though participants in such activities may not recognise themselves as learners. Brown describes community meetings where learning was taking place, although it is doubtful whether people who took part in these meetings would have characterised their experience in this way.

LEARNING FROM EXPERIENCE

Any discussion of animation must start with a view of what is being animated – learning from experience. While this brief introduction is not the place to canvass the lengthy debates about experience and learning in which philosophers have engaged over the centuries, it is appropriate to start with our own working assumptions about these ideas. In the discussion which follows we take experience to be the totality of the ways in which humans sense the world and make sense of what they perceive. Learning is the process which takes this experience and transforms it in ways which lead to new possibilities, which may involve changes in actions, ways of viewing the world or relationships. While there is no simple demarcation between experience and learning – making sense is always a learning process – it is convenient to adopt the assumption that learning is an act of becoming aware of experience, building upon it, extending it and in the process creating new experiences which become part of what we know. In an earlier book, one of us was involved in an exercise to identify and summarise key propositions about learning from experience (Boud, Cohen and Walker 1993). These, somewhat adapted, provide a starting point for the present discussion and are linked below to some of the implications for animators. These propositions are:

1 *Experience is the foundation of, and stimulus for, learning*

Experience cannot be bypassed; it is the central consideration of all learning. Learning can only occur if the experience of the learner is engaged at some level. Every experience is potentially an opportunity for learning – it is necessary to frame the experience as an event from which something can be learned. The effects of experience influence all learning: what learners are attracted towards, what learners avoid and how learners approach a task are all related to what has gone before.

Animators need to recognise the centrality of the experience of learners and to construct their own role in the light of this. Engagement of learners in matters of direct concern to themselves is fundamental. The uncritical celebration of experience needs to be avoided; it cannot be accepted as a simple given (Freire 1994).

2 *Learners actively construct their own experience*

Each experience is influenced by the unique past of the learner as well as the current context. Each individual is attuned to some aspects of the world and not to others, and this affects his or her focus and response. Learners attach their own meanings to events even though others may attempt to impose their definitions on them. The meaning of experience is not given; it is subject to interpretation. The major influence on the way learners construct their experience is the cumulative effect of their personal and cultural history.

Animators should take account of the prior experience of learners and acknowledge the ways in which this may frame their current learning. There must be opportunities in learning events for learners – alone and with others – to construct their own meanings, for example through reflective activities. There is also a role for animators in challenging interpretations and offering alternative ways of viewing knowledge.

3 *Learning is holistic*

Learning is normally experienced as a seamless whole; there is continuity between experiences even though they may be perceived as separate. It is impossible to dissociate learners from their own contexts, from the processes in which they are involved or from their past experience.

Animators should work with learners in ways which acknowledge the connectedness of knowledge and its many dimensions (for example, social, personal and transpersonal) and assist learners to make links between different kinds of experience and learning in different contexts.

4 Learning is socially and culturally constructed

While learners construct their own experience, they do so in the context of particular social settings, cultural values and economic and political circumstances. As well as being the foundation for learning, experience also distorts, constrains and limits. It is not possible to step beyond the influence of context and culture, although critical reflection on experience can expose some taken-for-granted assumptions. The most powerful, and generally invisible, influence of context occurs through language. The words which are available to describe experience frame it powerfully. The naming of experience provides a means for exploring and appropriating it.

Animators should be sensitive to the constructions within which learners operate and assist learners to work within the constraints of power and oppression which are present in all settings. Animators must be self-reflexive in accepting that they are also part of the culture and context and may act in ways which are oppressive and unawarely reinforce power, thus closing possibilities for learning, as well as acting to counter such effects. They can provide learners with options which extend and challenge dominant conceptions.

5 Learning is influenced by the socio-emotional context in which it occurs

Emotions and feelings are key pointers both to possibilities for, and barriers to, learning. Denial of feelings is denial of learning. It is through emotions that some of the tensions and contradictions between our own interests and those of the external context manifest themselves.

Animators have a responsibility for establishing a micro-context which (within any broader context) provides an opportunity (or space) for learners to investigate, disclose and construct meanings away from inappropriately oppressive or limiting influences, and which ensures these outcomes. The creation of a micro-context can provide a place where the expression and exploration of feelings and emotions is legitimate, distorting influences on experience can be acknowledged and channels of communication with others are open.

While the roles and concerns of animators need to be based on ideas about learning from experience, there are also other considerations. The final section of this chapter outlines the way in which the book is organised and the following chapter identifies some of the key themes in animating learning and links them with issues explored in the later chapters.

STRUCTURE OF THE BOOK

Following discussion of the themes, the book is organised around groups of chapters which centre on specific problems in working with experience and which explore the role of the animator in them. Each author describes his or her own practice in a particular context and draws wider issues from that practice.

Part 1 looks at reframing professional practice. In Chapter 3 Stephen Brookfield starts with the observation that the practice of some professionals can be unduly dependent on outside experts. He discusses how teachers can analyse and deal with the problems they meet through exploring together their own experience. John Smyth in Chapter 4 also focuses on teachers, but his emphasis is on the way in which critical reflection on the political and economic context in which they operate can assist them to confront and reconstruct their practice.

Part 2 takes the theme of challenging learners' perspectives further. Joyce Stalker (Chapter 5) argues that if adult educators are to work effectively with their students' experiences they must become familiar with the implicit theoretical bases which direct both educators and learners. She describes a framework which students can use for themselves to understand their own and others' experiences and ideologies. John Heron (Chapter 6), while acknowledging the importance of political dimensions of animation, points to the spiritual and emotional aspects of learning from experience through a rich account of his own practices in promoting what he terms 'whole person learning'.

Part 3 considers perspectives on gender and ethnicity. Jan Jindy Pettman (Chapter 7) approaches working with issues such as sexism and racism through consideration of how she helps students understand difference and the international. Elizabeth Tisdell (Chapter 8) also works with university students. Her chapter tells how her students learn about feminist theory through relating it to their own life experience.

In Part 4, the focus shifts away from formal educational institutions to an examination of trade union and community settings through socio-economic perspectives. Timothy Ireland (Chapter 9) describes his work with construction workers in Brazil. He analyses the important contribution of learners' experience to popular education and the way an animator like himself can relate to the context of workers to collaborate collectively with them. Jim Brown's setting in Chapter 10 is a project on a housing estate in which residents rejected an external economic development scheme and established a community council to improve the quality of their own lives. He takes a sober look at his own practice and confronts uncomfortable issues about limitations to the power of educators in the face of structural poverty and alienation.

The final part includes three chapters which explore in quite different ways the overcoming of barriers to learning. John Bernard Harris (Chapter

11) argues that animators should recognise that learning from experience is a normal human activity and seek to help learners remove their personal and social inhibitions against change and take responsibility for the matter and manner of their learning. In an organisational development setting he analyses team building activities as team learning whereby blocks and inhibitions to thinking and feeling are removed at both individual and societal levels. Jane Mace (Chapter 12) examines her practice as a literacy educator in terms of overcoming barriers to learning imposed by the need to write in an academic context. Writing is regarded as a means of thinking in which confidence can be developed through working in democratic learning environments where there is a shift of power relations between learners and tutors. Bob Johnson (Chapter 13) takes up the theme of emotional blockages to learning from his position in a context in which such responses are dominant and controlling: a maximum security prison. While such a setting may seem removed from most people's everyday practice, it provides a demanding context in which to test ideas about working with experience.

The book concludes with our reflections on our processes of learning in the course of constructing and editing the book, and with some examination of the relationship between our personal experience and the themes elaborated by the contributors.

REFERENCES

Boud, D., Cohen, R. and Walker, D. (1993) 'Understanding learning from experience', in D. Boud, R. Cohen and D. Walker (eds) *Using Experience for Learning*, Buckingham: SRHE and Open University Press, 1–17.

Boud, D., Keogh, R. and Walker, D. (eds) (1985) *Reflection: Turning Experience into Learning*, London: Kogan Page.

Boud, D. and Walker, D. (1990) 'Making the most of experience', *Studies in Continuing Education*, 12, 2, 61–80.

Freire, P. (1972) *Pedagogy of the Oppressed*, Harmondsworth: Penguin.

— (1994) *Pedagogy of Hope*, New York: Continuum.

Hart, M. (1992) *Working and Educating for Life: Feminist and International Perspectives on Adult Education*, London: Routledge.

Heron, J. (1989) *The Facilitators' Handbook*, London: Kogan Page.

— (1993) *Group Facilitation: Theories and Models for Practice*, London: Kogan Page.

Kolb, D. A. (1984) *Experiential Learning*, Englewood Cliffs, New Jersey: Prentice-Hall.

Lave, J. and Wenger, E. (1991) *Situated Learning: Legitimate Peripheral Participation*, New York: Cambridge University Press.

Marsick, V. J. and Watkins, K. (1990) *Informal and Incidental Learning in the Workplace*, London: Routledge.

Marton, F., Hounsell, D. and Entwistle, N. (1984) *The Experience of Learning*, Edinburgh: Scottish Academic Press.

Miller, N. (1993) *Personal Experience, Adult Learning and Social Research: Developing a Sociological Imagination in and Beyond the T-Group*, Adelaide: Centre for Research in Adult Education for Human Development, University of South Australia.

Miller, N. and Jones, D. J. (eds) (1993) *Research: Reflecting Practice*, Boston, Lincs.: SCUTREA.

Mills, C. W. (1970) *The Sociological Imagination*, Harmondsworth: Penguin.

Mulligan, J. and Griffin, C. (eds) (1992) *Empowerment through Experiential Learning*, London: Kogan Page.

Rogers, C. R. (1983) *Freedom to Learn for the 80s*, Columbus, Ohio: Merrill.

Stalker, J. (1994) 'The adult learner/teacher relationship and sexual harassment: demeaning tradition', *Canadian Journal for the Study of Adult Education*, 8, 1, 15–30.

Stanley, L. and Morgan, D. (eds) (1993) 'Auto/biography in sociology', Special Issue of *Sociology*, 27, 1.

Swindells, J. (ed.) (1995) *The Uses of Autobiography*, Basingstoke: Taylor and Francis.

Thompson, J. L. (1983) *Learning Liberation: Women's Response to Men's Education*, London: Croom Helm.

Tough, A. (1979) *The Adult's Learning Projects*, 2nd edition, Toronto: Ontario Institute for Studies in Education.

Weil, S. W. and McGill, I. (eds) (1989) *Making Sense of Experiential Learning*, Buckingham: SRHE and Open University Press.

2 Synthesising traditions and identifying themes in learning from experience

David Boud and Nod Miller

In this book we draw together two educational and social scientific traditions which have been important in the development of theories of learning from experience, and which have often been in conflict with one another. The first of these is that tradition of human relations training, counselling and adult learning which has its foundation in humanistic psychology and which has developed particularly strongly in North America. This has in recent years become the dominant paradigm in relation to learning from experience in formal settings. Concepts such as self-directed and lifelong learning and an emphasis on the individual learner have characterised the discourse of this tradition. The second tradition has developed in the context of collective social movements and political action. It focuses more on groups than on individuals. It draws on continental European thought, such as that found in critical social theory, and on the values and practices of participatory action research which have developed in third world countries as well as newer currents of feminism and anti-racism. Social structural features of experience and constructs such as power and oppression feature more than the psychological or the personal.

Until recently, much educational literature and practice have reflected divisions along these lines. Inappropriate polarities between the individual and the group, the psychological and the sociological and learning and control were emphasised at the expense of a deeper synthesis. Insights from one tradition were ignored or dismissed by those in the other. This has lead to fruitless debates between protagonists and the impoverishment of practice.

We hope that this book will contribute to a coming together of these traditions to inform educational practice. However, this process involves more than learning each other's vocabulary since the two traditions represent fundamentally different views of the world. Despite the difficulties of recognising valid components in both traditions, we should not be deflected from finding ways of making sense of the complex business of animating learning. In one context, insights derived from one of the traditions might be most helpful; in another, the situation might be reversed.

The contributors to this book take up widely varying positions within the two traditions identified. In this chapter we draw out some of the key themes developed in their texts and highlight some of the common ground between them.

RELATIONSHIPS BETWEEN ANIMATORS AND LEARNERS

The influence of animators is greatly dependent on the relationships which they establish with learners. Relationships may of course be shaped by factors outside the control of the individuals concerned and may pre-date them. For example, in educational institutions the fact that teachers make assessments of learners to which the learners are not party, and which can have consequences for the lives of learners beyond the immediate situation, introduces a constraint on the kinds of learning relationships which are possible. Teachers often do not control the assessment policies under which they are operating. Conversely, assessment may have the effect of promoting learning by providing opportunities which might not be utilised if assessment or accreditation factors were not present.

A number of the chapters which follow indicate how the economic context in which the animator works influences the nature of relationships with learners. In Chapter 10, Jim Brown shows how his position as a consultant employed by the local council set limits on the way in which he could work with the members of the community on a housing estate. His conception of his role could not be fully accepted by the people with whom he was working because of fundamental differences between himself and those with whom he worked: he was a relatively well-paid consultant operating on a working-class housing estate with high levels of unemployment. Jane Mace (Chapter 12) also demonstrates how the political and economic context in which animators operate sets inevitable limits on what can be attempted or achieved; her work as a literacy educator was halted by the enforced closure of the Centre of which she was co-ordinator. Timothy Ireland (Chapter 9) points to the marked differences in socio-economic class between learners and animators in the literacy project he describes and the consequent limits to the ways in which it was possible to work within this context.

While many practitioners have begun to acknowledge the influence of the social and political context of their work, John Heron (Chapter 6) argues for the importance of other considerations as well. The politics of animation and the ways in which animators make decisions on behalf of learners are significant in his view, but these concerns must be balanced against a recognition of the transpersonal and spiritual aspects of animation. Learners are whole persons with feelings and emotions, not just instrumental, social or autonomous beings, and must be treated as such.

The emphasis of animation is often a function of the framework of the animator. Humanistic practitioners tend to focus on autonomy, social activists on interdependence and oppression and those with a transpersonal emphasis on holism.

Habermas (1970) emphasises the importance of social communication as a means of addressing power differences in relationships. He introduces the notion of what he terms an 'ideal speech act' in which the pattern of communication is not distorted by differences of power and status. He argues that free communication is only possible in circumstances when it is reciprocal and when no barriers exist between the parties. This is, as he recognises, an ideal, but such an ideal suggests how communication might be improved in normal conditions and how the influence of power might be recognised (for example, by examining lack of reciprocity in communications). In some circumstances the existence of hierarchies and status differences are recognised and utilised for learning; the practice of mentoring is an example of this. Mentoring involves a relationship between an experienced, and often older, person and a less experienced learner who is guided in the ways of the world. Bob Johnson (Chapter 13) writes about his work in a context – a maximum security prison – which gave him considerable power over the well-being of his learners. It was only through making himself potentially vulnerable to attack that he was able to open communication between himself and the inmates with whom he worked.

Another key consideration is 'what are the intentions of the learners?' The intentions which learners bring may not be fully articulated, or even capable of being revealed to the other, but they provide the most important starting point for defining the particularities of the relationship between learner and animator (Boud and Walker 1990). Intent gives an indication of the personal foundation of experience of the learner and what the learner regards as a legitimate starting point for this relationship. It may not end there, but to start anywhere else is to deny the learner his or her autonomy in entering the learning relationship.

Stephen Brookfield (Chapter 3) argues that learners' experience constitutes a rich resource for problem-solving and suggests that an important task for the animator is to develop learners' confidence in the usefulness of this experience. Brookfield acknowledges that learners' expectations that they are going to be 'taught things by an expert' – which derive from a lifetime of being taught – need to be taken into account, but cannot frame the situation. If an animator wishes to take an alternative view to this then he or she must acknowledge learners' expectations and find a way of operating which meets with the agreement of participants. John Bernard Harris (Chapter 11) makes a similar observation in relation to his team-building clients. Animators need to operate in ways which make their own interventions increasingly redundant, thereby avoiding the use of their own power to create dependency and thus exercising control over learners.

A learning relationship cannot exist without a degree of mutual agreement about each party's expectations of the other in the given context. In some situations, when there may be ambiguity about whether the two parties are in a learner/animator relationship or one defined by other social roles, it will be necessary to formalise this by making explicit the nature of the mutual obligations. This can lead either to an informal contract between the two in which the relationship is negotiated and agreed or even a formal one when the details are committed to paper and signed by all parties. The latter may well be necessary where a monetary transaction is involved. Harris shows how his practice as an animator is characterised by the establishment of a clear contract at the beginning of a learning event or relationship.

At the heart of a learner/animator relationship are the patterns of engagement and interaction which it provides. For example, in discussing learning possibilities in higher education institutions, Barnett (1994) draws attention to the fact that 'the key actors, staff and students, will have some measure of freedom to determine the patterns of their engagements with each other and their mutual responses' (p. 30). Some degrees of freedom will always exist no matter what the context. In practice these will be limited on both sides, but any given relationship may be more open than either party is willing to admit.

Jane Mace's account of her practice in the field of democratic literacy education (Chapter 12) illustrates the dialectical relationship which may be seen to exist between the actions of animators and the responses of learners. Mace's thinking about the animation of literacy has been significantly shaped by her reading of students' writing.

THE SIGNIFICANCE OF FEELINGS AND EMOTIONS

Several contributors emphasise the importance of feelings and emotions in learning. The affective experience of learners is probably the most powerful determinant of learning of all kinds. According to Margaret Donaldson, emotions point to where learning might be had: 'feelings ... mark importance. We experience emotion only in regard to that which matters' (Donaldson 1992: 12). An event that is of no significance gives rise to no emotion. As well as being indicators of where we might focus attention, they are a necessary part of the way we make choices (Damasio 1994). If we had to make all decisions on the basis of rational weighing of alternatives, we would not be able to operate effectively in the world. Feelings and emotions provide the best guides we have to where we need to devote our attention. This may be uncomfortable for animators, especially if they are not reconciled to their own emotional agendas, and they may be set aside because of immediate circumstances, but we cannot learn if they are continually denied.

In addition to their vital role in facilitating learning, emotions can also act as substantial barriers (Boud and Walker 1993). Animators need to pay attention to participants' feelings and ways of dealing with emotion. Bob Johnson (Chapter 13) suggests that emotions have a powerful effect in distorting learning. He argues that understanding and dealing with fear – one's own, first and foremost – are of primary importance in animating personal change. He asserts that fear is allayed by the establishment of trust. Tim Ireland (Chapter 9) also focuses on trust. He raises the question 'why should they trust me?' as the key for forming his relationship across a class divide. Jane Mace (Chapter 12) emphasises the importance of overcoming fear – in this case, the fear of writing, and of the judgement of the reader.

CONTEXT AND DISCOURSE

Experience, as we have noted earlier, does not exist in a social and personal vacuum. It always has a context, which sets boundaries to the learning that is possible, whether learners or animators are aware of it or not. Any examination of learning needs to take account of that context. Our world is defined by the people and objects that surround us, the meanings with which they are imbued and the language which is used to represent them. This world manifests the political, social, economic and historical situation in which we exist. Significantly, the context of learning is not merely an external environment which provides the scenery and objects of learning. The world is mirrored within each individual. Learners create an internal representation of the world which influences all their thoughts and actions. They test their thinking on this internal representation and judge their actions accordingly. This internal world is a filter through which perceptions are modified.

In addition to the experience of the world that learners bring with them to any new situation, many other influences are present. An exclusive focus on learners and their needs and interests has led to a psychologically and individualistically determined view of learning which tends to ignore some of the most powerful influences which have an impact on learners. Learning often occurs in the company of other people, whether or not they can be regarded as co-learners. As John Bernard Harris demonstrates in Chapter 11, groups may be regarded as organisms in their own right, with internal processes and structures and stages of development which animators need to take into account in their interventions. John Heron's descriptions (Chapter 6) of his actions in initiating rituals and ceremonies in the course of his work as a group animator underline his belief in the importance of giving attention to the spiritual aspects of learning groups.

Learning occurs within a framework of taken-for-granted assumptions about what is legitimate to do, to say and even to think. It is influenced directly and indirectly by the power of others as well as by forces which constrain participants' views of what is possible. John Smyth (Chapter 4) suggests that the teachers with whom he acts as an animator are constrained by the economic and managerial discourse which he believes has shaped debate about education in recent years. Smyth sees as central to his practice the process of encouraging teachers to examine the political context of their activities, and to question taken-for-granted assumptions about the social world embedded in the dominant discourse of contemporary education.

The concept of discourse embodies the notion that language is not only a means of communication of facts and feelings, but also of ideology: the choice of particular words and phrases structures expectations and aspirations, and frames what is legitimate to think and to do. Parker summarises this idea in the following way:

> Language is so structured to mirror power relations that often we can see no other ways of being, and it structures ideology so that it is difficult to speak both in and against it . . . studies of language from a wide range of disciplines have shown how, for example, gender is constructed and women are silenced (Spender 1981), how colonialist visions of those outside the white West are elaborated in language as 'other' (Said 1978), and how notions of class, knowledge and stupidity are connected in the ways we speak (Andersen 1988).
>
> (Parker 1992: ix)

At any historical moment, some discourses are dominant. For example, we have already referred to Smyth's argument (Chapter 4) that the use of economic discourse is dominant at present in education and training. Metaphors of the factory, of inputs and outputs, and of efficiency, quality and accountability are seen to have taken over in public debate from earlier discourses such as the humanistic, which drew on horticultural and biological metaphors of growth and development, nurturing and fruitfulness. Joyce Stalker (Chapter 5) describes the model of ideological systems she uses to uncover the political assumptions and dominant discourses which guide learners' experience. She uses the model to encourage learners to confront and challenge the hidden curricula and power relationships they encounter in the classroom and in their wider lives.

CREATING THE MICRO-CULTURE

One of the central tasks of animators is that of establishing an appropriate micro-culture, climate and space within which to work. Although the relationship between learners and animators always exists within a broader given context, it is often necessary to create a domain – within the context but symbolically apart from it – which has local rules and norms which counter (or indeed, on occasions, reproduce) some of the structures and processes of the wider context. The creation of a micro-culture for animation is not just a matter of structuring a room, designing useful starting activities and opening channels of communication. It is a continuous process which always has to take account of the external context.

It is never possible to exclude the broader context fully. It will always intrude to some extent – through ways in which power is exercised by individuals, by the assumptions made by one person about another. However, if attention is drawn to how these features are operating at the local level, it may be possible to set them aside to enable more open approaches to learning to proceed.

John Heron's account of his practice (Chapter 6) shows the importance he attaches to climate-setting at the beginning of a workshop or learning event. Through careful and deliberate structuring of the environment and setting a particular interpersonal tone he creates a world in which a greater range of possibilities for learning is invoked. A fortnightly community meeting was a central feature of the work described by Jim Brown (Chapter 10), but the economics and politics of the community continued to dominate all strategies. Even within the ostensible learning orientation of a university, Jan Jindy Pettman (Chapter 7) stresses the desirability in her practice as an educator of creating a safe, congenial (and critical) space in order to counteract a potentially hostile environment. The variety of micro-climates which are discussed in the book and the ways in which they were achieved lead one to be suspicious of the simple prescriptions for climate-setting which are typically included in training manuals. What is clear from the illustrations here is that establishing the micro-context depends on a thorough understanding of the macro-context in which the animator is operating.

POWER AND OPPRESSION

The dynamics of power and oppression always exert some influence on learning. Their effects need to be explored. Animators need to recognise which features are pertinent in any given situation. Neither power nor oppression can be directly observed, but they are useful constructs to enable otherwise inexplicable phenomena to be explained. These dynamics operate even when participants appear to deny their significance. Jan Jindy Pettman (Chapter 7) points to the tendency for members of dominant groups to deny the importance of categories and group identities, illustrating this observation with reference to a remark she has often encountered in the course of her work as an animator that 'I've never thought of myself as white'. She also highlights the danger that minority students may be pushed into carrying the burden of speaking for all members of their group, and that they may be under constant pressure to educate the majority.

Power can also be exercised through the manipulation and distortion of communication. Different groups have different degrees of control over the construction of consensus (Habermas 1977). Power is thus used to structure the social framework within which interests, ideas and issues are formed and made known. As Lukes (1974) suggests, power is socially structured in that it does not depend on the capacities of individuals, although historically it may be seen in the actions of individuals. Power is also quite insidious. Furthermore, because it is socially and culturally located it may have the appearance of consensus (Hugman 1991).

Individuals or groups who exercise power in learning situations may be unaware of doing so and may even reject the very idea that they exercise power. When animators hold a professional role *vis à vis* learners then such structural issues of power are inevitably present; this does not mean that they are necessarily absent when the animator is in the position of a peer. Several of the contributors to this book make reference to the way in which their actions as animators are both enabled and constrained by aspects of their professional relationship with learners.

In Chapter 8, Elizabeth Tisdell suggests that animators inevitably hold greater power in relation to the people whose learning they are promoting by virtue of their institutional positions. She believes that this imbalance of power gives rise to ethical issues which need to be faced in describing and theorising about others' experience. Some parallel concerns are also raised by Jan Jindy Pettman (Chapter 7), who argues that working within a formal university setting places constraints on the extent to which co-operative learning is possible; her own location in an institution of higher education leads her to confront some tensions between her context and her ideological commitment to feminism and liberation. Differential power relations can be successfully challenged, as Jim Brown (Chapter 10) illustrates with respect to his consultancy in a working-class community group. The community redefined Brown's role, at the price of some discomfort to him, so that it focused exclusively on the community's agenda. Pettman also highlights some ethical issues in raising questions about how extremely difficult and painful aspects of experience (her examples include war and 'ethnic cleansing') are to be dealt with; she suggests that in some contexts it is desirable to place limits on self-disclosure.

Social divisions and 'difference' need to be taken into account in animation. Dimensions such as class, gender, ethnicity, culture and physical appearance influence how learners are perceived, the expectations placed on them and the oppression which they experience. Such expectations often remain unchanged even when the animator is a member of a similar group. As Pettman suggests, one of the insidious aspects of oppression is the way in which it can become internalised, and members of a given group may begin to take on the labels placed on them by those from other groups. Internalised oppression works when relationships of power and oppression operating in wider society are taken on by individuals and applied to themselves, thus reinforcing external oppression.

Recent years have seen a growth in the literature examining the effects of oppression and 'difference' on learning. Strategies have been proposed which take into account the learning approaches of different social groups (Coats 1994, Hayes and Colin 1994, Pettman 1991). These have focused particularly on issues of gender and ethnicity in learning. It is worth noting that many of the prescriptions for good learning strategies for women and for members of non-dominant groups are similar to those outlined in the general literature on adult learning. For example, the following are typical of the principles invoked in both kinds of literature:

- exploration of personal experience is validated;
- a holistic view is advocated;
- there is seen to be no division between the personal and the theoretical or academic;
- the creation of a safe learning climate with a non-judgemental stance on experience is seen as important;
- activities are designed to build self-esteem and a sense of personal responsibility for learning;
- links are made between the learners' experience and that of others;
- learners are encouraged to act as animators.

However, to list any strategies as if they were suitable for all members of a particular group, even when they have been articulated by members of a group, is potentially to reinforce stereotypes and to create new ortho-doxies, which can limit action.

Animators are often required to offer alternative perspectives to those held by learners. Such perspectives can act, metaphorically speaking, to exert leverage against reality, which the learner believes is a given, to show how things might be different. This can occur in many ways – by bringing concepts and language which name realities which are not visible within the dominant discourse, by bringing stories that show ways in which others have operated counter to the power constraints, by bringing personal testimony of how oppression can be overcome, and by showing through their presence and commitment that boundaries are more per-meable than is normally assumed. A number of the contributors to this book illustrate in their chapters the importance and value of developing processes of reflection and theory-building through the telling of personal stories to do this.

THE FOCUS OF LEARNING

It is important for animators to ask the questions 'who is the learner?' or 'who are the learners?' and 'what relationships already exist between us or will exist by virtue of our different roles and what we bring to our interaction?' Each different combination of roles and relationships offers possibilities for learning as well as constraints on what might be possible.

The focus of learning is significant. In some of the chapters which follow the focus is on helping *individuals to learn in groups*, in others on helping *groups as whole systems to learn*. This distinction is an important one to consider in any analysis of animation and learning. The learning outcomes can be quite different in each, and the animation role and the assumptions which the animator brings will necessarily be different.

A major theme which is developed in the book is the importance of working with experience in order to move beyond individual learning so as to promote wider change. Change at a group or societal level involves more than change in individuals. Assisting learners to uncover the forces that inhibit and constrain them and working to change those conditions are seen to be important tasks for animators. As John Smyth (Chapter 4) observes, change is a social and collective phenomenon and it 'starts with us'. Learning and animation may necessarily start with the learner, but if it is to take account of the wider influences of power, oppression, emotion and trust we have discussed here, it cannot end with the individual. Learning will demand change not only of ourselves but the context in which we operate.

At the beginning of this chapter we argued for a synthesis of the educational and social scientific traditions which have informed ideas about learning from experience. In our discussion of the themes which run through the book, we have drawn from theories of the social and of the individual and from the discourses of political action and personal development. We believe that understanding of the processes of both individual learning and wider social change will be helped by a move beyond the dichotomy of the two traditions.

REFERENCES

Andersen, R. (1988) *The Power and the Word: Language, Power and Change*, London: Paladin.

Barnett, R. (1994) *The Limits of Competence: Knowledge, Higher Education and Society*, Buckingham: SRHE and Open University Press.

Boud, D. and Walker, D. (1990) 'Making the most of experience', *Studies in Continuing Education*, 12, 2, 61–80.

— (1993) 'Barriers to reflection on experience', in D. Boud, R. Cohen and D. Walker (eds) *Using Experience for Learning*, Buckingham: SRHE and Open University Press, 73–86.

Coats, M. (1994) *Women's Education*, Buckingham: SRHE and Open University Press.

Damasio, A. R. (1994) *Descartes' Error: Emotion, Reason and the Human Brain*, New York: Putnam.

Donaldson, M. (1992) *Human Minds: An Exploration*, London: Allen Lane, The Penguin Press.

Habermas, J. (1970) 'Towards a theory of communicative competence', *Inquiry*, 13, 4, 360–376.

— (1977) 'Hannah Arendt's communications concept of power', *Social Research*, 44, 1, 3–24.

Hayes, E. and Colin, S. A. J. (eds) (1994) *Confronting Sexism and Racism*, New Directions for Adult and Continuing Education No. 61, San Francisco: Jossey Bass.

Hugman, R. (1991) *Power in Caring Professions*, London: Macmillan.

Lukes, S. (1974) *Power: A Radical View*, London: Macmillan.

Miller, N. (1993b) 'How the T-group changed my life: sociological perspectives on experiential groupwork', in D. Boud, R. Cohen and D. Walker (eds) *Using Experience for Learning*, Buckingham: SRHE and Open University Press, 129–142.

Parker, I. (1992) *Discourse Dynamics: Critical Analysis for Social and Individual Psychology*, London: Routledge.

Pettman, J. J. (1991) 'Towards a (personal) politics of location', *Studies in Continuing Education*, 13, 2, 153–166.

Said, E. (1978) *Orientalism*, London: Routledge.

Spender, D. (1981) *Man Made Language*, London: Routledge.

Part 1

3 Helping people learn what they do
Breaking dependence on experts

Stephen Brookfield

'Helping people learn what they do' is how the adult educator Myles Horton describes what I have been trying to do in my attempts to get teachers to take their experiences seriously when they're searching for answers to their problems. When I heard Myles speak this phrase to a group of educators in New York I was taken immediately with how it captured what I saw happening in the best kind of teacher reflection groups. In these groups people come to realise the value of their own experiences, they take a critical perspective on these, and they learn how to use this reflection to help them deal with whatever problems they face. In Myles' words,

> I knew that it was necessary ... to draw out of people their experience ... it was essential that people learned to make decisions on the basis of analysing and trusting their own experience, and learning from what was good and what was bad ... I believed then and still believe that you learn from your experience of doing something and from your analysis of that experience.
>
> (Horton 1990: 57)

In recent years, as I've worked more and more with helping teachers take their experiences seriously so that they begin the process of problem-solving with collaborative and critical reflection on these experiences, Myles' words are always at the front of my mind. The process I want to describe in this chapter – the Good Practices Audit – is my attempt to put Myles' advice into effect by providing teachers with a structure for collaborative critical reflection.

The Good Practices Audit (or GPA) is a three-phase process helping people to search their experiences as a way of coming up with good responses to common problems they encounter. It involves a mix of individual reflection and collaborative critical analysis and is focused on helping people deal with difficulties they have themselves identified. On the surface it appears as highly task oriented and instrumental enough to satisfy the most sceptical, resistant, left brained, insecure, anal compulsive educator. What could be more focused than an actuarially inclined process of auditing? In fact, once the GPA gets going, the reflection, sharing and analysis become much more spontaneous and unstructured than the method seems to suggest. The conversations that ensue are open and unpredictable, yet they happen under the guise of a well-structured series of tasks.

PHASE 1: FORMULATING THE PROBLEM

The GPA starts with the problem formulation stage. The problem formulation exercise is an activity I use in a great many workshops as a way of helping a group of teachers who work in different situations and disciplines, with different kinds of students and very divergent constraints, discover and prioritise common problems of practice they might work on together. The exercise is designed to elicit people's own definitions of their own worst problems as they themselves perceive them. This is by way of contrast to most professional development activities where people focus on problems that a well-meaning dean, president, superintendent, policy analyst or principal thinks they should attend to. If the problem formulation exercise succeeds in getting people to externalise and prioritise their most deeply felt problems, then it builds a natural enthusiasm for participating in the rest of the process. Knowing that the problems to be worked on are the problems that they have selected gives teachers the sense of being authentically engaged in a project that is in their own best interests to see through to the end.

The problem formulation exercise begins with educators individually and privately listing the problems that drain the most emotional energy from their lives and that they regard as being the most impenetrable. I ask them to think about the part of their practice that they would most like help with – the aspects of their work that they would most like to get 'fixed'. One approach that works quite well is to ask people to imagine that they've rubbed Aladdin's lamp and that a pedagogic genie has appeared to promise them that he will rid them of any one of the problems that they face in their work. Whatever problem they choose is the one that they should nominate to be explored by the whole group. Another way is to ask them to complete the sentences 'what I most need help with is ...' or 'what I most need to work in my practice is ...'

I've also had some luck with the 'Survival Advice Memo'. In this memo I ask educators to imagine that they're in their last hour of their last day at work and that they have not had the chance to meet their successor. Because they've been left a billion-dollar inheritance by a long-forgotten aunt, they have decided to leave their job and never to worry about financial security again. Before they walk away from their desk, they have the chance to take a few minutes to write a confidential memo to their successor who will be starting the next day. In the memo they are to write down their best advice to their successor on how to survive in the job, and to focus particularly on avoiding certain problems that stymied the new billionaire when she was trying to do what her successor must attempt. As well as helping people surface what they feel are their most pressing problems, the survival advice memo also helps them become aware of the foundational assumptions that undergird how they think about their work and the essential, core knowledge that they feel is necessary to what they do.

Still another approach to doing problem-formulation is to use a critical incident method. I ask people to think back over the last six months and to pick out the day when they felt most vulnerable or depressed, the day when they felt as though they were on the verge of quitting. A common response to this instruction is for people to say 'that happens to me every day', in which case I ask them to do their best to grade the relative levels of discomfort they felt. When they've got the worst day clear in their minds I ask them to write a paragraph describing what happened that day, making sure that they include details of where and when the incident in question happened, who was involved, and what it was about the event that was so particularly distressing. As they review what they've written, I ask them to reframe the event in terms of a generic difficulty or problem that can be addressed with colleagues. For example, a teacher who wrote movingly about the devastation he felt in a staff meeting when his enthusiastic comments about a new curriculum model were met by a colleague unexpectedly cursing him and castigating his naïveté, reframed this incident as the problem of 'avoiding cultural suicide'. An incident in which a teacher wrote about her class staging a mini-revolt and absolutely refusing to complete what she felt was a reasonable course requirement was reframed as 'understanding and responding to students' resistance'.

I usually ask that the people take some time – maybe a few days – to think about the problem they wish to choose, and then to make some private notes about it. This helps avoid the danger of the 'crisis de jour' determining the problem they select. Then I ask them to gather with colleagues to read out what they've written to each other. This often happens in some kind of faculty development workshop or professional day, though there's no reason why it has to be so formal. It could just as easily happen in an informal weekly reflection group meeting over coffee or lunch. I ask them to work in groups of about five or six: if the group gets much larger than this it takes too much time to articulate and sift through all the responses, but if it's much smaller there's the risk that not enough important experience will emerge, or that a form of groupthink will develop. After each person has read out their problems, I ask the group to look for commonalities, for general kinds of difficulty that are embedded in the individual crises described.

Now comes the difficult part. I ask the group members to nominate the top two problems that a reasonable majority can agree on as the problems they would like to address in more detail. Since a six-person group will usually generate at least fifteen problems (despite my guidelines teachers usually come with considerably more than the one or two problems I've asked them to focus on) it's important to try and prioritise what we look at first. Sometimes group members take votes as a way to help them prioritise their problems. They allow each participant to choose three problems from the list compiled and then assign three points to every first choice, two to every second choice and one to every third choice. Then the top two problems that have accrued the most votes are the ones the group nominates. I try to counsel against this mechanistic way of reaching consensus, however, arguing instead that if teachers talk through how they choose what are the real problems they face they will become much more aware of the structural constraints to their practice. Often that argument is met with a lot of frustration and the desire to 'get going', in which case I feel I have to honour that wish. It's always a delicate balance but I try to keep in mind the advice of Paulo Freire and Myles Horton that you can never start from where you are as an educator, you must always start from learners' own definitions of their needs.

When all the groups have nominated their problems I ask each group to write its problems on newsheet and tape them on the wall of the room in which we're meeting. Because I work in workshops with quite large groups of teachers a lot of the time this is the method that makes most sense for me, but it could just as easily be done through newsletters, electronic bulletin boards or other means. As I and all the workshop participants wander around the room looking at what problems the different groups have posted up on their newsheets, commonalities start to emerge. Words or phrases are repeated, situations 'jump out' at us, shared problems start to be recognised. After a while we gather together as a whole group and discuss what common themes and shared problems are revealed. Usually, four or five are settled on, typically dealing with difficulties caused by students' resistance to learning, educators' feelings of being isolated, incompetent and overwhelmed, the problem of how to respond to the diversity of ethnic, class, gender and ability factors in just one group of students, the difficulty of keeping students engaged in learning, the struggle of balancing a commitment to process with a concern for content, and the problem of how to motivate what seem to be uniformly sullen students. When the four or five problems have been defined I ask for suggestions as to how they can be worded as a focused project for action; for example, 'understanding and dealing with resistance to learning' or 'engaging students in learning unfamiliar skills or knowledge'. We then discuss some of the most specific indications that show us that such a problem exists (for example, students' blank looks, students putting on Walkmans when teachers start speaking, students failing to hand work in on time despite repeated requests to do so) and list these underneath the general problem heading.

When the problems to be worked on have been identified I ask everyone

BEST/WORST EXPERIENCES MATRIX

WORST EXPERIENCES	*BEST EXPERIENCES*
AS A LEARNER	AS A LEARNER
OF COLLEAGUES	OF COLLEAGUES
AS A TEACHER	AS A TEACHER

SUMMARY OF GOOD PRACTICES

Figure 3.1 The best/worst experiences matrix

to volunteer to work on a team responding to one of the problems listed. As people join their respective teams they often find it to be comprised of people who were not members of their problem-formulation groups. They find themselves working with colleagues from very different situations and enjoying the advantages this experiential richness confers. One advantage of the GPA technique is that it doesn't really matter if everyone involved in the process chooses to work on the same problem. For example, I've seen the entire faculty of a college choose to work on 'dealing with resistance to learning', even though for many of them this was not the problem they originally posed in the problem-formulation stage. When this happens I just tell participants to form groups of five or six and to think how many more good responses will be generated if more than one team is working on the same problem.

PHASE 2: ANALYSING THE EXPERIENCE

As educators struggle to discover good responses to the problems that bedevil them they have three categories of educational experiences available to them, each of which is indicated in the 'best/worst experiences matrix' (Figure 3.1).

The three categories in the matrix comprise teachers' experiences as learners, their experiences as observers of colleagues, and their experiences as teachers with their own practice. Each of these categories can be investigated according to their best or worst dimensions. This means that every person can view the problem to be worked on through at least six possible experiential lenses. Three of these focus on the *worst* things that they have experienced as regards the problem chosen – things that either created the problem where it need not have existed, or that made it much worse than it otherwise would have been. The other three of these focus on the *best* things they have experienced as learners, colleagues or teachers – things that addressed the problem and helped them keep it under control. I generally begin by asking teachers to focus on the worst responses to the problem as I have found this often produces more useful and unexpected insights than the best responses. As Horton recognised, 'if you analyse them, you can learn more in some ways from failures than successes' (1990: 176). After all, if we could quickly generate a list of best responses to a situation, the chances are that the situation would never have emerged as the problem it is. If we identify things that create the problem or make it worse then we can work back from these to consider what the opposite response would be.

When I ask people to complete the matrix, the first experiences explored are the worst responses to the problem chosen that individual teachers have ever suffered when they have found themselves in the role of learner. These would be responses to the problem that, from their viewpoint as learners, either created the problem in the first place or made it much more serious than it really need have been. Most of us periodically find ourselves in the role of learners or participants in staff development programs, graduate study, academic conferences, faculty institutes, professional days and various kinds of recreational or avocational learning. These learning experiences can be a rich source of insight into the dynamics of teaching, alerting us to strategic mistakes and unchecked assumptions that otherwise would have eluded us completely. From learning to swim and drive I learned a great deal about how to calm the fears of nervous learners, the importance of specific and regular affirmation, the need to set realistic goals and the importance of continually monitoring how people were reacting to their learning. Of the six lenses of experience contained in the best/worst practices matrix, our autobiographies as learners are by far the most neglected by educators.

After having examined their worst experiences as learners, participants are then asked to consider the worst responses to the problem they've ever seen a colleague make. In other words, are there things they've observed colleagues doing that created the problem where it didn't originally exist, or that made a relatively insignificant problem into a much more serious one? These might be the actions that colleagues took in response to the problem that were so disastrous that while you felt bad for your colleague you were grateful for the fact that you had learned a valuable lesson about exactly what *not* to do if you found yourself in a similar situation. For example, having seen colleagues change rules about curriculum, methods or evaluative criteria in mid-course, and the anger and resentment this causes in students, has had the beneficial effect of alerting me to the need to avoid doing this at all costs. When I've felt that doing this was unavoidable, I've realised that a great deal of disclosure and negotiation about this change was going to be necessary if I was not to create irreducible hostility in students. That has had the effect of ensuring that I leave plenty of non-teaching time in the sessions around the time that this change is happening to make full disclosure about what's happening, and why, and to engage in good faith negotiations about it.

The last worst experiences category is the worst response we have ever made to the problem under consideration in our own practice as teachers. Into this category come the mistakes that, even as we're in the middle of making them, we know to be disastrous, though we may not know right at that moment exactly why they're so awful. This category also includes miscalculations that we become aware of only after the fact: for example, those occasions when it becomes apparent that our readings of what we thought was happening in a situation are dramatically different from what actually was happening (at least in the eyes of others involved). For example, I have redesigned whole courses on the basis of what I thought was significant resistance from a majority of students, only to find out later that resistance came from a small but vocal minority with the silent majority of students feeling too insecure to speak. As a result of becoming aware of this worst practice as a teacher I now make sure that I keep a systematic record of how students are feeling about the class by collecting anonymous weekly critical incidents.

After compiling the worst experiences of the problem in the three categories examined, people now examine their best experiences. First, they review things that have happened to them as learners that seemed to reduce the significance or harmful effects of the problem for them. For example, one of the chief blockages to my own learning is my fear of public humiliation, of not doing everything perfectly and of looking a complete fool in front of my peers. Consequently, I don't do well in situations where teachers place a premium on an early public performance by learners in front of their peers. However, if I know that my mistakes as a learner are a private matter between myself and a sympathetic, non-judgemental teacher, I am much more ready to take risks, stretch myself, and attempt things that I would have avoided at all costs in a more public setting. Knowing this alerts me to the importance of ensuring that student failure is experienced as privately and non-threateningly as possible.

When teachers turn to the best responses they have observed in colleagues they are looking for actions by colleagues that either kept the problem under control or stopped it developing in the first place. For example, through watching colleagues who used personal storytelling capture the attention of apparently bored learners, I have made a deliberate attempt to incorporate personal anecdotes into my own teaching in the last few years. A decade or so ago, the idea of doing this would have horrified me because of my culturally inbred sense that personal revelations were indulgent, subjective and embarrassing (I am English, after all). No one was really interested, I thought, in my private life. Yet, having seen colleagues connect with large groups of students through good personal stories that illustrate some aspect of the ideas or skill experiments they are trying to convey, I know that this can be very effective in capturing students' attention. Of course, I should have known this from reflecting on my own experiences as a learner. Whenever I hear an academic talk about her private struggles with her work, her moments of revelation and the things that have taken her totally by surprise in her scholarly autobiography, I am hooked. Much more so than if the presentation stays at the level of distanced, objective reportage. It's the incidental, throwaway comments, the little asides about how she felt as she tried something out or had a breakthrough in her learning or thinking, that I remember most clearly.

Lastly, people reflect on the best things they have ever done as teachers in response to the problem identified. Usually, this is the least useful source of analysis. After all, if teachers had good responses to the problem they're examining, they probably wouldn't have identified it as a problem in the first place! However, most of us can probably point to situations in dealing with a problem where we realised afterwards that if we'd done or said something different, the problem would have been eased. Those realisations can be built on as we speculate on what might have happened had we followed an alternate course of action. Also, in the midst of the worst problems we face, we have occasional moments of clarity and hope when we sense that we are doing something right, even if these moments are fleeting. For example, from among my darkest experiences of dealing with students' resistance, anger and boredom, I can usually recognise moments of illumination when I felt I was on the verge of getting it right, moments when I knew that if only one or two things had been changed the problem would have been much reduced.

PHASE 3: COMPILING THE SUGGESTIONS

The final stage of the process focuses on teachers working collaboratively to analyse their individual matrixes and to generate useful responses to the problems. I ask group members to take turns to go round the group and to read out the best and worst responses to the problem that they've experienced as learners. If more than one person mentions something like the same response, this is noted down. I ask them to focus on the educational approach, technique, method or practice that this common response suggests that they either employ or avoid. For example, if the group is examining the problem of how to keep students coming back to class, and 'feeling ashamed in public' is a common worst response that teachers offer as a reason why they dropped a course when they were students themselves, then the approach to employ is 'making evaluation private' and the approach to avoid is 'using public forms of evaluation'. The group is then asked to take this general insight to a level of specificity and to talk about different approaches to assessing students' progress privately (for example, by using learning journals, weekly learning audits, individualised narrative evaluation, or having students submit videos of their performance that are for teachers' eyes only).

Next, group members take turns to go round the group and read out the best and worst responses to the problem that they've observed in their colleagues. If more than one person mentions something like the same response, this is noted down. Again, participants are asked to focus on the educational approach that this common response suggests they either employ or avoid, and then to specify particular techniques, methods or practices that would realise this.

The same procedure is repeated as people read out the best and worst responses to the problem that they've made in their own work. The process ends with participants listing all the ideas of good things to do in response to the problem (in other words, the good practices) that their group has suggested.

The hardest part of this third phase is getting people to convert their general insights into specific practices. I suggest to people that for every idea that they list in the audit, at least three concrete, specific suggestions of how this might be put into practice are given. For example, one group that decided that 'connecting learning to students' lives' was a good practice in response to encountering student hostility or resistance, proposed (i) starting off a new course with a panel of former students talking about the value of the course for them, (ii) using a simulation, role play or case study in the first week or so of the class where it becomes clear to students that only by their learning the skills or knowledge taught in the course will they be able to negotiate real life crises or proceed successfully through their studies, and (iii) informing students that one third of the way into the course they will be doing an anonymous critical incident evaluation to find out what's working for them and what needs to be changed or emphasised differently.

OVERVALUING EXPERIENCE AND THE CORRECTIVE ROLE OF THEORY

Despite my enthusiasm for the GPA approach to analysing teachers' experiences (the enthusiasm all inventors feel for their creations) I don't want to claim too much for it. Individual experiences can be distorted, self-fulfilling, unexamined and constraining. Simply having experiences does not imply that they are reflected on, understood or analysed critically. In fact, it is a mistake to think that we have experiences in the sense that our own being stands alone while the river of experience flows around us. Experiences are constructed *by* us as much as they happen *to* us: the meaning schemes and perspectives we employ to assign significance to events shape fundamentally how we experience them. Neither are experiences inherently enriching. Experience can teach us habits of bigotry, stereotyping and disregard for significant but inconvenient information. It can also be narrowing and constraining, causing us to evolve and transmit ideologies that skew irrevocably how we interpret the world. A group's pooling of individual experiences can be a swapping of mutually reinforcing prejudices. Even when cross-disciplinary groups work on the same problem (for example, when teachers of mathematics, psychology, athletics, literature, theatre and engineering join in the same group to look at how they can respond to the diversity of ability levels and learning styles in their classes) there can still be a form of groupthink caused by these teachers being drawn from the same class, cultural group and geographical area, and by their having gone through similar educational experiences.

There is also the possibility that we can analyse our experience enthusiastically to help us deal with problems that we think are the chief obstacles to pedagogic fulfilment and happiness, but that this analysis can be superficial and can ignore the political and cultural constraints we face. What seem to be urgent short-term problems requiring our immediate attention can divert our attention from longer-term disturbances. What looks like a little local difficulty confined to our particular classroom, subject area or students is often symptomatic of an underlying structural problem. We can focus on changing external classroom conditions and ignore the fact that our deeply ingrained ways of perceiving our students and colleagues are what really need to be changed. So the analysis of experience must always benefit from an interaction with critical theory. Literature, research, philosophical speculation and theoretical analysis helps to keep us alert to structural constraints and distortions, to different perspectives and to the possibilities of self-deception.

Like it or not, we are all theorists as well as practitioners. Our practice is theoretically informed by our implicit and informal theories about the processes and relationships of teaching. Our theories are grounded in the epistemological and practical tangles and contradictions we seek to explain and resolve. The educational theory that appears in books and journals might be a more codified, abstracted way of thinking about universal processes, but it is not different in kind from the understandings embedded in our own local decisions and actions. As Usher suggests, formal theory serves as 'a kind of resource and sounding board for the development and refinement of informal theory – a way of bringing critical analysis to bear on the latter' (1989: 88).

Reading theory can assist us in naming aspects of experience that elude or puzzle us. When we read an explanation of a contradictory experience that interprets it in a new and revealing way, it makes it comprehensible.

As a result, we feel that the world is more accessible, more open to our influence. When someone else's words illuminate or confirm a privately realised insight we feel affirmed and recognised. In her study of classroom chronicles, Isenberg (1994) shows how reading others' depictions of the crises, anxieties and dilemmas that she thought were uniquely her own, helped her put her own problems in perspective. Also, seeing a personal insight stated as a theoretical proposition makes us more likely to take seriously our own reasoning and judgements. This does wonders for our morale and self-confidence. It also strengthens our ability to state clearly the rationale informing our actions.

Theory can also help free us from falling victims to the traps of relativism and isolationism. To quote Freire, 'Reading is one of the ways I can get the theoretical illumination of practice in a certain moment. If I don't get that, do you know what can happen? We as popular educators begin to walk in a circle, without the possibility of going beyond that circle' (Horton and Freire 1990: 98). By studying ideas, activities and theories that have sprung from situations outside our circle of practice, we gain insight into those features of our work that are context-specific, and those that are more generic. Embedded as we are in our cultures, histories and contexts, it is easy for us to slip into the habit of generalising from the particular. Reading theory can jar us in a productive way by suggesting unfamiliar interpretations of familiar events and by suggesting other ways of working.

For teachers who lack the opportunity to belong to a conversation, reflection or GPA group, and who are unable to benefit from listening to the contrasting perspectives and interpretations of colleagues, the written word may be the only source of alternative viewpoints available. By reading books and articles we can engage in a simulated conversation about practice with interested colleagues. A conversation with a book is written, not spoken. Books which end up with comments scrawled throughout the margins, pages turned down and peppered with yellow slips, are books we have talked with. Even for teachers lucky enough to belong to a reflection group, reading educational literature still serves an important function. It supplies provocative elements of dissonance that can shake up comfortably settled frameworks and assumptions. Teachers in GPA groups often display an ideological homogeneity. They share paradigmatic, framing assumptions about purposes and methods of education that are so deeply embedded that their existence is hardly even realised let alone subjected to critical analysis. Members of these groups tend to value the same ideas and resources, disagreeing only on technical matters concerning how best to realise common aims. In such groups the prospect of groupthink – of an uncritical adherence to certain formal beliefs and informally developed norms – is very real. There is a mutual reinforcement of pedagogical correctness, and a corresponding dismissal of inconvenient points of view as irrelevant, immoral or ideologically unsound.

To stay intellectually alive, GPA groups may need the stimulus of unfamiliar interpretations and perspectives. Having the study of educational literature as a regular feature of a GPA group's existence reduces the likelihood of groupthink and intellectual stagnation. This is especially true if group members deliberately seek to expose each other to ideas and materials that have previously been considered off limits, radical or contentious. Viewing common practices through the lens of an alternative theoretical critique can expose contradictions of which we were previously unaware, and can help us make explicit those paradigmatic assumptions that are part of our intellectual furniture.

Without the regular and serious study of theoretical literature we can easily remain immersed in a pragmatic fixation on the puzzles of our own practice. We struggle with the problem of how to use participatory and experiential methods in classes of over a hundred members, or of how to connect with every one of our widely diverse students. We agonise about how we can catch teachable moments, diverge from our lesson plan, and build on spontaneity, while still getting through the syllabus. Theoretical literature helps us remember that these puzzles are not just procedural kinks or tangles to be unravelled, but politically sculpted situations illustrating the internal contradictions of the systems in which we work. Critical theory views these problems as the predictable consequences of having teachers work alone in arbitrary periods of time under a centrally controlled system. Reading this literature means that we reframe what we consider to be the 'problems' in our practice. Our 'problems' become defined as the refusal of the curriculum council or accreditation agency to let us develop materials specific to particular contexts, or the educational institution's placing of intolerable burdens on teachers who are expected to take on more and more students with no additional help.

CONCLUSION

The limitations of the GPA for actually achieving change should be acknowledged. By itself, the audit cannot alter how teachers, administrators or indeed students behave. All it can do is indicate potentially useful directions for action. Moreover, the audit is limited by its focus on pedagogic process. For problems that are political and cultural in nature – the most important and most intractable of all – the audit is of limited use. It can highlight the fact that these problems exist, but it can do little to suggest how they might be addressed. This is a question of political analysis and political action. But the structured, critical analysis of experience that the GPA enables does have three undeniable benefits that, taken together, explain its appeal to beleaguered teachers searching for help wherever they can find it. First, it gives teachers a sense of being focused on what really counts, on concerns that feel close to home. Because the responses in the matrix are focused on the problems they have nominated there is the feeling that any time and energy spent doing the GPA will be worth the effort. Second, in giving a structure to the analysis of experience, it reassures the cynics and sceptics who have been burned by endless workshops in which 'sharing experiences' is a synonym for self-obsessed, superficial analysis, for idiosyncratic war stories or for ego-maniacal grandstanding. Third, once the exercise has been tried and found to work, it introduces teachers to the ideas that their experience really should be taken seriously and that they, and not people who write books on teaching, are really the experts on their own problems.

To finish, let me give one brief example that illustrates how working teachers can find this exercise useful. I recently worked over a period of several months with a hundred or so teachers who wanted me to be the featured presenter at a series of 'in-service' days. Half way through my time with them I introduced the good practices audit process which was met with the usual reactions of one part irritation and two parts puzzlement, usually expressed in the question 'Why don't you just tell us what to do?' However, because I had spent two to three months working with them before trying this out, they were willing to suspend their disbelief long enough to give the method a try. They went through the problem-formulation stage, completed the best/worst experiences matrix at home and then came together in groups to develop their audits. Throughout the weeks that this process took, I sensed a real scepticism that was exemplified by one participant who read the paper quite a lot during my presentations, rarely made eye contact with me and who looked (to me, anyway) thoroughly bored with what seemed from his lack of facial animation to be considered by him to be an obvious waste of time.

On the last day of several months' work with these teachers I was wrapping up by telling them (yet again) that my agenda had not been to appear as the visiting expert or pedagogic dignitary dispensing disconnected, decontextualised advice on the nature of good teaching. Instead my intention had been to come in and introduce them to a process of experiential analysis and critical conversation (the GPA) that they could take and apply in the future to the analysis and resolution of the as yet unknown difficulties they were bound to face. As I was turning off the overhead projector and gathering my papers prior to walking out of the room the paper reading, eye avoiding, bored looking participant suddenly spoke up to make the last comment of the whole four months. Thanking me briefly for my efforts this person summed up everything I had been trying to do by saying 'We came here expecting a Walleye dinner and you taught us how to fish.' (Walleye pike is a Minnesotan cod-like fish much favoured at Friday night fish fries.) I was astounded. From a person I would have picked out as one of those most disconnected from the process had come a summary of exactly what I was trying to do. As I walked away from the school I thought, yet again, about how I can never trust the evidence of my own eyes when it comes to interpreting people's facial reactions or body language. But mostly I was grateful for the fact that someone (and an apparent sceptic at that!) had finally expressed so succinctly exactly what Myles Horton was trying to do in his work, and what the Good Practices Audit was trying to accomplish.

REFERENCES

Horton, M. (1990) *The Long Haul*, New York: Doubleday.
Horton, M. and Freire, P. (1990) *We Make the Road by Walking: Conversations on Education and Social Change*, Philadelphia: Temple University Press.
Isenberg, J. (1994) *Going by the Book: The Role of Popular Classroom Chronicles in the Professional Development of Teachers*, New York: Routledge.
Usher, R. S. (1989) 'Locating Adult Education in the Practical', in B. P. Bright (ed.) *Theory and Practice in the Study of Adult Education: The Epistemological Debate*, New York: Routledge, 65–93.

4 Developing socially critical educators

John Smyth

Before I launch into 'what I do', it may make more sense to the reader to have a broad orientation on where this chapter is headed. I want to report on a 'project' I have been involved in for more than a decade, in which I have been working with teachers (as a university academic) individually and collectively, to analyse and reflect on what they do as classroom teachers, what it means, the wider forces shaping it and what they see as the limits and constraints emerging from the broader contexts in which they operate. I do this, at the outset, by making the point that in Australia we have become besotted with economic discourse to the point that it virtually saturates almost all discussions about matters educational. The consequence, I argue, is that in this country there is an educational discourse of a very decided genre, that powerfully shapes and informs educational possibilities. I go on to explain, as the chapter unfolds, how I have worked at trying to develop a counter-hegemonic discourse of teaching, and how this operates in practice. It is true that I don't have the space to go into all of the detail required to provide a comprehensive account on teachers' terms (and that is one of the disadvantages of case study styles of rendition – they are very wordy), but I hope I am able to give at least a glimpse of the alternative public sphere within which this discourse might occur. The process I describe is one that is *descriptive* of what is occurring within their teaching, while being *informing* as to the generalities and the specifics, *confronting* in terms of how it arrests the taken-for-grantedness, while providing the spaces within which the *reconstruction* of transformative action can occur.

WHAT DO I DO?

'What we do' is not a question we often get asked or are even given a chance to answer, except in the most superficial of ways. I teach and do research in a country that is more obsessed with matters economic than any other country in the world – yet most Australians are blissfully unaware of that. The observation was made by the Deputy Governor of the Reserve Bank that 'There is no country in the world that is as obsessed with economic issues as Australia. In other countries, the front pages of their newspapers are full of stories about civil wars, riots, racial tensions, constitutional crises, etc. Ours are filled with balance of payments statistics, unemployment statistics, Budgets, etc.' (cited in Evatt Foundation 1994). In the preface to a recent book entitled *The State of Australian Government 1993–94* by the Evatt Foundation, Peter Groenewegen, Professor of Economics from University of Sydney, explained it this way:

> This obsession with economics is not, incidentally, something of recent years. When Crauford Goodwin produced his history of nineteenth century Canadian economics, he could do so in about 200 pages. When Goodwin wrote a similar history of Australian economics for the same period it took 650 pages, and this, despite the fact that Australia's population was a third that of Canada's ... [This obsession is partly explained] by the vagaries of Australia's economic dependence on overseas events making economic issues of direct interest to a large section of the population.
>
> (Groenewegen 1994: vi)

The full realisation of this has only started to impact on me in recent times as I have increasingly engaged in a meta-analysis of what I do as a teacher and an academic, and the way in which external forces are profoundly shaping the nature of all aspects of education in Australia (and elsewhere). While I was trained as an economist and economic historian, I do not work in that area, but rather in teacher education and educational policy, and my interests focus around what is now fashionably termed 'reflective practice', although when I began working with these ideas nearly two decades ago it was much more modestly described as 'school-based teacher development' and 'teachers theorising about their practice'. My interests and mode of work is that of a sociologist, social theorist and policy analyst concerned with the way in which the broader social, economic and political structures are increasingly coming to shape and sustain what passes as teaching and learning.

The work I engage in with experienced teachers is founded on a view that what is taught and learned is a social, historical, political and economic (as well as a pedagogical) act, and that these are crucial framing and contextual facets of the work of teaching and learning that must be reflected upon and acted upon by teachers themselves. In other words, teaching is an avowedly political activity. Having said that, teaching has a largely cognitive and psychological (as distinct from a sociological) legacy, that is not always fully acknowledged – a factor that is not altogether unimportant in determining how teaching is defined, what constitute shortfalls in teaching, what gets looked at and what are deemed to be solutions to proposed problems. Framing teaching in essentially individualistic ways means that matters of broader import, such as the structure of society and how power is used and in whose interests, are issues that conveniently get pushed off the agenda of reflective practice in education. My work has been involved in trying to put this political dimension back on the agenda for teachers and education generally, in ways that enable teachers to see the nature of their own implication and complicity in those broader structures.

The forces shaping the work of teachers are being driven by a largely economic agenda and the lexicon of business and the corporate sector. Schools and teachers are simultaneously blamed for the uncompetitive state of our economies, while at the same time being held up as the mechanism by which our problems might be solved – provided that a particular narrow instrumental view of teaching is strictly adhered to. The claim is that if teachers engage students in more basic skills, set more homework, enforce discipline more rigorously, require teachers to be better at covering content, while testing teachers and appraising their work more closely – then all our problems will dissipate. The claim is one that has a good deal of community currency to it, especially when backed up by anecdotal evidence of *some* disgruntled employers who are able to cite *some* instances of functional illiteracy among *some* of their employees. It seems not to matter that schools are at the sharp end of trying to deal with an increasing range of complexities brought about by the disintegration of social, institutional and family structures.

'What I do' can be broadly characterised as trying to work with teachers so that they can come to see themselves as having agency as 'political actors' (see Ginsburg 1988, White and White 1986, Stevens 1987, Carlson 1987), and who *can* and *do* have a stake in changing the work of teaching. Referring to teaching in this way is not a form of nomenclature, however, that rests easily with many teachers, who have been enculturated into ways of thinking and acting that leave them as little more than implementers of other people's agenda. Teaching is a conservative occupation shaped largely in the image of how teachers were taught themselves as students.

In Australia, teachers have been subjected for more than a decade to an orchestrated rhetoric by media and politicians about the pre-eminence of instrumental ways of regarding schooling. They have been assailed with all manner of ways in which it is argued they ought to change the work of teaching to fit with systemic needs and national priorities. Schooling is put to teachers as being fundamentally about vocationalism, skills formation, flexibility, responsiveness, competitiveness and the international market place – in a context in which educational providers are expected to become leaner and meaner, while producing educational outcomes that are acceptable to local communities who are expected, at the same time, to pick up responsibility for local decision making.

The notion of 'devolution' of responsibility, but not power and control (and there is a fundamental difference: Martin *et al.* 1994), is rapidly becoming the *sine qua non* of educational governance, as politicians divest themselves of responsibility for education while continuing to steer at a distance through the retention of the power to make and enforce policy. The difficulty with the way devolution is being spoken about, is that it reads and sounds logical and persuasive, and for many teachers it has a certain surface appeal to it. The need to have 'effective' and 'well-managed' schools is not something that many of us would want to challenge. What is much less clear, however, is whose views of what is effective will prevail, whose views will be marginalised, and whose ultimately denied or silenced. Students of non-English-speaking and working-class backgrounds are the ones most likely to be homogenised and oriented towards middle-class values and standards.

Much of what I have been doing for the past decade and a half has been associated with working with teachers to in some ways reclaim their teaching.

HOW DID I COME TO DO THIS?

This is not an easy question to answer. Being a former high school teacher and teacher activist in the 1960s, and seeing that things could indeed be changed through collective action, left a profound mark on me. Certainly, the period of the 1960s in Victorian high schools were interesting times, as teachers who had been educated in universities began to exercise their minds and their industrial muscle on what constituted reasonable standards of professional preparation for people wishing to be teachers. It was the teacher union movement in Victoria, at least in high schools, that forced employing authorities to comply with minimum standards of training for anyone deemed fit to be competent to be a secondary teacher – this was at a time when the only employer requirement was to be upright and breathing! Many high school teachers had four years of university education, but this was not a requirement and many had no post-school education at all. So, there was a significant issue beginning to emerge as teachers themselves began to form a view about what kind of occupational group they saw themselves belonging to.

The other related issue which galvanised many teachers of this era was the question of who had the right to pass judgement on what was a competent teacher. The practice was to use inspectors, who periodically invaded the psychological and working space of teachers, often in ways that were totally ineffectual so far as making any changes to teaching. Looking back, I can see that the seeds were sown for me at this time, that there had to be better ways of dealing with the question of how teachers might make sense of their work. It was not simply a question of how to make technical changes to teaching, but how to understand something about the wider forces operating to shape and influence the work of teaching.

One of the things that struck me early on as a teacher, even after we had been successful in having the inspectorial system abandoned, was that the work of teaching was still quite closely framed by a number of factors (many of which are very much taken for granted) that operate to constrain what it is we do and how we do it. I was reminded of this only recently through the experiences of someone I was working with in assisting her to reflect on her work as a teacher. She had been giving a lesson to a group of grade 3 students in which she wanted them to see that how we view things depends on what perspective we hold. She had the class perched on their desktops when a parent knocked at the door to collect her son to take him to the dentist. The teacher spoke at length and in detail in her journal of her concern about what the parent thought was going on in the classroom, and whether she should be using such unconventional approaches. The point is, how teachers teach is largely framed by what they believe is the acceptable norm (children being passive, sitting in desks, with the teacher 'in charge' at the front of the room), regardless of whether other approaches might be pedagogically more effective.

The work of teaching and teacher education is heavily predicated upon instrumental questions. 'How-to' questions – like how to 'plan' a lesson; how to 'control' an unruly class; how to handle questions of 'equity and social justice'; how to choose among a range of possible 'teaching methods'; and how to 'assess' whether learning has occurred – are not only questions of technique, as they are often construed. They are heavily imbued with all manner of *moral*, *ethical* and *political* choices, most of which are not on public display. How we choose to structure a lesson; what perspectives we decide to allow to be included in content; what perspectives we exclude; even where we start and where we finish: these are all matters that have to do with values – whose knowledge is important? (and by implication, whose is not?); who is included in the way we structure a lesson or use a particular method? (and who is excluded?); and what kinds of images and impressions are we conveying to students about what we consider to be important, or worthless? These are not questions that are always apparent to us, nor are they ones that we are likely to regularly ask ourselves as we embark on the work of teaching – *but they are there*, and how we address them (even if we don't ask them) is still going to convey messages to our students.

Peter Elbow summarised what I am alluding to when he said teaching is a process of 'embracing contraries'. It is a continual struggle:

> because it calls on skills or mentalities that are actually contrary to each other and thus tend to interfere with each other ... [T]he two conflicting mentalities needed for good teaching stem from the two conflicting obligations inherent in the job: we have an obligation to students but we also have an obligation to knowledge and society.
>
> (Elbow 1983: 327)

The contraries Elbow refers to take the form of coming to grips with the fact, as Carr (1992) put it, that there are not 'simple, final and conclusive answers to complex questions'. According to Carr, 'any teacher who has ceased to think further about such matters is no longer able to see the entire enterprise of education as ... inherently problematic, [and] is no longer properly functioning or progressing as a mature professional' (1992: 248). Because many of the questions surrounding teaching and teacher education are 'open-ended' and therefore not amenable to 'straightforward answers and solutions', what we are really dealing with is something that, at its heart, is a 'moral practice which is deeply implicated in values and conflicts of values, more than a technological enterprise directed towards the optimum achievement of pre-determined or agreed ends' (p. 248). He makes the point through an example:

> If my car comes to a dead stop because of a broken timing chain, it may be a lengthy, complex and expensive business to dismantle the car and replace it, but given that I need that car and want it repaired there are no real problems about what I should do other than how to get it done. But, on the other hand, if I want to exercise discipline over an unruly class and have discovered that wiring the children's desk seats to the national grid and administering short sharp shocks to recalcitrants secures the necessary order, the discovery of this straightforward pragmatic solution to a practical educational problem hardly concludes matters but raises considerable further problems about what I am up to in educational terms.
>
> (Carr 1992: 248)

The argument is that in teaching our *means* are related to our *ends*, not in a technical, but rather in a moral and political way. Put another way, in a moral practice like education:

> ... our aims and goals are not logically separable or distinct from the procedures we adopt for their achievement. Presumably we do not just require *any* order of discipline in the classroom but a particular sort of order or discipline. We ought not ... to want order and discipline which is based on fear, resentment and discourtesy, because presumably ... confidence, trust and courtesy are some of the qualities that we want children to acquire.
>
> (Carr 1992: 249)

Hextall *et al.* (1991) argue that what we need to do to break the 'circuit of power' (Clegg 1989) are 'imaginative projects' – that is to say, ones that genuinely engage with what it means to be a 'reflective teacher' in terms of a range of competencies that extend considerably beyond the candidates normally considered for appraisal in teacher education. Such a profile of items might include:

- A reflective teacher tries to stand back from their own practice and identify and specify from within that practice features, areas or skills which call for further development;
- A reflective teacher can articulate and defend their own purpose as a teacher and relate this to other professional opinion;
- A reflective teacher recognises that within practice, dilemmas will arise which must be honestly confronted, analysed and acted upon and which, although they may be managed, may not be resolved;
- A reflective teacher observes and records the social and learning processes in the school and the classroom, as a basis for reflection upon development and action;
- A reflective teacher treats teaching as an experimental process – recognising the necessity of turning reflection into action, choosing between alternatives and critically evaluating the process;
- A reflective teacher can produce coherent accounts of their practice in terms of their intention or purpose and defend this view in relation to another's perception of practice and purpose;
- A reflective teacher can produce accounts of how their actions in the classroom are coherent with their personal, professional stance.

(Hextall *et al.* 1991: 87)

Construed in this way, being competent takes on a wider mantle of not only acknowledging 'on-the-spot, thoughtful and consequential decision-making, based on an interpretation of what is happening in the classroom at any given moment' (p. 86), but that it is embedded in an awareness of the 'constant struggle' – the recognition of conflicts, the weighing of the evidence, the consideration of possible responses, the strategic acts (p. 87).

Part of the process of doing this, Hextall *et al.* argue, lies in developing different kinds of partnerships and close co-operation between schools, employing authorities and universities, in which the partners are prepared to negotiate and recognise, in a mutually respectful way, the contributions others in the network can make. It is not a kind of partnership that leads us in the direction of 'more classroom contact' nor 'more observation of practice work [by] the student', because that is a false version of what it means to be 'practical' – it is a 'training model built on technical, low level skills which separates, artificially "doing" from "thinking about doing" or action from reflection upon it' (p. 91).

The other point to be made in all of this, is that how we choose to teach is not something that can or should be regarded as the outcome solely of individual will, disposition, preference or style. Hursh (1992) puts it that because education is political 'in the sense that the organisation of the school, curriculum content, and practices are outcomes of contested political goals' (p. 5), then how we operate in classrooms is always constrained and mediated by the 'discourses, practices and structure of the school' (p. 5). His claim is that teaching is the outcome of political, moral, historical and ethical differences, rather than quirks of style, and that what we need are ways of exposing and exploring the interests served and denied within particular forms of classroom organisation and pedagogical technique.

SPECIFICALLY, WHAT DO I DO?

One of the methods I use in trying to get teachers (and intending teachers) to think and act more expansively (that is to 'problematise' their teaching – see Smyth 1987 for a full treatment), is to look for the wider connections in their work and the social context in which it occurs.

One clear way of doing this is to listen to teachers' voices more, and less to the captains of industry that lie behind so-called 'educational reforms'. Much current educational restructuring, for instance, is being driven from places other than classrooms, and as a consequence the question needs to be asked and answered as to why there is such a lack of emphasis on not only acknowledging but loudly celebrating teachers' theories about what works. Working in ways suggested by the latter is to treat teachers in ways that acknowledge that teaching is a form of 'intellectual struggle', and that teachers are not unthinking technicians – which is the impression left when change is externally initiated. It also involves being more trusting of teachers, and not treating them in ways that are implicitly distrustful.

The extremely complex nature of the work (and that teachers are dealing with greater ranges of abilities, backgrounds, social, emotional and physical needs than ever before) ought to be recognised, putting to rest the view that teaching is something that anybody can do! This also means that when students don't learn as expected, those outside of schools should be less hasty in pointing the finger at teachers, and look more closely at the context within which teachers work, asking if the work of teaching is being properly supported.

Another way of achieving the kind of status for teachers and students being aspired to here is in terms of curriculum being constructed around the 'lived experiences' of children and teachers, rather than crafted around national profiles that are allegedly aimed at restoring sagging international competitiveness. What is needed, above all, is encouragement of 'deliber-ate improvisation' in teaching, so as to move beyond processes that produce 'compliant' and 'defiant' kids. This means providing the kind of circumstances in which teachers feel comfortable and compelled to call into question the basic assumptions about teaching and learning – and to radically change those if experience tells them otherwise. Construed in these terms, teaching ought to be about engaging with the 'big questions' that fire the 'imagination', the 'spirit', the 'feelings' and the 'intellect' (Clifford and Friesen 1993).

To be more specific, the project in which I have worked with teachers has them frame their thinking and actions (individually and collectively) with such questions as:

1 Am I prepared to endure discomfort?
2 Am I willing to challenge taken-for-granted (even cherished) assumptions and beliefs?
3 Am I willing to begin to 'describe' and 'theorise' about what is going on here?
4 What, then, is actually going on here?
5 How do I know what's happening here?
6 What else do I need to know about what is going on?
7 Who says this is the way things should happen?
8 How did things come to be the way they are?
9 Whose interests are served by having things this way?
10 Why do I teach this way?
11 Whose interests are served in these circumstances?
12 Whose interests are silenced or denied?
13 What are the impediments to change?
14 How might I work differently?
15 What kind of resistance might I expect?
16 How do I intend to tackle that?
17 How can I create different social relationships in my classroom and in the school at large?
18 What hierarchies (authority, gender, race, class, etc.) exist around me?
19 Schools are never neutral value-free sites – whose politics are served?
20 What's educationally worthwhile fighting for here?

While these are questions that apply in my case to teachers and my own work as a teacher educator, they could equally well apply to adult and community educators generally.

WHAT, THEN, IS IMPORTANT, AND WHAT IDEAS HAVE INFLUENCED ME?

To engage one's work in a socially critical way is to start from the presumption that schools *ought to* exist for reasons other than reproducing dominant (and supposedly neutral) viewpoints, ideologies and sets of social and economic relationships. Through curricula intentions and the ways in which these are translated into practice through materials used, conceptions of teaching that accompany them and the status attributed to students, educational institutions *should be* about developing practices that not only enable, but require, that we empower students to draw upon 'their own cultural resources as a basis for engaging in the development of new skills and interrogating existing knowledge claims' (Sultana 1990: 19). In other words, being socially critical is to be concerned with teachers and students (however we choose to define them), working to decode and interpret their everyday realities in the quest for alternatives that are 'more humane, just and equitable' (Sultana 1990: 19). In this, we are speaking about three interrelated moments:

> First, ... knowledge [is viewed] as socially produced, legitimated, and distributed and seeks to make explicit the ways in which such production, legitimation, and distribution take place. Second, knowledge is apprehended as expressing and embodying particular interests and values, implicating issues of power and ethics in all expressions of knowledge. Third, seeking to negate the 'objective' nature of knowledge and forcing the educator to confront the relation between knowledge, power and control, [critical pedagogy] additionally requires the articulation and consideration of transformative action – that is, action that would alter the distribution of power and increase the range and scope of possibilities for individually and collectively defined projects.
>
> (Simon 1985: 1119)

The fact that corporate managerialism is rampant in schools and educational institutions, and is antagonistic to teachers, politicising their work, discouraging them from reflecting on the linkages between their work and issues of power and control, is no reason to shy away from the issue; if anything, it bolsters the case for the reverse. It is the press for vocationalism that makes it even more imperative that as teachers we engage in problematising our work (Smyth 1991a). As Orlando Fals Borda (1979) said, you have to 'investigate reality in order to transform it'.

If teachers are to uncover the forces that inhibit and constrain them, and work at changing those conditions, then they need to be assisted to engage in four forms of action best characterised by several moments (which I have described elsewhere – see Smyth 1991b), and linked to a series of questions:

1 Describe ... what do I do?
2 Inform ... what does this mean?
3 Confront ... how did I come to be like this?
4 Reconstruct ... how might I do things differently?

Broadly speaking, the project in which I have been engaged is concerned with facilitating the process of teachers theorising about their practice, in a context in which they seek to locate that practice in the broader social, political and economic context in which it is inextricably embedded. In doing this change is regarded by all participants in the project as starting with each of us personally – it is not (as often tends to be the case) something which is good for somebody else. But, having said that, this is not to suggest that change *must* continue to reside in the individual – but it needs to *start there*, and then move to others. Change is a social and collective phenomenon.

The teachers with whom I have been working start out the reflective process at the level of their practice as classroom teachers. One of the requirements (although it may seem paradoxical to have an element of 'compulsion' in what is a 'voluntary' activity) is that they have a preparedness to begin to reflect in collective, collaborative and participatory ways with others similarly engaged in the project. On occasions this has meant participants establishing and sustaining contact with colleagues over quite long geographic distance for periods of several months, as they share experiences – often in other than face-to-face ways, using phone, mail, fax and other electronic means. The important point is that nobody engages in this reflection without a sustained sharing of it with other people – there must be a preparedness to do this from the outset, sharing insights as well as frustrations with others.

To put this another way, individuals undertook to 'describe', 'inform', 'confront' and 'reconstruct' their teaching, but they did this in a context in which they continually conferred with one another, comparing, contrasting, supporting, critiquing and working to sustain the energy and enthusiasm necessary for authentic change. In other words, there was a collective dimension to the activity, built on people engaging themselves individually and *then* moving to share that dialogue with others. It is important to know this because what follows could otherwise be seen as an individualistic process, which it was not.

1 Describing

Starting with teaching as a text to be described and then untied for the meaning it reveals, provides a form of accessibility which has a lot of appeal. Articulating the principles that lie behind teaching (as a prelude to critiquing them), teachers must start with a consideration of current practice as the way of gaining access to the 'knowledge, beliefs, and principles that [they] employ in both characterising that practice and deciding what should be done' (Elliott 1987: 151). Written codification can be a powerful guide to engaging in reflective deliberation.

As we reflect about our own (and one another's) teaching and the context within which we enact it, what we are doing is describing concrete teaching events. The teachers I have worked with (Smyth 1991b) have used journals or diaries (Holly 1984, Holly and Smyth 1989) as a way of building up an account of their teaching as a basis for analysis and discussion. Writing a narrative of what occurs in confusing, perplexing or contradictory situations has been a help to them organising accounts of their teaching in ways which were crucial to them finding and speaking their own voices (Fulwiler 1987). These descriptions do not have to be complex or in academic language – on the contrary, if there is to be genuine ownership, it is important that such descriptions be in teachers' own language. If teachers can create a text that comprises the elements of their teaching, then there is a likelihood they will have the basis upon which to dialogue with one another so as to see how their consciousness was formed in the first place, and how it might be changed. In Shor's (1980) terms, when teachers keep journals they are able to 'extra-ordinarily re-experience the ordinary', in a manner that enables them to see how the elements of particular situations alienate and confuse them, and impose real limits on what it is possible.

2 *Informing*

When teachers describe their teaching it is not an end in itself – rather a precursor to uncovering the broader principles that are informing (consciously or otherwise) classroom action. As Kretovics (1985) put it, it is a way of beginning to confront the 'structured silences' that abound in teaching. Creating narratives is a way of uncovering what Tripp (1987) calls 'local theories'. When teachers engage in unpicking descriptions of their teaching, they begin the process of recapturing the pedagogical principles of what it is they do. They are in effect seeking to develop defensible practical principles 'grounded in a largely tacit knowledge of complex and particular situations' (Elliott 1987: 152). Such theories may fall well short of being generalisable, but the contradictions and binary oppositions they contain are highly significant in explaining the nature of idiosyncratic work contexts. What teachers are trying to do is to move teaching out of the realm of the mystical, so as to begin to see through discussion with others, the nature of the forces that cause them to operate in the way they do and how they can move beyond intellectualising the issues to concrete action for change.

Educational research assumes that theories about teaching are developed by people outside of classrooms, then transfused into classrooms to be applied by teachers. Such a view of research is highly problematic in that it takes no account of the extensive experiential wisdom possessed by most teachers. The problem, then, is a political one of who has the right to define what counts as knowledge about teaching. As Kohl said:

> Unless we [as teachers] assume the responsibility for theory making and testing, the theories will be made for us by ... the academic researchers and many other groups that are simply filling the vacuum that teachers have created by bargaining away their educational power and giving up their responsibility as intellectuals.
>
> (Kohl 1983: 30)

3 *Confronting*

Theorising one's practice and the circumstances of its enactment is one thing, but being able to subject those theories to interrogation and questioning that establishes their legitimacy is another matter. Yet, if we are to be clear about what it is that we do as educators, and why we do it, then it is imperative that we move to this stage. We need to regard teaching not as idiosyncratic preferences, but as the product of deeply entrenched cultural norms. Locating or situating teaching in a broader cultural, social and political context amounts to engaging in critical reflection about the assumptions that underlie methods and classroom practices. Teaching thus becomes less of an isolated set of technical procedures, and more of a historical expression of shaped values about what is considered to be important about the educative act. When teachers write about their own biographies and how they feel these have shaped the construction of their values, then they are able to see more clearly how social and institutional forces beyond the classroom and school have been influential.

It is possible for teachers to approach this confrontation of their theories of teaching through a series of guiding questions, that might include the following:

- What do my practices say about my assumptions, values and beliefs about teaching?
- Where did these ideas come from?
- What social practices are expressed in these ideas?
- What is it that causes me to maintain my theories?
- What views of power do they embody?
- Whose interests seem to be served by my practices?
- What is it that acts to constrain my views of what is possible in teaching?

(Smyth 1987)

This amounts to a way of problematising teaching by asking poignant questions about the 'social causation' (Fay 1977) of those actions. Untangling and re-evaluating taken-for-granted (even cherished) practices requires breaking into well-entrenched and constructed mythologies that may not always be easily dislodged.

4 Reconstructing

Locating oneself personally and professionally in history so as to be clear about the forces that have come to determine one's professional existence is the hallmark of a teacher who has begun to act on the world. Seeing teaching not as immutable givens but as being defined for them by others enables teachers to see the tenets of teaching as being contestable. If teachers are to experience their lives in authentic terms, then they have to expel the internalised images that researchers, administrators and policy makers are so deft at perpetuating. By constructing portrayals of their own teaching that are embedded in the particularities of that teaching, they are able to exercise control through self-government, self-regulation and self-responsibility. Acting in these ways is to deny the artificially constructed separation of thought from action, of theory from practice, of mental from manual labour, and to jettison the false and oppressive view that people outside of classrooms know what is 'best' about teaching.

When teachers begin to link consciousness about the processes that inform the day-to-day aspects of their teaching with the wider political and social realities within which it occurs, then they are able to transcend self-blame for things that don't work out and to see that perhaps their causation may more properly lie in the social injustices and palpable inequities of society – which is to say, deficiencies in teaching can be caused by the manner in which dominant groups in society pursue narrow sectional interests. Only when teachers take an active reflective stance are they able to challenge the dominant factory metaphor of the way schools are conceived, organised and enacted. Being socially critical, therefore, means starting with reality, with seeing injustices and contradictions, and beginning to overturn reality by reasserting the importance of learning.

HOW IS MY OWN PRACTICE REFLEXIVE OF ITS AGENDA?

The process of my own reflection, and the wider forces that shape and form how I work with participating teachers, is not a matter that ought to go unexamined. I must admit, however, that as a formal process this was not a part of this chapter until the editors challenged me to include such a section. This is quite intriguing because on other occasions (Smyth 1989) I have gone to some lengths to include such material; suffice to say, that reflection suffers significantly because it is frequently deemed to be a process that is good for others, and its most erstwhile advocates somehow escape having to model what it is they so ardently propose.

In my case, the process of journalling works in a way that is sufficiently dialogical and open as to enable both myself and the teachers to reflect on how the process of reflection is working for all of us – indeed, we often consciously pose this as a deliberate question to be addressed on occasions. The consequence is that the very act of reflection is continually in the process of being re-focused in the light of collective experience, and particularly in respect of how the participating teachers believe it might work better for them. An illustration may serve to make my point. Early on, it became clear that teachers keeping journals individually was a useful but extremely limited activity – there was a need, I believed, to explode the walls of privatism that placed such strictures on the work of teaching, and to make teaching into a genuinely collaborative, sharing community. Fine ideal, but it was grossly at variance with the way teachers were socialised and the self-images they had of themselves as competent stand-alone practitioners. What I was trying to do in having them share their journals (and admit on occasions to failure and being inadequate) transgressed one of the most deeply entrenched norms of teaching – namely, appearing to be in control and competent to colleagues at all times. The journalling process, and the kind of public disclosures I was suggesting, had all of the portents of severely undermining this. I therefore had to grapple hard with the dilemma of how to simultaneously sustain one of the most fundamental norms of teaching that endorsed individual self-efficacy, while at the same time working to actively interrupt if not completely supplant it. This was a contradiction I struggled with at some length, and even now have only partially resolved it.

Likewise, my own status and location in the process of working with teachers to critically reflect on their teaching is continually in a process of re-definition. On the one hand, I am the instigator of the process (albeit at their request), but nevertheless in a position of power, and yet I am continually reminded that in processes of this kind nothing occurs unless teachers give me provisional authority to work with them in ways that they find personally and professionally satisfying. It is the continually changing nature of this provisionality that has to be negotiated and re-negotiated, for without it nothing is possible beyond the most instrumentalist and shallow of activities. In the final analysis, the lived experiences that are reflected upon by the teachers must be owned by them even if I have difficulties (as I often do) with the profundity of what it is that is being reflected upon. I try, where possible (and when invited to do so), to open up what I consider might be robust and fertile possible candidates for reflection – but they are always imbued with my own biases and predilections, and to get teachers to own them means being prepared to give up part of themselves to my view of the world. In the end I only ever resolve this tension too in a limited way by openly acknowledging my experiences, motivations and aspirations and inviting teachers to do likewise. In the end, this is what reflection must ultimately be about – a preparedness to be open about one's experiences, and to share those in a context of dialogue, contestation and debate, even if that means having to justify what it is we do in a much more public way. For to do that is to be open to possibilities that might be beyond our range of vision, and to see our biases, preferences and assumptions in a different light.

NOTE

Some of the ideas contained in this chapter draw heavily on my 'Socially critical approach to teacher education' (Smyth 1993), which is reproduced in part here, with permission.

REFERENCES

Borda, O. F. (1979) 'Investigating reality in order to transform it: the Columbian experience', *Dialectical Anthropology*, 4, 1, 33–55.
Carlson, D. (1987) 'Teachers as political actors', *Harvard Education Review* 57, 3, 283–306.

Carr, D. (1992) 'Practical enquiry, values and the problem of educational theory', *Oxford Review of Education*, 18, 3, 241–251.

Clegg, S. (1989) *Frameworks of Power*, Newbury Park: Sage.

Clifford, P. and Freisen, S. (1993) 'A curious plan: managing on the twelfth', *Harvard Educational Review*, 63, 3, 339–354.

Elbow, P. (1983) 'Embracing contraries in the teaching process', *College English*, 45, 4, 327–339.

Elliott, J. (1987) 'Educational theory, practical philosophy and action research', *British Journal of Educational Studies*, 35, 149–169.

Evatt Foundation (1994) *The State of Australian Government 1993–94*, Sydney: Evatt Foundation.

Fay, B. (1977) 'How people change themselves: the relationship between critical theory and its audience', in T. Ball (ed.) *Political Theory and Praxis: New Perspectives*, Minneapolis: University of Minnesota Press, 200–233.

Fulwiler, T. (ed.) (1987) *The Journal Book*, Portsmouth, NH: Boynton/Cook.

Ginsburg, M. (1988) 'Educators as workers and political actors in Britain and North America', *British Journal of Sociology of Education*, 9, 3: 359–367.

Groenewegen, P. (1994) 'Foreword', in *The State of Australian Government 1993–94*, Sydney: Evatt Foundation.

Hextall, I., Lawn, M., Menter, I., Sidgwick, S. and Walker, S. (1991) 'Imaginative projects: arguments for a new teacher education', *Evaluation and Research in Education*, 5, 1 and 2, 79–95.

Holly, M. (1984) *Keeping a Personal/Professional Journal*, Geelong, Australia: Deakin University Press.

Holly, M. and Smyth, J. (1989) 'The journal as a way of theorising teaching', *The Australian Administrator*, 10, 3 and 4, 1–8.

Hursh, D. (1992) 'Re-politicising pedagogy: developing ethically and critically reflective teachers within the liberal discourse of teacher education programs', *Critical Pedagogy Networker*, 4, 4 and 5, 1–7.

Kohl, H. (1983) 'Examining closely what we do', *Learning*, 12, 1, 28–30.

Kretovics, J. (1985) 'Critical literacy: challenging the assumptions of mainstream educational theory', *Journal of Education*, 167, 2, 50–61.

Martin, R., McCollow, J., McFarlane, L., McMurdo, G., Graham, J. and Hull, R. (eds) (1994) *Devolution, Decentralisation and Recentralisation: The Structure of Australian Schooling*, Melbourne: Australian Education Union.

Shor, I. (1980) *Critical Teaching and Everyday Life*, Montreal: Black Rose Press.

Simon, R. (1985) 'Critical pedagogy', in T. Husen and N. Postlethwaite (eds) *International Encyclopedia of Education: Research and Studies*, vol. 2, London: Pergamon Press, 1118–1120.

Smyth, J. (1987) *Rationale for Teachers' Critical Pedagogy: A Handbook*, Geelong, Australia: Deakin University Press.

—— (1989) 'A critical pedagogy of classroom practice', *Journal of Curriculum Studies*, 21, 6, 483–502.

—— (1991a) 'Problematising teaching through a critical approach to clinical supervision', *Curriculum Inquiry*, 21, 3, 321–352.

—— (1991b) *Teachers as Collaborative Learners: Challenging Dominant Forms of Supervision*, Buckingham: Open University Press.

—— (1992) 'The practical and the political dimensions of teaching', *Education Links*, 43, 4–8.

—— (1993) 'A socially critical approach to teacher education', in T. Simpson (ed.) *Teacher Educators' Annual Handbook*, Brisbane: Queensland University of Technology, 153–165.

Stevens, P. (1987) 'Political education and political teachers', *Journal of Philosophy of Education*, 21, 1, 75–83.

Sultana, R. (1990) 'Towards a critical teaching practice', *Journal of Further and Higher Education*, 14, 10, 14–30.

Tripp, D. (1987) 'Teachers, journals and collaborative research', in J. Smyth (ed.) *Educating Teachers: Changing the Nature of Pedagogical Knowledge*, Lewes: Falmer Press, 179–192.

White, J. and White, P. (1986) 'Teachers as political activists', in A. Hartnett and M. Naish (eds) *Education and Society Today*, Lewes: Falmer Press, 171–182.

Part 2

5 Sharing the secrets of perspectives
Operating honestly in the classroom

Joyce Stalker

How do I deal with learners' experiences? One might well ask, since as a Senior Lecturer at the University of Waikato in New Zealand I stand in front of classes that vary in size from two or three hundred students to 'small' groups of twenty-five. Furthermore, as a Canadian standing in front of both Maori and Pakeha New Zealand students, I cannot relate directly to many of their experiences even in the smaller classes. The Land March, Bastion Point, Rugby League, Christmas on the beach – there is an endless array of experiences which have shaped the perspectives of my students, yet which are miles away from my experiences of peace marches in Vancouver, skating across the lake and Christmas afternoon walks through snowy woods.

My strategy, faced with this potentially alienating situation, is to introduce students to a framework which they can use independently to understand and to analyse their own and others' experiences. Theoretically, one might not expect a framework to create critical reflection. After all, it represents a fairly rigid representation of ambiguous, dynamic and complex concepts. None the less, pedagogically, this framework accomplishes that difficult task.

Introduced at the beginning of my courses, it gives students the tools to undertake informed analyses of their environments. Regardless of their academic level, students learn to recognise the subtle manipulations which occur in the classroom, through readings and during activities. Indeed, they often extend these analyses and examine the ways in which media, government, religious and family structures skilfully direct their lives. In other words, they become thinkers who are truly critical. They locate sites of power, authority and control and explore the mechanisms by which those phenomena are maintained.

It makes for a complicated situation to have students become critical within institutions and a wider society which are guided by rules and regulations. Such insights can encourage them to challenge us and the institutions for which we work. Fortunately, this framework also seems to foster more honest encounters among learners, and between learners and myself. Healthy, positive discussions, challenges and negotiations are more possible in a learning situation when the 'secrets' of the assumptions which underlie the learners' and my approaches to the learning experience are evident. Dichotomous, defensive and confrontational debates are less frequent if we all understand the different bases from which our comments emerge.

In view of the above, the purpose of this chapter is to present the framework which helps learners to understand and to analyse their own and others' experiences. The four categories within this framework, for the most part, parallel my own perspectives and practices as an adult educator over the years. This is to be expected, since each perspective was dominant at the same time as I grew into the world of adult education. Indeed, it is an interactive and interrelated relationship in which as adult educators we both create, maintain and reflect the dominant perspectives in society. Therefore, I present the four categories as I experienced them and as they influenced my practice as an adult educator. Perhaps this will help readers to connect their experiences and practices with mine and thus to locate themselves within the framework. The presentation of the four categories are followed by a brief discussion of the caveats which accompany them. The chapter then describes selected activities which are useful for reinforcing and clarifying the concepts and closes with a brief conclusion.

A FRAMEWORK FOR UNDERSTANDING AND ANALYSING EXPERIENCES

Consensus perspective

When I look back, it was inevitable that as a young woman I would hold a consensus perspective of the world. I grew up in a large, happy, farming family in a conservative, rural area. The charitable underpinnings of our involvement with the church, my parents' unflagging belief in hard work and effort, all were congruent with this perspective.

Sharing many of the elements and characteristics of functionalist and structuralist viewpoints, the consensus perspective evolved during the 1950s and early 1960s (Karabel and Halsey 1977) – my childhood years. It dovetailed neatly with the optimism and social stability of the years in which 'first world' job opportunities flourished, economies stabilised and confidence in the future grew. At the same time, money was allocated generously to educational institutions for new programmes and for innovative approaches. There was hope that these increased opportunities would attract those who were traditionally less likely to participate. My childhood reflected these good times. I remember, for example, that during these years we acquired a speed boat and I began practising my slalom waterskiing style on the bay in front of our house!

The consensus view of society is of a harmonious, stable, balanced and static form which functions successfully. These represent the situation in which some individuals have more power, authority and control than others. Regardless of their dominant perspective, most people acknowledge these differences. It is, after all, impossible to ignore the contrast between those who live in mansions and those who live beneath the bridges. For those who hold a consensus perspective this hierarchical relationship is viewed as completely normal. There is a sense that 'the poor will always be with us'. Indeed, on the way to my one-room school in Adolphustown, it never crossed my mind that things could be different for the unemployed family who had a lawn full of broken down cars and dogs who nipped at my legs as I peddled frantically past. It was 'just the way it was' and, like most in our community, I had a strong belief that this family had an attitude problem and could make it if they tried.

Theoretically this differential power is seen as essential for the continuance of a smoothly operating society in which some are more able to lead and others more suited to follow. Society is similar to a smoothly operating, living organism in which each element is unique, but interdependent on each other element. Continued equilibrium and survival of the society as a whole are of paramount importance. Consensus individuals suggest that these differently empowered groups of individuals interact smoothly with each other. They recognise that disputes and tensions may exist and that change might occur. However, change is viewed as a process which happens smoothly, slowly, gently. Somewhat like differently sized ball bearings moving in thick fluid, the differently empowered groups nudge each other and slight changes occur gradually over a period of time.

Consensus theorists acknowledge that a slightly modified form of society might result; however, they believe that the preferred resolution fundamentally perpetuates and maintains the status quo. In other words, those with a consensus view accept, maintain and perpetuate the existing social, political, cultural and economic structures.

In my own life as a child and a young adult, certainly I was proud of the Canadian system. I viewed changes as more a matter of tinkering with a democratic system which fundamentally worked well than a matter of significant changes. After all, Canada bragged of its high standard of living and clearly provided 'the good life' for those who applied themselves.

This stress on the responsibilities of individuals is typical of those who hold the consensus perspective. They point to the rewards which are achievable and deserved by those who work hard and persevere. This sentiment lends itself to an emphasis on the notion of equality of opportunity. All individuals are deemed to be acting on a level playing field. In other words, equality is about treating unequals equally, providing equal access to all. Individuals' efforts determine the winners. By the same logic, consensus theorists regard poverty, unemployment or non-participation, for example, as the individual's lack of effort. Often, these individuals are labelled as 'disadvantaged' and emphasis is placed on their 'special needs'. There is a hint that they are somehow deviant or abnormal and their behaviour is often explained in psychological terms as the end product of learned behaviour and socialisation.

This is not to suggest that people who hold a consensus view are without warm hearts and sincere interest in the well-being of others. That is far too harsh a judgement and never fit the reality of my parents' generosity and concern for others. What is clear, however, is that members of my childhood community, in typical consensus fashion, based the solutions to these situations in a charitable approach. Sometimes this meant a beneficent distribution of gifts from those who had resources to those 'in need'. Decades later, and on the other side of Canada, I watched this same phenomenon as my mother was pressured to donate her handworked quilts to the poor of their island community.

Increasingly, this top-down charitable approach is institutionalised and focuses on remedial courses and programmes to improve the attitudes, behaviours and skills of those individuals who have 'failed'. I was involved with an adult basic education course in northern Canada when I held this consensus perspective. It was a remedial programme designed in modularised, competency-based, individualistic units. The content, based in white middle-class values and experiences, was used by mostly First Nations' women students. Their experiences of culture, tradition and language were not incorporated into the programmed units. I enthusiastically encouraged my students to complete the course and discussed with the counsellor ways in which I could maintain and improve their motivation, attitudes and social skills. We inserted career counselling sessions and résumé writing sessions. There was a high completion rate among the students and we established a warm and supportive environment which we all enjoyed.

Slowly, however, I began to seriously question this way of working with students' experiences. I read statistical information that indicated my First Nations' students were less likely to find work than my white students – and then I saw that statistical information realised in the experiences of my students. I recognised too that the experiences of First Nations' people paralleled the poverty and oppression within so-called 'third world' countries in Central America where I had recently travelled. With my new insights, I was amazed that my fellow Canadians were as proud as ever of our system, for I felt a deep shame.

Simultaneously I enrolled in a 'Life Skills' course. It stressed the importance of one-to-one communication and listening skills and we 'shared' our experiences and feelings with each other endlessly, the better to facilitate it among our students when we returned to our classrooms. Somehow, it did not make sense to me. I knew these students' lives and I knew that improved communication skills were unlikely to stop their abuse and harassment by some of the local police. My consensus tendency to focus on the individual's potential to create their own experiences continued to shift.

Around the same time, I moved to Australia and worked as an equal employment officer in the public service in New South Wales. I began to read statistical information about the pay levels, employment possibilities and so on for women and for Aborigines. I saw programmes that I judged to be truly helpful to women cut back and less useful ones continued; I began to recall instances where I had been turned down for jobs because I was married; I felt the isolation, humiliation and alienation of an immigrant; I talked to the Aboriginal project officer and noticed how much less support his unit had than many of the others. Finally I understood, too intimately it seemed, experiences of racism, patriarchy, sexism. I was no longer comfortable with the consensus approach to students' experiences.

Conflict perspective

As my perspective was changing, concurrently, the dominant consensus perspective of society was changing. At the end of the 1960s and into the 1970s, this was fostered by three situations. First, internationally recognised research projects (e.g. Bowles and Gintis 1976, Jencks 1972) consistently demonstrated that those who were less likely to participate in education were continuing not to participate. The promises based on equal opportunity and improved access had not been realised. Second, sophisticated statistical computing techniques began to trace the issue of non-participation and drop-out to socio-economic variables. This helped to shift the dominant view away from a focus on the individual to a concern for social issues and structures. Third, there was growth in ideological conflicts. There was a 'sharpening of antagonism between classes, races and nations' (Karabel and Halsey 1977: 29). The Vietnam War, the women's movement and the civil rights movement were three of the more visible conflicts of those years. The conflict perspective became dominant. Specific variations of this view are labelled Marxist, radical, neo-Marxist and critical. For the purposes of providing students with a handy heuristic device, however, I present this, and each of the other perspectives, as an amalgam of the dominant characteristics of those variations.

This view emphasises the dynamic, ever-changing nature of society. Unlike the harmonious, balanced and static society of the previous perspective, the conflict society is viewed as volatile and energised. It is an unstable form within which different kinds of groups exist in a state of tension and confrontation.

Once again, it is possible to identify different groups, the elite and the lower classes, and their differential levels of power, authority and control. However, unlike those with a consensus view who believe that 'the poor will always be with us', those with a conflict view find the differentials of power and authority unacceptable. They strive to create an alternative society based in equally shared power, authority, control and resources.

Change towards that goal is seen as a sharp and destructive process rather than a slow and evolutionary one. It is based in societal struggles in which the elite have the advantages of power, authority, resources and the ability to allocate resources according to their own criteria. The struggle for change becomes obvious when those with less power, authority, control and resources challenge the status quo and harsh confrontation often results.

When I looked at the North American society, I saw scenarios which mirrored and supported this view. Students were killed for their role in the anti-Vietnam movement; Martin Luther King was assassinated as he led the civil rights movement for Afro-Americans. These struggles uncovered the enduring nature of the social, political, cultural and economic structures which ensured the perpetuation of less power among groups such as the working class, the poor and women. It became obvious to me that there were larger forces at work than individuals' attitudes and commitments to work hard. It was clear that being a member of a group with particular ethnicity, race, gender, ability or sexual orientation was enough to condemn even the brightest and most capable person to a second-class status in society.

As I moved into this conflict perspective, I saw social problems and the solutions to those problems in new ways. With others who shared the view, I no longer blamed my students for their experiences of poverty, unemployment or non-participation. We no longer saw them as 'disadvantaged'. Instead we recognised that power structures existed and that these students existed within a context which held the 'oppressed' captive to the advantage of the elite – generation after generation after generation. The problem became one of conflicting macro-level group interests rather than individual inabilities.

These social, political, cultural and economic explanations felt incongruent with the consensus, psychological explanations of 'learned behaviours' and 'socialisation'. The alternate notion of hegemony was more suited to this perspective. It explains individuals' behaviours and attitudes in relation to the political, social, cultural and economic control exerted by the dominant class over the less powerful classes. This control occurs in such a way that the oppression becomes accepted as commonsense and natural. Hegemony is buried deep inside ourselves and it is hard to extricate ourselves from its force. It guides our experiences and our understandings of those experiences in ways which are difficult to pinpoint. Although hegemony and socialisation appear to be similar, the emphasis has shifted from an explanation at the micro, individual level to one at the macro, societal and economic level.

Once the problem of oppression is defined as one of group interests of the elite and hegemonic control, new solutions are created. Such solutions focus on notions of justice and rights rather than on the concept of charity. They replace the maternalistic/paternalistic top-down consensus approach to working with others' experiences with a grassroots, bottom-up emphasis on the rightful and equal claim of oppressed groups to power, control, authority and resources. These claims are seen as valid, legitimate and genuine.

This view lends itself to an emphasis on the notions of equality of outcomes and equity. This is a shift away from the consensus emphasis on equality of opportunity. In order to achieve equality of outcomes, equity must be practised. This means that unequals are treated unequally in order to redress the imbalance of power and the injustices of the past and present. In practical terms, this means targeting members of less powerful groups to give them assistance. My work as an equal employment officer in Australia involved me in this approach. We created workshops and networks to foster the careers of women in the public service. As one might expect, those who held a consensus view of 'you can make it if you try' argued that such programmes gave some people undeserved advantages over others.

While I held this view as my dominant one, working with students' experiences seemed very straightforward. With a largely female student body, it was easy to discuss sexism and the oppression associated with it. In addition, there were few students who had not experienced the powerlessness associated with issues like unemployment, pollution, violence and poverty. I constantly asked students to reframe their analysis of their experiences at the societal rather than at individual or organisational levels. As a result, students became aware of their own dominant perspective. Often this meant that dedicated adult educators were shocked to discover that although they proudly had identified as radical educators for years, their approaches actually were consensus based. Frequently they reassessed their charitable, individualistic approaches. They understood their experiences intellectually through a study of Freire's conscientisation processes and through sociological literature which explored theoretically both the consensus and conflict perspectives (e.g. Jarvis 1985, Rubenson 1980, Thomas 1982). They sought for new models of practice in the community development and 'third world' development literature.

Slowly the clarity of this perspective began to be muddied. I became uncomfortable with the dichotomous identification of categories like elite/working class, man/woman, powerful/powerless. For example, I realised that as a woman I was oppressed, yet as a white woman I held considerably more power than Maori women. I realised sexism was a patriarchal and male-based phenomenon, but I knew some men who were struggling to be something other than patriarchal. The conflict model seemed to give little room for these complexities. It seemed too reductionistic and simplistic. I also found the macro-level discussions, although intellectually stimulating, impractical and unable to explain continuing inequalities. It was one thing to identify the elite as the enemy in the class struggle, but in the end, weren't those groups composed of individuals – and where did the responsibilities of individuals fit into this model? I saw my students struggling with the same issues – fitting their experiences into this model, yet finding the incongruencies unsettling. Added to this for many was a dis-ease with the model's seeming support of direct and conflictual methods of change. I read academic critiques which supported my dis-ease. Like many others in academia, I sought deeper understandings through the interpretive perspective.

Interpretive perspective

To hold an interpretive perspective is to view both the consensus and conflict views as too unequivocal, rigid and simplistic. Rather than perceive society and how it functions in such clear, deterministic ways, one sees the world as a complex place of negotiated understandings. Within this context, groups and individuals create and maintain shared rules and understandings. These are influenced by social, political, cultural and economic contexts. Thus, in one context, a set of keys may indicate wealth, while in another it may represent the torture associated with imprisonment.

From an interpretive perspective, society constantly reshapes itself according to its context. Groups with differential power do not represent a social structure required to make society function well, nor do they represent the oppression of some to the advantage of others. Rather, they represent complex structures which are interrelated and constantly interact to form the particular nature of a society at a particular moment. Interpretivists are intrigued by the shared practices, beliefs and spoken and unspoken agreements among different groups and individuals which guide that society. This is dissimilar to the consensus preoccupation with society's good and the conflict concern for group interests.

This interpretivist preoccupation with the complexities, the intricacies and different dimensions of concepts and situations dovetailed with my growing involvement in academia. It seemed every word or concept I could think of had generated hundreds of books in the English language alone – each with a slightly different interpretation of the concept. At the same time, post-modernists and post-structuralists encouraged and continue to encourage us all to seriously re-examine and re-analyse our experiences and our understandings of them.

From an interpretivist perspective, we examine notions of both equality and equity and extend it to consider equality of conditions. We analyse the many meanings, implications of and interconnections among these concepts. We explore the contexts within which each thrives, fails, is resisted or accepted and so on. These interactions and the changes they engender, or not, are interesting in and of themselves. In other words, one can say that while the consensus view is about maintaining the status quo, and the conflict view is about challenging it, the interpretive view is about examining it and valuing the differences we uncover.

As one might expect, these theorists have a unique interpretation of an individual's or group's situation of poverty, unemployment or non-participation. They are unlike consensus and conflict theorists, who define these situations from their perspectives in terms of 'disadvantage' or 'oppression'. Rather, they see their task as one of uncovering and analysing commonsense understandings and shared systems of meanings of these terms within particular cultures. They are curious to understand them from the position of those who experience them. This emphasis on subjective understandings is also evident in interpretivists' solutions to these situations. Fundamentally, they deem these phenomena to have different meanings and different levels of desirability in different contexts. Thus solutions are not about charity, justice or rights. Rather they are about people's subjectively determined solutions. They are about understanding, accepting and valuing the differences among these solutions.

These elements of the interpretivist perspective are congruent with my own experiences. As a new emigrant to New Zealand, I need to understand a new way of life. History books and local writers provide some insights, but I rely heavily on the experiences of my Maori and Pakeha students. As I further my own understandings of the tensions and possibilities within the country, they simultaneously further their understandings. As we work through role plays of Maori seeking housing accommodation, of unemployment of youth and poverty among the aged, the students use their experiences and extend their knowledge of their country. We explore those problems together and true to the interpretivist paradigm I use to work with their experiences, we explore possible solutions based in consensus, conflict and interpretive perspectives. However, I have never been comfortable with only analysing and understanding problems and solutions. Thus, I combine the interpretive and conflict perspectives. I encourage students to uncover deep understandings and to retain a commitment to social action and the alleviation of oppression. Increasingly this approach is happening within a New Right context.

New Right perspective

The New Right view resembles neo-conservatism, neo-liberalism, Thatcherism, Reaganism and Rogernomics. Like the three previous views, this perspective is not new. Rather, it rose to prominence during the early 1980s. In response to economic crises in the 'first world', the increasing power of women in society, a continuing disenchantment with existing perspectives and an upsurge in moral imperatives, it offered a clear way forward.

A basic premise of this view is that the state has no role intervening in the life of society. Those who hold this view believe that a healthier society results when it is market rather than state governed. Thus they promote the privatisation of state services. They argue that the quality and nature of these services will be regulated best by the market. They believe that only those providers who offer top quality outputs will survive in an open, flexible market place.

This notion of corporate freedom to compete extends to their emphasis on the sovereignty of the individual. They emphasise the absolute freedom of individuals within a New Right society. They believe that individuals' achievements must be uncontaminated, unrestrained and unhampered. As a result, they argue against state interference in the lives of individuals (for example, through benefits for the unemployed) or the false protection of special interest groups (for example, through affirmative action programmes). For those with this perspective, the New Right environment gives the ultimate equality – absolute, unrestricted freedom to achieve success.

In the view of the New Right, it is not useful to label people as poor, unemployed or non-participating. These labels are restricting and inhibit people's potential. Rather, it is important to highlight the freedoms and opportunities for achievement that are possible in the open market place. Similarly, notions of socialisation, hegemony and shared rules are irrelevant. These terms are interesting but do not deal with the reality of a competitive global market in which there are solid economic opportunities for those who identify and pursue them.

It follows that they view poverty, unemployment or non-participation as individuals' lack of imagination in determining the needs of the market place and participating accordingly. Similarly, there is not a designated elite or poor – rather there are simply those who have judged the needs of the New Right environment correctly and those who have not.

These strong emphases on the market place and the sovereignty of the individual are complemented by the promulgation of Christian norms, values and attitudes. Those who hold this perspective argue for a 'return to basics' and the morals associated with the traditional family of the 1950s and heterosexual relationships. Voluntary involvement in the community is encouraged – a scenario which converges nicely with withdrawal of state support for social services.

In New Zealand, the New Right environment is palpable. Funding cutbacks to education, government statements which focus on the importance of education in the global market place, the vocationalisation of education, the increased competition for jobs – students have on-going experiences of the New Right in the 1990s. As the 'lived-in' experience of the moment, this perspective is hard to analyse. It is as if we are too close to examine its subtleties and implications. None the less, it is identifiable and it is firmly entrenched. The challenge I present to students is to draw from the perspective the potentials for creating that more just social world which, from my unrepentant conflict perspective, I continue to hold as a possibility.

CAVEATS

These, then are the four perspectives which I present to students so that they can work independently to understand their own and others' experiences. Sometimes I have thought that the four categories are so reductionistic as to be useless and so simplistic as to be repetitious of things people surely can see for themselves. However, students remind me of their importance. Many comment on how helpful it is to have a framework which allows them to classify their readings, lectures and lecturers, to understand the tensions between their views and those of others and to simply understand their worlds. Indeed, some final year and graduate students have been outraged that they were not explicitly told that these different perspectives existed. They feel they were unnecessarily naïve and unable to fully evaluate the information and skills which they assimilated over the years.

I deliver this framework with several caveats, however. I try to ensure that students understand that these are four ideal, falsely tidy categories which are culturally bound. I warn them that these categories are not developmental steps. One view does not naturally evolve out of the other, nor does one have more value than another. Further, no one of us will adhere to one category only throughout our lives. I warn them that their dominant view may shift as they become more critical and that this may feel uncomfortable and disorientating (Kuhn 1962). None the less, I emphasise that I believe a single dominant perspective guides our understandings and behaviours at any one stage of our lives.

I also clarify my position relative to these categories. I locate myself on the conflict/interpretive line and demonstrate how even my explication of the four 'secret' categories fits that location. I talk too about my search for more satisfactory categories – ones which are not dominated by Western values and norms as these ones are. I speak of the need to see the spaces, the possibilities within each perspective. I encourage them to think creatively of new ways of using the best of the four perspectives to create a new perspective which also acknowledges spirituality, intuition, partnerships and love.

For some students, these categories are merely four truisms to be memorised and regurgitated somewhere along the way. Indeed, it is possible to create a tidy, digestible chart which represents the major concepts within each view (see Figure 5.1). However, as stated earlier, my intention is for students actually to use this framework to understand and to analyse their own and others' attitudes and behaviours. Interestingly, I find this aim to be less problematic in New Zealand than in Canada. Many Maori students and some Pakeha students grasp the notion of different

CONSENSUS	CONFLICT	INTERPRETIVE	NEW RIGHT
static	dynamic	complex, shared understand-ings	global
equality of opportunity	equality of outcomes	equality of opportunity, outcomes, conditions	absolute freedom
equality	equity	equality, equity	individual freedoms
society's good	group interests	shared rules, negotiations	for the good of the market place
charity	justice, rights	different mean-ings in differ-ent contexts	state has no role to intervene
special needs, disadvantaged	oppression	subjective understand-ings	labelling limits
socialisation	hegemony	shared rules	irrelevant
maintain status quo	challenge status quo	examine status quo	there is no status quo

Figure 5.1 Four perspectives for understanding and analysing experiences

perspectives almost instantly. New Zealand's on-going and very visible dialogue around indigenous issues of domination and oppression appears to create lived experiences of the concepts which make them easier to understand and use. At any rate, to ensure that all students can use this framework in their analysis of their everyday lives, I have devised several activities which reinforce and clarify the perspectives.

REINFORCING AND CLARIFYING THE PERSPECTIVES

In order to have students see the application of these perspectives to their everyday lives, I present them with a problem. In my larger classes, I divide the lecture hall into four groups which extend lengthways from the lectern to the back of the hall. Each group represents one of the perspectives.

Among each group I distribute about a dozen comments typical of members within that group. I then present my 'problem'. Often I use the latest statistical data and say that my problem is that I am a woman who earns so many cents relative to the man's dollar in wages (in the particular country where I am teaching). As I stand before each group in turn, students read their individual comments. A dialogue between myself and the students occurs. I find this usually works well, since students are assured of safety by reading a scripted comment and, at the same time, there is a sense of reality about the exchanges. In addition, the unique nature of each perspective becomes clearer.

In smaller classes, I once again divide the students into four groups and assign a perspective to each group. This time I present them with a case study which resembles the following:

> Powhiri is a 35-year-old mother of two children: Rangi who is ten and Janet who is three. Powhiri separated from her partner five months ago. When she was first married, she worked as a clerical assistant for several years, and when she had her first baby she and her partner agreed that she should work at home.

I ask students to identify the problem and advise Powhiri on what she could do. I suggest they think of themselves as social workers/mothers/friends in order to find new ways of discussing the problem. Each group reports back to the larger group. After all groups have reported back, I have groups react, staying 'in role', to other groups' responses. These exchanges highlight the tensions and miscommunications which occur among different perspectives.

This activity is frequently useful on two levels. On the one hand, most 'first world' students slip comfortably into a consensus logic and have difficulty working from a conflict perspective. This activity thus helps them to identify their dominant perspective. On the other hand, facilitators and learners alike are no longer bound by the experiences held by individuals within the classroom. The notion of 'learners' experiences' is extended and it is possible to create and experiment with the experiences, attitudes and activities of each view.

There are numerous other ways to help students understand these perspectives at a deep level. In the beginning, one of the most straightforward ways is to present concepts from each of the four perspectives. Thus 'adult education' is presented as a concept with four possible definitions and questions about it are answered from the four different dimensions. Defining all concepts in four dimensions throughout a course is an unwieldy and somewhat frustrating enterprise, however. Thus, I reveal my dominant perspectives and facilitate the courses accordingly. None the less, beginning with this emphasis seems to help students understand the perspectives and their utility fairly quickly.

To build on these understandings, we analyse the dominant perspective of television shows, movies, newspaper editorials or academic articles. Sometimes we then recreate these presentations from alternate perspectives. I play tapes of songs which promulgate each perspective, give assignments which ask the students to identify the perspective of a particular organisation, institution and, indeed, my own lectures. As a result of these kinds of activities, most students become proficient at applying the perspectives to their own experiences and to analysing the activities and behaviours of others.

CONCLUSION

In this chapter I discussed the framework which I present to learners so that they can work with their own and others' experiences. I hinted at the complexity of the four views which constitute the framework and offered some cautionary comments. Practical activities for reinforcing and clarifying the four views also were included.

In conclusion, I would like to emphasise that adult educators who reveal to learners these 'secrets' give their students an authoritative tool. The framework is a basic first step to understanding the complex world which they face in their intellectual and day-to-day lives. It allows them to make thoughtful, informed decisions about the nature and direction of their learning and of their lives. Presenting these perspectives is, in other words, a basic step for working with students' experiences and operating honestly in the classroom.

REFERENCES

Bowles, S. and Gintis, H. (1976) *Schooling in Capitalist America: Educational Reform and the Contradictions of Economic Life*, New York: Basic Books.

Jarvis, P. (1985) *Sociology of Adult and Continuing Education*, London: Croom Helm.

Jencks, C. (1972) *Inequality: A Reassessment of the Effect of Family and Schooling in America*, New York: Basic Books.

Karabel, A. H. and Halsey, J. (eds) (1977) *Power and Ideology in Education*, New York: Oxford University Press.

Kuhn, T. (1962) *The Structure of Scientific Revolutions*, Chicago: University of Chicago Press.

Rubenson, K. (1980) 'Background and theoretical context', in R. Hoghielm and K. Rubenson (eds) *Adult Education for Social Change: Research on the Swedish Allocation Policy*, Lund: Gleerup, 1–45.

Thomas, J. E. (1982) *Radical Adult Education: Theory and Practice*, Nottingham: Department of Adult Education, University of Nottingham.

6   Helping whole people learn

John Heron

THE SETTING FOR A SHIFT IN STYLE

This chapter describes what I do in practice to help whole people learn. It covers work done since January 1991, in a particular place – New Zealand – where I have done over 140 days of two-, three-, four- or five-day workshops over the last four southern summers. These workshops have covered a wide range of titles: facilitation skills (the focus of this chapter), radical and holistic education, whole person learning, learning contracts, self/peer and collaborative assessment, peer review audit, six category intervention analysis, co-operative inquiry, one-to-one counselling, co-counselling, transpersonal experience, authentic manhood, team development, soft revolution. These events were hosted, variously, by universities, institutes of technology, polytechnics, private institutes and alternative networks. There were also side trips to Australia, for universities in Sydney and Perth.

Prior to January 1991, I had taken a four-year break from facilitation, starting in November 1986, in order to lie fallow after sixteen non-stop years, to change my lifestyle, and write some books. The fundamental shift in my facilitation since my return to active work in 1991 has been to make fully explicit and integrate the use of transpersonal interventions as an integral aspect of the workshop. While this dimension has always been present in my work, it was often more tacit and intermittent than is now the case.

What I mean by 'transpersonal interventions' are proposals which invite people to explore their spirituality, a variety of inner and altered states of consciousness, as an explicit part of their learning and as a ground of the whole person learning process. These states may be manifest outwardly in expressive, ritual actions; or they may be entirely inward, involving rearrangements, deepenings and expansions of consciousness. A comparison may make the notion of transpersonal or spiritual interventions more telling.

When I was at the British Postgraduate Medical Federation in the University of London, I initiated a co-operative inquiry into whole person medicine with a group of sixteen doctors. It ran through 1982–1983 and one of the working principles the doctors adopted was that the patient is a being of body, mind and spirit. However, they felt that it was no good if the concept of spirit here just remained a matter of cloudy rhetoric, meaning nothing in practice. So they set out to clarify through action what would constitute appropriate and effective spiritual interventions in relation to their patients in their consulting rooms. In the same way I make practical use of spiritual interventions as part of the facilitation of whole person learning, and invite the learners to inquire into this practice with me.

What makes New Zealand a relevant setting for the use of such interventions is its active biculturalism. Traditional Maori beliefs and practices, sustained on the many *marae* throughout the country, have made a significant impact on those working at the leading edge of educational development. Thus the Education Centre, the staff development unit at the Central Institute of Technology near Wellington, has within its building a special room set aside to host a semi-sacred space bequeathed to the Centre by the local Maori community for the affirmation and expression of Maori values. In the many workshops I have run for the Centre on educational themes, the use of this room for in-depth personal, interpersonal and transpersonal work has been an integral part of the learning process, alongside the use of a conventional seminar room.

What a discriminating minority of the non-indigenous people in New Zealand absorb from the ethos of Maoridom, without being bound by its traditional authoritarianism, are the following: the use of ritual for affirming the spiritual integrity and solidarity of human beings; respect for the spirit of place and the living presences of nature; the concept of *mana*, personal charisma and power; the continuity of life beyond death and the relevance to human society of ancestral light; the importance of community, collective support, or what the Russian mystics call *sobornost*, togetherness.

HOW I PREPARE MYSELF TO DO WHAT I DO

There are three aspects to this. The first is to prepare coloured wall charts, incorporating graphics, of the various conceptual models I will be using. The second is to visualise the proceedings of the group as if they have already been completed in a richly fulfilling manner for all concerned. The third is to focus my attention on an inward place in the psychological heart which is pregnant with all the relevant interactions with the group that are to come. I do not have a set programme devised in detail in advance of the workshop, but a broad and flexible strategy together with a wide array of detailed alternative options. It is the interaction of this with participants' presence, needs and interests that shapes what occurs.

WHO ARE THE PARTICIPANTS?

In the main section that follows about what I do in practice, I focus on workshops on facilitation skills, and so I will write here about who comes to these. They have all been sponsored by a department, in an institute of technology or in a university, which is concerned with both staff development and professional development in the outside world. So the people who attend are facilitators and trainers in higher and continuing education, in management, in medical and therapy settings, in organisational and community development, in personal development, and so on.

The participants cover a wide range of competence from those with considerable facilitative skill and experience to those who have just started to launch themselves beyond didactic teaching. Likewise there is wide variation with respect to personal growth experience: some have attended a wide range of personal development workshops over a long period, others have never been to any. Each workshop delivers a different and unpredictable mix along these two parameters.

The age range is from the twenties to the sixties with the mean age for any one workshop being somewhere in the late thirties or mid-forties. Normally, at least 60 percent of the participants are women; but occasionally this ratio is reversed.

Attendance is entirely voluntary: participants are self-selected and no one has been sent or pressured into enrolling. They are there because they have been to and valued other workshops I have run, or because they have had the workshop recommended by past participants, or because they have read something I have written, or because they have heard of me and are curious to experience what I do. All this adds up to a lot of positive expectation intermingled, in the case of people attending an event of mine for the first time, with varying degrees of normal anxiety about the unknown.

Participants will return to institutions with varying degrees and kinds of constraint on what can be practised within them. So a popular and valued part of the facilitation skills workshop I call 'Techniques of soft revolution'. Participants consider carefully what they can and cannot take back, and strategies for introducing change, both within the classroom or group room, and politically on the wider institutional front. These entail not confusing inner anxiety with assumed external constraints; and conversely not letting excess enthusiasm obscure real constraints. We also discuss the moral issue of introducing change where there is no contract to do so with the recipients of it.

WHAT I DO IN PRACTICE

The following items are the main ones that occur to me at the time of writing this chapter. I expect there are several others, but these are sufficient to provide an outline of my practice. In order to give the list coherence, I have chosen items *all* of which I would use in a workshop on facilitation skills, and I describe them in terms appropriate to that use. The models which I use in my work have been written in a recent series of books (Heron 1989, 1990, 1992, 1993). I have alluded to these models in some of the discussion which follows.

Introductions

I usually start a workshop with the following: a simple ritual, a round of introductions, an overview of the nature of the workshop and of possible events to come, a clarification of my role, and setting the culture in terms of proposed values and ground-rules. The round of introductions affirms the principle of participation by all from the outset: each person is invited to share, very briefly, their name, occupation, facilitative work, prior facilitation and personal development training, reasons for attending this workshop and anything else that the group thinks is pertinent to what we are about. This also gives me a working grasp of the range of facilitation skills and of personal development experience present in the group.

Culture-setting

I find culture-setting to be of prime importance among the proceedings at the outset of a workshop. For me it means commending and seeking assent to a set of values as the basis for our being and learning together. A typical set would include the following: being co-operative and non-competitive; creating a safe, supportive and trusting climate; being experientially risk-taking and non-defensive; being vulnerable, open to areas of inner pain, chaos, confusion and lack of skill; being open to our personal presence and power; exercising autonomy and the voluntary principle; participation in the political life of the workshop; adopting a spirit of inquiry without dogmatism and authoritarianism; exploring multi-modal, multi-stranded learning; having an open, transparent workshop process; enjoying ourselves; affirming confidentiality.

When group members find the space within themselves to assent to these values, I note that a deep affective climate, one that advances holistic learning, is inaugurated. As part of this process, I will also commend and elaborate on the view that personal development, the cultivation of professional facilitative skills and organisational development go hand to hand.

I make a deliberate choice to propose and seek assent to these values, rather than invite the group to generate its own set of values. This because the group is still an aggregate of people not an integrated group, because initial anxiety and discomfort in a group can distort its selection of values, and because the propose-assent model, as I have suggested, generates a certain security that bodes well for future learning. It also permits the following.

Suggestion and permission-giving

Culture-setting is not only seeking rational assent to values that respect persons and their capacity for change and mutual support. When I facilitate it with a measure of charismatic presence and voice, it brings about a light trance state, and so it is also a way of empowering people with positive suggestion. I find that these two planes, of seeking rational assent and of empowering with entranced suggestion, are not at odds: rather they enhance each other.

An incidental and powerful effect of some of these positive suggestions is that they give permission to the hurt child within the adult to embark on a process of being recognised, accepted and healed. This is important for subsequent learning, since some of the blocks to learning will reside in the fixated pain of old and unresolved experiences of wounding and oppression. A related effect is the permission given to disinhibit the charismatic and spiritual core which social conditioning has repressed in many people.

Healing the wounded child

In our emotionally repressive society, where everyone seems to carry around more or less unresolved emotional pain from their childhood which restricts their adult functioning, I find it irresponsible and counter-productive to teach professional facilitation skills in divorce from personal work on the hurt child within. So I will seek to create a safe and trusting climate within the group which gives space for this kind of work to occur.

As I said earlier, participants show a wide variation with respect to personal growth experience: from those who are already well established in their own healing and recovery, to those who have scarcely identified it as relevant. For the latter in particular, I will stress the interdependence of personal healing, facilitation skills and organisational development. When the climate in the group matures, then old pain will unexpectedly claim present attention in some group members, especially those who are still busy repressing it. I will facilitate a little healing work with this, affirm its legitimacy and relevance, and point those involved on the path of follow-up after the workshop through the use of local resources such as a co-counselling network.

While this personal healing is not extended in time or taken to great depth, and is a relatively small part of the total workshop proceedings, I regard it as an integral part of the whole learning process. It makes strongly the point that past trauma can be an emotional block to learning present life-enhancing skills; it affirms the importance of emotional competence as a necessary basis for interpersonal and facilitative competence; and it shows that such competence is a matter for main-line education and training, not the cultural backwater of psychotherapy.

For participants who are new to all this, it can be a turning point in their own general development, hence the importance of showing the way to, and encouraging, post-workshop follow-up. For someone who is on the brink, shows signs of breakthrough, but chooses in the moment to put his or her defences against past pain back together again, I affirm their choice and their absolute right to make it. No one should give up their defences until they really choose to do so. In this area the voluntary principle reigns supreme.

The use of ritual

I introduce a ritual as part of the opening sequence of events in a group, sometimes at the very outset before the round of introductions, at other times, for example, after culture-setting. It all depends on the group, the mood, the climate. I also use them at the start of each subsequent day, and sometimes at the end of a day. I devise rituals that are as free as possible of overt theology and transpersonal doctrine. Their purpose is to affirm spiritual openness, groundedness and mutuality of presence, each to each. I seek the assent of the group to try them out in a spirit of holistic inquiry. I also seek feedback and comment afterwards, giving space both for those who want to affirm and for those who may have been discomforted.

My belief and experience is that appropriate rituals subtly transfigure the whole subsequent learning process by opening up individuals and the interactions between them to deep potentials in persons for participative awareness. They legitimate each person's charismatic presence. And they enhance positive emotional arousal and imaginal awakening, both of which, on my current models, are also key elements of holistic learning.

One example, among many, of such a ritual: the group stands in a circle holding hands; one after another, going round the circle, each person takes hold of the same flower, turns to the one on their left and says 'May you flourish in the belly, in the head and in the heart', at the same time tapping the recipient with the flower in each of those three places. The rest of the circle continue to hold hands while the two who are active disengage from the hand link to face each other. I start the process giving the first evocation, and end it receiving the last evocation. What makes this a spiritual ritual is the benedictory, evocative language, and the bestowing gesture of empowerment. Alternatives for the verb 'flourish' are 'learn' or 'grow'.

A nonverbal ritual I frequently use is to stroke a piece of wood around the rim of a Tibetan bowl, lent to me by a participant in New Zealand, while the group enters into a state of meditative attunement in and through the pervasive, omnipresent sound.

I have found in New Zealand a remarkable degree of openness to these rituals, with a lot of sensible evaluation of them. I think this is because of the active biculturalism, which I have already alluded to. Elements of Maori ritual and protocol are honoured in quite a few meetings of different kinds in the wider society, so the whole idea of ritual procedure is no longer culturally odd. In one three-day team development exercise I ran for staff from a hospital, they had launched the first meeting with a Maori-based ritual before I had got my own ritual proposal off the ground. The same kind of acceptance applies to the next three items.

An imaginal focus

At the very start of the workshop, before any proceedings begin, I will often place on the floor, in the middle of the circle of chairs, some symbolic object – without making any comment at all about it. For quite a number of different workshops, this was a small black rubber mouse. Mainly, the object sets the imaginal mind going through metaphorical drift and association. It promotes group interaction through shared conjecture and unfettered whimsy. It can also elicit arousal through emotional projection. It works as a fruitful yeast in the group unconscious.

Sooner or later the unconscious process breaks out and there is a sustained discussion about the significance and relevance of the mouse to what we are about. It then provides a useful experiential focus for the grounding of conceptual learning in the multivalent processes of symbolism, metaphor and analogy in the deeper imagination.

Tibetan awakening

In an accessible place in the workshop there stands a bell, which I or anyone else can ring every once in a while, whatever is occurring in the sessions or in breaks between them, in order to remind us to wake up from the sleep of identifying with the immediate content of experience. The invitation of the bell is to regain mindedness, inner alertness, knowing what is going on as a form of our awareness rather than as an occlusion of it. This state of consciousness which fully includes and indwells what is happening and at the same time transcends it, is in my view a precondition of insightful learning. It involves a felt participation in immediate events and an intuitive, transcendent grasp of their whole pattern.

Holonomic focus

The holonomic principle, thought by radical physicists, systems theorists and others to be fundamental in the scheme of things, asserts that the whole is represented in the part: the whole hologram is represented in any part of the holographic plate; the whole of the tacit universe is represented in any part of the explicit universe (Bohm 1980). There certainly seem to be occasions in which the group is represented by one of its members: one person will contribute in a way that focuses the learning of all. I seek to be sensitive to this phenomenon and to be alert to make way for it when it is about to manifest. And from time to time I will be a holonomic focus for the energy, needs and concerns of the whole group. Tuning in to the shared experiential field is a way of enabling that to happen.

I sometimes work with the holonomic principle through ritual. Everyone writes their own name on a piece of paper, which is put into a basket. Then each in turn picks one paper, reads the name and hands the basket to the person whose name is on the piece of paper. The last person's name to be picked out is the holonomic focus. Once this person is selected he or she goes ceremonially round the group, shakes each member by the root of the nose and says 'I empower you to learn and grow'. It is surprising how well people will engage with this unusual activity as a form of inquiry. And the effect can be quite extraordinary, producing a total shift of consciousness in the group. The whole is more than the part and can be revealed through the part. The whole group can get in touch with its full power when that power is focused through one person and bestowed through that person to everyone in the group.

Flexibility in the use of decision-modes

I exercise unilateral political authority about learning when I take a meta-decision about whether to make decisions – for example about the programme of learning – hierarchically for the group, co-operatively with the group, or to delegate this decision-making to the group, or some combination of these. Even when I consult the group about whether to make planning decisions hierarchically, co-operatively or by delegation, I have still made, at a higher meta-level, a unilateral, hierarchical decision to do so. (I have discussed this matter most thoroughly in Heron 1993: Chapter 1.)

No facilitator can avoid the exercise of unilateral decision-making at these meta-levels. I make it clear at the start of a workshop what meta-decisions I have taken. I work with this most explicitly in a five-day facilitation skills workshop. So I start the workshop proposing (i) that for the first day or so I will decide hierarchically on the training programme, both in order to present the trainees with issues which I think are fundamental, and in order to model such decision-making; (ii) that some time into day two or day three, I will shift over into co-operative decision-making to negotiate a contract between participants' needs and interests and what I have on offer; and (iii) that on the last day or two we will have an autonomy lab, in which participants post up what they have to teach and what they want to learn, then everyone plans their own learning on a basis of self-direction and peer negotiation, and I will be a resource and learner alongside everyone else.

Then I consult the group as to whether this three-part proposal is acceptable. The assent usually given is inclined to be more nominal than substantial because of participants' relative unfamiliarity with the issues. The second consultation, after a day or so, about whether it is time for me to shift, as originally proposed, from hierarchical to co-operative decision-making about the programme, is altogether more substantial in its outcome. If this outcome is to move over into the co-operative decision mode, then in a further day or two I will consult for a third time about the final shift into an autonomy lab, and by then the participants are fully immersed in the relative merits and demerits of moving between the three basic decision modes with respect to the programme of learning.

What I am doing is deciding unilaterally at the higher meta-level to consult participants at the lower meta-level in deciding whether (and when) I, or they and I, or they, should decide on the programme of learning. By making the issues simultaneously experientially and theoretically explicit about directive, consultative and autonomous decisions at different levels, a great deal of learning about the facilitation of learning is going on. And I will extend this not only to the programme of learning, but also to the more detailed method to be adopted within any specific learning activity.

While a facilitation skills workshop is the obvious place for me to exercise a high degree of political, i.e. decision-mode, flexibility, in all other kinds of workshop I will also apply appropriate versatility in moving between modes or staying in a particular mode, and I will make it clear what I am doing and why. The purpose of all this is to elicit and empower both autonomy and peer support in learning. I notice that this autonomy and support emerge strongly in a context where the facilitator prepares, or intermittently tills, the soil with the right kind and degree of direction and negotiation, and is transparent about it.

Wall charts as patterns

In a facilitation skills workshop, usually of five days, before the proceedings begin I will cover the walls with a large number of wall charts which in words and graphics give an account of different aspects of facilitation, holistic learning, models of personality, group dynamics and so on. Some charts are multi-coloured in an arbitrary and/or aesthetic way; some are both multi-coloured and colour-coded according to conceptual content.

I recommend that from the outset group members practise regarding the charts as background patterns, like wall paper, and this whether looking at them directly or being marginally aware of them at the periphery of the visual field. Sometimes I will lead the group on a slow tour round the room walking past the charts, inviting each person to keep focusing the eyes off the charts, while being aware, at the edge of vision, of the pure pattern of each chart while passing by it.

My purpose is to underline experientially the point that propositional knowledge is grounded in the matrix of imaginally grasped patterns, and that the learning of conceptual content is enhanced by a prior and purely imaginative immersion in the visual and auditory patterns that carry it. Some, but not all, of the charts will later be used in terms of their conceptual content; but not until they have been soaked up as peripheral pattern.

Charismatic presence and voice

I have written elsewhere at some length about charismatic training (Heron 1993), and I must refer the reader to that book for a full account of what I can only allude to in this section. Charismatic presence is about relaxed and aware posture and movement; charismatic voice is to do with tone and timing, especially moving between a more rapid information-giving clock time, and a slower more rhythmic and evocative charismatic time which empowers what is said with human depth and significance. The purpose of both combined is to facilitate learning by engaging with the substrate of participative feeling, the 'ocean of shared feeling where we become one with one another' (Alexander 1979: 294), and with the intuitive mind of the learners who can then enter most fully into the imagery of what is being said and how it is being said, as the ground for understanding its conceptual content.

As well as using this combination myself as and when appropriate, and when I am alert enough to remember it, I also introduce it as part of the facilitation skills training. This has proved to be one of the most effective parts of the training, and is very popular with participants. It gives participants immediate access, through a simple behavioural rearrangement of conscious use of the self, to an inner wellspring of personal empowerment, which also facilitates the empowerment of others.

Use of the experiential learning cycle

At the heart of the learning process I use versions of the experiential learning cycle, which engage the whole person construed as a being of feeling and emotion, intuition and imagery (including perception, memory and imagination), reflection and discrimination, intention and action. I take the view that holistic learning involves an up-hierarchy, in which what is above is grounded on what is below. So the practical (intention and action) is grounded on the conceptual (reflection and discrimination), which is grounded on the imaginal (intuition and imagery), which in turn is grounded on the affective (feeling and emotion). When these four modes are construed as a cycle, the affective mode is the wellspring of the cyclic interaction (Heron 1992, 1993).

A good example of this at work, illustrated in Figure 6.1, is in one-to-one facilitation or counsellor training, where the trainee (female) is practising counselling skills with another trainee (male) who is being a real client. The four modes – affective, imaginal, conceptual and practical – are shown as circles generating motion in each other in that order.

Stage 1: affective   The trainee feels empathically the presence of the client, while attending to and managing her own emotions.

Stage 2: imaginal   The trainee notices the whole pattern of the client's behaviour, both what he is saying and all the nonverbal cues, intuitively divining its meaning as a whole.

Stage 3: conceptual   The trainee discriminates selectively among all this data, rapidly classifying it, and with quicksilver reflection evolves a hypothesis about the client's process.

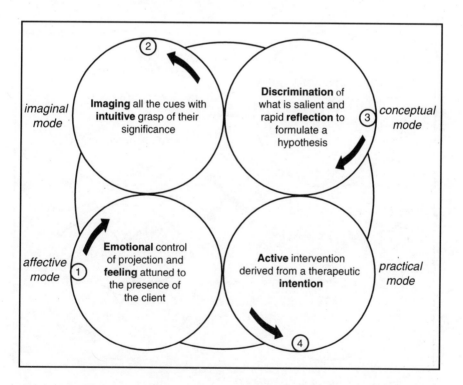

Figure 6.1 The trainee's primary cycle

Stage 4: practical She converts her hypothesis into a practical intervention based on an underlying therapeutic purpose. She is using intention and action.

This is an inquiry and learning cycle since the client's response, noted in stages 1 and 2, to interventions made in stage 4, can modify hypotheses generated in stage 3, which alter interventions in stage 4, and so on.

This primary training cycle, managed within by the trainee, is set within a secondary cycle which I manage as the trainer, as illustrated in Figure 6.2, and use to prepare trainees for the primary one and to digest it afterwards. It differs from the primary one in reversing the order between the imaginal and the conceptual modes. For more detail on this see the relevant books (Heron 1992, 1993).

Stage 1: affective The trainees work on their negative and positive emotional responses to the impending exercise of counselling practice.

Stage 2: conceptual I give an analytic input on the counselling process, its stages, the different whole person aspects involved, followed by discussion with the whole group.

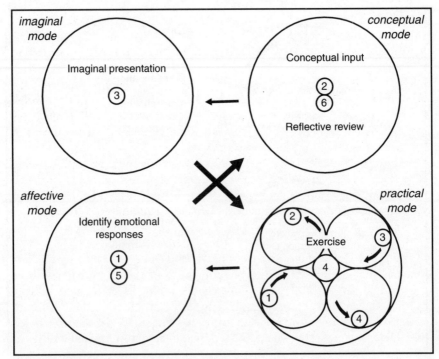

Figure 6.2 The facilitator's secondary cycle

Stage 3: imaginal I then demonstrate or illustrate the whole process and also the training exercise which is to follow.

Stage 4: practical The trainees do a practice counselling session using the four stages of the primary cycle, as described earlier. The primary cycle as a whole is within stage 4 of the secondary cycle. After a turn as counsellor, each trainee gives feedback to self and receives feedback from the client.

Stage 5: affective The trainees process the positive and negative emotions involved as counsellor and in response to the other as counsellor.

Stage 6: conceptual Trainees as a group discuss the issues arising from the practice, and relate these to the theoretical model put forward in stage 2. Learners here are doing one or more of four things: they are cultivating a personal view of counselling practice, one that expresses their own stance in life; they are testing for a valid view, one that is consistent with their experience; they are developing a coherent view, one that is internally consistent; and they are unfolding a practical view, one that is effective in and for action.

Multi-stranded activities

When I use various versions of the experiential learning cycle, different aspects of the whole person are integrated in a coherent way *within* the learning of some facilitation skill or conceptual model. The holistic method is internal to the learning. But I will also have strands of activity which variously affirm different aspects of the whole person *alongside* the learning of specific skills or content, providing a holistic ground or context for it. Three, at least, of the items already mentioned fall within this category: the use of an opening ritual, of an imaginal focus in the middle of the group, of a bell for Tibetan awakening.

Other examples which include the whole group are: free form dancing to music, musical improvisation with percussion and other instruments, theatrical improvisation, games, energetic movements, loud noise, time for unfettered reflection, moments of silence and attunement.

Switching and integration

I switch, or negotiate switches in, or delegate the management of switches in, group energy for the purposes of sustaining a variegated holistic momentum in learning, and at the same time of releasing the tension of sustaining only one mode of human functioning. The secondary experiential learning cycle, the one managed by the facilitator, is itself a series of switches between affective, imaginal, conceptual and practical ways of being. The use, alongside the learning, of one of the multi-stranded activities mentioned above will involve a switch of energy from what was previously going on.

Classic switches are moving both ways between the conceptual and the imaginal, between the conceptual and the practical, between the conceptual and the emotional/interpersonal, between each of these and physical action/sensory awareness, between any of these and felt spiritual attunement, participation consciousness, resonance. Switching spotlights the different modalities of human functioning, development and learning, but only to highlight them for their subsequent and more conscious harmonisation in multi-modal ways of being.

The polarity of light and strong

I may take your hand lightly or I may grasp it strongly. As a facilitator of group energy, I use the polarity of light and strong: some interventions have a light, deft touch that elicits laughter and an 'up' climate of positive emotional arousal. Others are stronger in their mode of delivery and more stringent in their content: they generate gestation – a brooding, meditative, reflective mood. I find that the creative use of this polarity is central in sustaining a good learning curve in a group.

PARTICIPANTS' RESPONSE

Shona Todd followed up polytechnic tutors some months after they had attended one or other of my two facilitation skills workshops in Auckland in the summer of 1991–1992 (Todd 1992). What they gained included: feeling fully accepted and valued with the resulting freedom to explore whatever were the real issues for them; personal validation and empowerment through finding one's inner beliefs affirmed in the workshop; 'being made whole' by integrating personal development and professional development; effective facilitation as requiring emotional competence; managing the power dynamic in the learning situation by moving between hierarchy, co-operation and autonomy; involving different aspects of the whole person in the learning process. One tutor typically wrote:

> I overtly use his whole model on control and power in terms of being hierarchical or cooperative or autonomous and I overtly talk to students about that whole thing at the beginning of the course ... In my general planning of classes I am much more conscious of the need to acknowledge the multidimensional nature of people and that tends to prevent me getting hooked into just didactic, cognitive teaching, but to try and incorporate, where it is possible and appropriate, a more balanced session that taps into the emotional aspect, or the political aspect, or the spiritual aspect of people. I think I did some of those things before, but I

can now more overtly do them and do them for a particular reason which I like.

(Todd 1992: 44–45)

KEY ISSUES AND CHALLENGES FOR THE FUTURE

There are in my experience and practice three big issues that stand out as challenges for the future.

The integration of autonomy and holism in learning

In the present educational climate, there is a considerable tension, in higher education, between introducing student autonomy in learning and initiating students into holistic learning methods. Most students, moving from secondary to tertiary education, come from a very non-autonomous and non-holistic background. If they are encouraged early on in a tertiary course to use learning contracts and thus to plan their own learning to a significant degree, then they are likely to do so in terms of the old familiar non-holistic learning methods they have brought with them. If, however, they are going to be initiated into holistic methods, then their facilitators will have to plan a lot of the learning until the methods are internalised and students can manage them autonomously.

Too much student autonomy early on will be at the expense of holism in learning; and directive initiation into holistic methods will be at the expense of student autonomy. This tension between autonomy and holism in learning is, I believe, a major issue in the educational revolution that is afoot, and one that is not yet fully grasped. So some teachers are pioneering with student contracts in a manner that is relatively non-holistic with respect to learning methods; and others are busy with holistic methods, as in suggestive-accelerative learning, in an unawarely directive way.

The resolution of this tension lies in a greater command by teachers of the decision-modes of direction, negotiation and delegation in planning their students' programmes of learning; and in using these modes to establish a gradient from directive initiation into holism at one end towards increasing student autonomy in planning the sequence and methods of learning at the other.

Spiritual immanence as a principle of learning

The relevance of transpersonal psychology, both theory and practice, to experiential learning awaits future development. One problem has been that the transpersonal or spiritual self has too often been construed only as transcendent, beyond ordinary consciousness. Special steps have then to be taken to get ordinary consciousness to connect up with it.

It is more fruitful for experiential learning to work with the model of divine immanence, of spirituality that is the foundation of psychological processes. I have expressed this in my account of feeling, distinguished from emotion, as the capacity for participative union with being and beings while retaining a sense of own's distinct identity (Heron 1992). Related notions such as experiential focusing (Gendlin 1981), entelechy (Houston 1987), E-therapy (Kitselman 1953), ground-unconscious (Wilber 1990) and actualising tendency (Rogers 1959) are useful sources for enhancing our model both of autonomy and holism in learning.

In less technical language all this points to the view that the spiritual dimension is deeply within the human being, an inner ground of everyday mental and emotional states, and can be accessed through opening to this inward source; and that this is a much needed complement and counter-balance to the way that goes up and out and beyond to some all-encompassing transcendental reality.

A self-generating culture

Another challenge for the future is to prepare to take experiential learning out into the world. What this entails is individual and co-operative commitment to a learning culture: each person in various aspects of his or her daily life, personal and professional, adopts a set of primary experiential learning cycles. Torbert (1991) calls this action inquiry: an extended consciousness-in-action, encompassing your vision of goals, your strategies to achieve them, your current actions and their outcomes, and what is going on in the world around. It also means noticing and amending, either through action or internal revision or both, incongruities between these components of your lived inquiry.

In the wider canvas of life, such action inquiry will have its idiosyncratic private strands, its shared and face-to-face strands with people at home and at work, and its more collective strands within organisations as learning systems. It will involve primary cycles of living and learning, with time out in secondary cycles for review, reflection and goal setting. The totality of all this I call a self-generating culture, a society whose members are in a continuous process of learning and development, and whose forms are consciously adopted, periodically reviewed and altered in the light of experience and deeper vision (Heron 1993).

REFERENCES

Alexander, C. (1979) *The Timeless Way of Building*, New York: Oxford University Press.
Bohm, D. (1980) *Wholeness and the Implicate Order*, London: Routledge and Kegan Paul.
Gendlin, E. (1981) *Focusing*, London: Bantam Press.
Heron, J. (1989) *The Facilitators' Handbook*, London: Kogan Page.
—— (1990) *Helping the Client: A Creative, Practical Guide*, London: Sage.

—— (1992) *Feeling and Personhood: Psychology in Another Key*, London: Sage.
—— (1993) *Group Facilitation: Theories and Models for Practice*, London: Kogan Page.
Houston, J. (1987) *The Search for the Beloved*, Los Angeles: Tarcher.
Kitselman, A. L. (1953) *E-Therapy*, New York: Institute of Integration.
MacMurray, J. (1957) *The Self as Agent*, London: Faber and Faber.
Rogers, C. R. (1959) 'A theory of therapy, personality, and interpersonal relationships, as developed in the client-centred framework', in S. Koch (ed.) *Psychology: A Study of a Science*, vol. 3, New York: McGraw-Hill.
Todd, S. (1992) *The Process and Practice of Facilitation: Empowering the Educator*, Auckland: Auckland Institute of Technology.
Torbert, W. R. (1991) *The Power of Balance*, Newbury Park, CA: Sage.
Wilber, K. (1990) *Eye to Eye*, Boston: Shambhala.

Part 3

7   Making the difference/teaching the international

Jan Jindy Pettman

There are dilemmas enough in teaching as a feminist within the university – and they are compounded when teaching 'the international' to mainly young, mainly local (Australian) students. In this chapter I reflect on my attempts to encourage students to locate themselves in and think about 'the world', to move from the local to the global and back again. I focus on particular challenges within this vast task: making the international accessible in terms of students' own experiences and understandings; and the ethical and political difficulties of teaching 'difference', without domesticating it or reducing it to bland diversity. I pursue these challenges within an explicitly feminist agenda.

The contradictions between a formal university degree setting and a feminist and liberatory political commitment are severe. Universities are individualistic, competitive, hierarchal, male-dominated, elitist institutions. The students who now inhabit them in Australia are increasingly under pressure from the job market, and from financial constraints that also often affect their families. Political pressures to disguise youth unemployment mean a younger student body. First-year students mainly straight from school are herded into huge foundation-year units, with harassed, overworked and often part-time or temporary contract lecturers and tutors, though some senior academics do make a special point of assuming some responsibility for first year. Students face too a fragmentation of knowledges through discipline territoriality, especially in older and/or more conservative universities like mine. Department and faculty rules formalise and bureaucratise organisation and assessment procedures; the two-lectures-and-one-tutorial-a-week format rules, and much energy needs to go into subverting these constraints.

Here I explore 'Gender and International Politics', a second- and third-year undergraduate unit in a political science department, though it also attracts women's studies undergraduates and, with different assessment arrangements, honours and postgraduates as well. This means that while most of my students are young and often have only just completed first year, some come with experience in international relations (IR) theory and others as old hands in women's studies. My students are overwhelmingly female, though there are always some, usually young, men.

Feminist critique has come very late to IR (Pettman 1993, 1966a), among the most masculinist and resistant to new social theory of all the social sciences. Until very recently, women have been invisible in IR, as if they are actually not there, as if states and wars and markets are men's business; or as if women are equally and similarly affected by international relations and processes. In the standard texts, it's very difficult to see where women – indeed, where most people – might possibly fit, for IR takes as its focus a world of states, and relegates women doubly away from that world – first to within the state, as the business of other disciplines, like sociology, and further, within a wider social science tradition, into the private, the domestic, leaving the public/political space as male. Female students could get all the way through many IR courses with only occasional references to a women leader, or to women as victims of wars or of the World Bank.

IR is currently a popular choice among Australian students, precisely because, it seems, the international is so far away: different, exotic, dramatic – and dangerous. Knowledge about the international appears overwhelmingly drawn from popular media, especially television, and to a lesser extent films and newspapers. It doesn't seem, then, that students come here to learn about themselves; though there are always some who have travelled and come back more curious about difference, and others who are themselves migrants or the children of one or more migrants – as currently one third of the Australian population is.

SETTING OUT

Academic studies are apparently constructed around reading and writing, on the whole, but in my experience the key dimension is talk – mine and theirs. Collaborative learning means, among other things, negotiating teaching/learning relations with students, and encouraging co-operative learning. I try to prod the latter along, against the formal constraints, by urging students to bring in gems and useful materials, share gleaned insights, talk together about their assignments and meet outside the classes and my presence, in library crawls, coffee chats and reading groups – though it is often students in their twos or threes, or women's studies students, who make this work.

In lectures, my formal authority position is marked, but I attempt to talk up a tone that is inclusive, respecting, exploratory, questioning. In tutorials we talk more, though an hour once a week with thirteen or fourteen students is hardly sustained intimacy. I set up smaller groups and tasks so no one leaves without having spoken to at least two others – and then tell them what I am doing. This begins the habit of routine discussion with them: why I ask them to do certain things and how they perceive the process and its effects. Early on, I try to get some sense of who they are, and why they are here. The diversity, in academic backgrounds and personal experience, is daunting. My reputation and the course name signal that it is a feminist unit, though there is no obvious agreement about what this means, either for the unit or for our interactions.

We begin by plotting what, in their experience, makes for a good tutorial class. The responses are usually familiar – one where one or two students don't dominate, where everyone participates, does the reading. There's less agreement about what I should be doing – set a structure and give explicit questions and direction; don't; encourage personal anecdotes and let them wander off the topic; don't. I'm reminded again that it might be better to have different sorts of tutorials for different students, but doubt that I could really be all things on cue. Only a few students know any others so the first task is to get the conversations started, to build towards a safe, congenial space with a critical edge, to make it clear that reading is required. (I've found that being seen as radical or woman or student-friendly can be read by some students as soft or uninterested in intellectual or rigorous thinking.)

The problem of connecting students' own experiences, observations and images to what we'll do means drawing out stories and responses and always trying to link these back to themes, issues, concepts in the unit, to build an accessible and use-able shared language. This makes me quite interventionist, especially early on, a translator-interpreter who is forever stressing that every interpretation is political, encouraging critique. It's already clear that the international for most students is 'out there' – a dichotomous world of home and away, though some students are clearly from somewhere else. Foreign, other, alien, outsider – a world that invites and intrigues us precisely because it is not us.

MAKING IDENTITIES

In the lectures, I sketch a framework, draw a map and begin building a language for working together more closely on bits and pieces in tutorials and assignments. More cynically, it looks like me spinning a web to draw students into meanings and conversations that edge us towards where I think we should be going. I begin audaciously with 'The making of the world', in fifty minutes (see Appendix for lecture outline), tracing the huge processes of industrialisation, colonisation, imperialism and integration, unequally, into the international political economy. In the first lectures I locate Australia within these processes, make us part of the world we are studying. I look at colonisation, immigration, nation-making, name gender relations as power relations, and ask about how men and women experience these processes differently. Already we are talking too about differences between women, between white colonising women and

Aboriginal women in Australia, for example. So alongside gender we already have 'race', class, culture, nationality.

In the first tutorial I ask students to respond in writing, first to the question 'Who are you?', beginning the answer with 'I am ...'. I put three or four together to compare notes, and bring us all back, to reveal (shared exploration or directed discovery?) that, on the whole, those of dominant or majority identities don't 'see' those identities, but take them as givens. So, despite the IR focus of the unit, almost no one identifies in terms of nationality except American exchange students or Japanese overseas students, who mark their difference from the norm. Almost no one says white, except one young American woman. Several of the minority of (young) men identify as male, but on prompting say they do so because they're conspicuous in a gender unit (which is at this stage being used by many students as a codeword for woman – as if to demonstrate the point). Some women do identify in gender terms, for example as a wife or mother, and a couple of younger women do as a daughter. (Do I remind them of their mother? One did go to school with my daughter.) Several of the women's studies students identify as feminist, which might also be an answer to why they're in this unit. Quite a few identify in terms of age – young – and as students. A few give more political or affiliation names – one youngish man defiantly and a little triumphantly declares as 'conservative' and lays down a challenge he'll pursue for some weeks. Interesting discussions follow on multiple identities, who we are, on what basis we recognise connections with others.

This becomes even more interesting in the next week. I set up a census-type questionnaire and ask them to write down, first, 'What is your citizenship?', then, 'your nationality?', 'race?', 'ethnicity?' We take up detailed discussion, after they've briefly exchanged answers with one or two sitting next to them. Discrepancies emerge between some namings of citizenship and nationality, for example as Australian and Croatian, or Scottish, and some give multiple answers, though the hyphenated identity is not as common here as in the USA. 'Race' is always a problem. In my experience, a few refuse to answer on the grounds that it encourages belief in something that isn't 'real', or say the human race. Most, especially again those of the dominant groups, are confused and do not know what to name themselves here – Caucasian, Anglo-Saxon, European, occasionally white? Racialised students are more specific, and give both self-selected and other imposed identities. Ethnicity is even harder, and some students have given 'Australian' for almost all the questions.

TEACHING/LEARNING 'RACE'

What becomes very conspicuous is the naturalisation/normalisation of dominant group identities; that for many 'race' means not-white, ethnicity means migrant or minority. Discussion runs then about essentialism, on making selves and difference, and after that we come to say 'we' in quotation marks and who 'we' are in any instance. What is quite sudden and dramatic is the number of students, particularly young women, who say 'I've never thought of myself as white.' This is said in all kinds of ways, and becomes a part of locating 'race' in structuring the international, and ourselves as inscribed through race as well as gender. There's quite a bit to draw on, about the personal and political significance of whiteness in particular societies, for example in exchanges between African-American and white feminists, and in 'third world' women's writings, in scrutinising – or uncovering – our own experiences of race (for example Mohanty *et al.* 1992, Frankenburg 1993).

I push this further when I ask in tutorials, 'Where are *you* located in the gendered politics of colonisation and race in Australia?' This is a difficult question and one which in my white experience requires constant working over (Pettman 1991, 1992). It is not a question that most students expected to be asked in this unit. There are readings to help the search here, including Aboriginal women addressing white women: 'Just because you are women doesn't mean you are necessarily innocent. You were, and are, part of the colonising force' (Huggins 1991: 506).

This is a personal challenge for many, including those women's studies' students whose focus on gender and personal/political commitment to notions of global sisterhood have encouraged them to see what women share; some cannot easily imagine themselves as part of the oppressor. The difficulty of teaching difference becomes clear here, as most students have no personal experience with Aboriginal people, and have gathered their views largely from media and sometimes from study. Learning from experience is here read across into recovering experience, that of being white in a racialised society and world, of owning one's own social location and identity. Australia as a settler society has thrived on forgetting, on repressing memory of invasion, dispossession and on-going racism. Aboriginal people's everyday experience is of being Aboriginal (although of course each of them is much more than this), and they are acutely aware of the political significance and power of whiteness in Australia. Whiteness is a potent identifier in the international, too.

We're already onto difficult issues – how to respect difference without essentialising or 'fixing' it, without reinforcing the very boundaries of us/ other that lock 'us' in and 'them' out of our particular community. Starting close, in the society around us, raises questions about responsibility and complicity. For those of us who are white, it may be a temptation to relegate race to history, onto our great-grandfathers, or to individualise – I am not racist. Guilt tripping is not a helpful strategy. Historicising and politicising, how the past makes the present, and how present political projects remake the past; how whiteness structures our everyday; learning to listen to Aboriginal anger, and generosity; asking how others see us, mightn't change much, but it does expose power relations, and systematic privilege and penalty. It also unsettles a certain largely unintended arrogance of dominant group knowers (though many, especially younger poorer students, don't feel very powerful), for it emerges that in many cases the slave or the underclass still know the master better than the master knows (him?)self.

I'm surprised, often, by students' good will and the readiness to 'hang in there', though sometimes it is curiosity and a distance-making intellectualism that allows this. Those dominant group students who have had relations, especially difficult or disappointing ones, with Aboriginal people, or who might find convincing accusations of Aboriginal ungratefulness or reverse racism, can explore their responses. There's always a danger that my own politics set the pace, although most students seem to have no difficulty in disagreeing or calling me to account. Another danger is that, narcissistic as most of us are, the conversation will again focus on us, on what we think about us, and marginalise or silence the others once again. These discussions also take a rather different track – or series of them – than they might if Aboriginal students were present. Given their very low numbers at our university, and their concentration in Aboriginal studies and service courses – education, social work, community development and law – they tend not to be here. When they are, other students often remain silent on these issues lest they cause offence, or some ask questions that do cause offence. Aboriginal students also find themselves in the situation that the Croatian, Japanese or Argentinian student does, of being foisted with the burden of representation – assumed to speak for all their 'group'. Called to interpret all the culture and politics, their words may be given an unquestioned authority. Indeed, the fewer there are, the more representative they are expected to be. Here too minority students become a general resource. Some get very tired of being endlessly expected to educate and inform their fellow students, though others may enjoy the momentary authority. Some, especially shyer or newly arrived overseas students, find becoming the centre of attention and being asked constantly to reveal their experiences and views unnerving. So while I'm trying to set up an easy to be in and easy to talk in environment, I need to signal the right to remain silent, as well.

THE INTERNATIONAL IS PERSONAL?

We talk a lot about difference and identity, about where we get our ideas from, against an early on combination of relentless individualising of self and routine overgeneralising about others. We talk about the politics of representation – about how people or differences are represented, about who represents or makes knowledge about them, about what representations of others are available to us. Here I'm teaching, often, against the grain, and encouraging students to critically reflect on what they know, about themselves and others. As we move further from home, sources include films, books, stories, news and current affairs shows. One tutorial activity is a media file, with students bringing in newspaper articles, cartoons, reports on last night's television, in a kind of show and tell. Here we search for evidence of constructions of difference, of views of the world, to illustrate in the everyday the things we are analysing through using academic texts and life stories, about relations of domination or exploitation, of militarisation or resistance.

Surprisingly perhaps, given how economics has managed to mystify and dehumanise, placing itself apparently beyond ordinary people's understandings or experiences, students do relate to our readings of the international political economy, especially its casualised, feminised global assembly line, and to talk of restructuring and economic rationalism. There is some rethinking of the first world–third world dichotomy, as for example our purchase of cheaper products from large local supermarket chains rely as much on exploitation of cheap piecemeal rates paid to homeworker Vietnamese women migrants in Melbourne as on transnational corporations and sweatshops in Asian states. There is disagreement again in terms of complicity or action, as some suggest 'ethical' shopping and boycotts of goods made through abuse, while others are of the opinion that the only thing worse than capitalist exploitation is not being exploited, in circumstances where poorer workers or regions have little choice and no social security. Students draw directly on their own personal beliefs and political experiences in the green movement, well supported here, where they do have understandings of 'one world' and of reciprocal relations disregarding state boundaries – a kind of localised 'we're all in this together' that does not necessarily get called up in other sections of the course.

TEACHING/LEARNING WAR

There are other areas, especially, where the distance between what students (think they) know and what we are talking about becomes a chasm, and the challenge becomes how to teach/learn beyond their/our experiences, while not appropriating other people's pain for our learnings.

My scene-setting in lectures – a performance – aims to entice, amuse, make connections, look for nods or clicks of recognition, quarrels or drifting off. I watch how I authorise my account – sometimes telling stories of my own experience as a researcher in other places, or of colleagues or political allies elsewhere, or referring to the writings of others. I note too whose accounts I set as readings, used to bolster my own: most obviously, also feminist, or at least woman-friendly.

But in the face of the most difficult and painful of topics, of war, ethnic cleansing, communal violence, I am in danger of floundering.

War is the foundation motive and ethical centre piece of IR, which was founded in 1919 in the ruins of World War I Europe in the hope of finding reasons for, so as never again to have, such a war. By the time of the next one, IR had lost its idealistic hope, and was captured by 'realists' who told of an amoral world of power politics, of national self interest, of security in military preponderance and success in clever strategy and diplomacy. But for me, war, the readiness to use organised and deliberate large-scale violence against others for political ends, remains the central problem. It cannot be separated from nationalism, from identity politics and boundary making that place others outside the limits of the moral community (even though those others might recently have been neighbours, as in Bosnia; and though in 'safer' states like Australia most people experience violence at the hands of those they know – those who are or were their intimates, and claim to love them).

For a while we keep a safe distance by exploring our and the readings' ideas about the causes of war, the gender of violence. This uncovers deep convictions about human nature, and of gendered difference. The tutorial topic 'Are women more peaceful than men?' is provocative, and generates very strong feelings and much argument. Here self identity as male or female becomes especially pertinent, though the splits are not along gender lines. The one, two or three young men in each tutorial shift uncomfortably in the face of some others' assertions of a masculine-aggression connection, either innate or socialised. There is talk about whether masculinity (I suggest, rather, certain kinds of masculinity?) makes for danger. How not to implicate the young men in findings that 95 percent plus of violence cross-culturally is perpetrated by men – though many of the victims are also male. Those who choose to do this unit are hardly likely to be typical?

My question 'When, if ever, is the use of political violence justified?' also reveals strong views, and most wish to include psychological and emotional violence. But the discussion quickly gets bogged down, as the scenarios being offered seem a long way from most people's experience and we are in danger of moralising. I try to bring it back with the question 'When, if ever, would *you* use violence?' and make it worse. There are some uncertain responses including 'in self defence' or 'in defence of my children'; but then admissions that they cannot actually imagine such a situation (and I am left wondering whether those who have dropped out of the discussion *can* imagine, and find this all too close for comfort). In the end, someone usually says 'How can we know? We've never experienced that.' And most agree.

I worry about the silent ones, and whether my own intrusive questioning is unsettling memories that may threaten them. I know on the law of averages that some in the class will have experienced violence, though more likely from parents, lovers or friends than from political enemies. I know, given the very large numbers of refugees and other escapee immigrants, from displaced persons camps in Europe after World War II, from Greece in civil war, Lebanon, Vietnam, ex-Yugoslavia and war-torn

Central American states, that political violence is the personal and family experience of many Australians, and that the children of survivors are not unaffected. Am I exposing personal and family troubles, often the very reason for coming to Australia – often, in the hope of forgetting?

But we must talk also of women and war, trying to avoid the recurrent images of women as victims, as dependents, as those to be protected (along with children), while lacking any control over the terms of their protection. I tell stories, and encourage students to find more, of women warriors, agents in liberation struggles for example, even while I myself remain fearful about the consequences of use of any violence. Those women may be of left or right, in support of inclusive or of exclusivist nationalist causes – there is no virtue simply in being a woman, nor any inevitable or necessary feminist commitment either. Some students, especially some women's studies ones with a considerable personal investment in themselves as women and in women as nurturers and peacemakers, as life givers with a special association with and responsibility for peace, struggle here.

TEACHING/LEARNING TERROR

Silence, women's absence, repressing women and sex, writing their experiences out of IR, is something that this unit is explicitly set against. So I must talk about what happens to women in wars. Much that happens to men; and, often, more.

Rape in war has a long history, though it is rarely named in war reporting, at least until Bosnia and the witnessing of those forced to act as 'comfort women' for Japanese troops. We maintain a certain distance by asking how and why such issues come onto the political agenda, in what language, whose views and whose experiences are being taken seriously? There is a brave feminist project here, to name private secrets and dangers to women's bodies, and do so in a way that focuses on the women themselves. Much feminist and women-centred work has paid off, really only since 1991, in the emergence of a strong stand on women's rights as human rights on the international scene. We read reports of, and where possible by, those women who have themselves experienced war rape – often systematic, multiple, in front of family and apparently with the complicit support or active direction of the leaders involved.

In Bosnia, and from the evidence in every other war, though in some more widely and officially endorsed than others, war rape is commonplace. The gendered and body politics of nationalisms, of difference, are crucial to our understandings of war. Women's relations to the nation and other political identities, as reproducers of its members, as cultural transmitters and as symbols of difference, so often located in culture and especially in women's and gender roles, make women particularly susceptible to violence as other/men's women. Sexual violence against them often appears as a way of getting at other men, of humiliating them by demonstrating that they are not real men, cannot protect 'their' women. 'Their women' are violated, so we have the extraordinary notion, from German-occupied France in World War I to Bosnia today, of 'enemy babies', and public, nationalist and religious debate about the desirability or otherwise of abortion in these circumstances.

It is difficult to find ways of talking about such horrors. I have written elsewhere:

> feminists seeking to help break the silence, but not wishing to speak for or dangerously expose other women, struggle to find ways of writing that do not appropriate their experiences and pain in ways that those women may not recognise, or in interpretations they themselves might reject. There are more dangers of writing, for fear that the endless repetition of the appalling is ultimately numbing and will 'turn off' the reader. Worse, it may turn some of them on, as women's own pain becomes 'warnography' (Gibson 1993: 258).

(Pettman 1996b)

There is no sign here that this is turning anyone on, though some draw down the blind and stoically let it (apparently) flow over them. In lectures, I stop for a moment.

I think other things. Did the women of whom I speak give permission for me to 'use' them? I refer only to public accounts. Am I using their pain to illustrate other things, other kinds of political project? In any student group there is likely to be one or more from ex-Yugoslavia, probably Croatian given the Australian demographics, and probably with relatives still there. I'm careful to say 'those who support the Greater Serbian project', rather than blame all Serbs. Research has revealed that 85 percent of women refugees in Australia have experienced sexual torture, and some of them have not told family members or now wish to forget. Some others in the room will have experienced rape or have friends who have – am I trespassing on dangerous territory? Am I responsible for the emotional effects of my teachings?

A feminist colleague has been doing work with Salvadorian women in Melbourne who are survivors of sexual torture (McIntyre 1993), who tell of nightmares and flashbacks following on news reports of Bosnian rapes, and on seeing misogynist soft porn in the ordinary news stands, like a recent one with a woman (model) naked on her knees with a dog collar around her neck.

I know too that some men also experience sexual violence in wars and identity conflicts. We talk about this, and push back to the dangerous connections between manhood and nationhood, between masculinity, militarism and domination practices.

BODY POLITICS

By this later stage of the course, I have put a lot of work into building a congenial space, a place where students' own knowledges and experiences are valued, where they feel safe to talk. This is now dreadfully disrupted, and there is distress, and anger too. Some women, especially younger ones, try to locate themselves in all this by turning discussion to women's physical vulnerability, about public space and the dangers, even here, of being seen to be 'out of place', or else fair game in a culture which sexualises women's bodies and puts them on display for men's use and pleasure. Here almost every woman has a story to tell, and for some the personal becomes political as the universality of their experiences is underlined.

Some say it's all too much; it's too depressing. They will repeat this as we go on, for example, to a section entitled 'The international political economy of sex' (Pettman 1996c). Part of experiencing the world – ours and others – is that we all experience it as gendered, and embodied, beings. The huge international processes that early on seemed so far away impact on everyday lives, and impact differently in part, in terms of raced and sexed differences inscribed on bodies. Sex tourism and international child prostitution are much in the news currently, as Australia and some other 'sending' states introduce legislation to prosecute the men (why is it always men?) on their return from abusing children in Thailand and the Philippines for example (often not seeing themselves as paedophiles, but seeking younger sex in part on the assumption that it is 'cleaner' in an AIDS endangered world). Indigenous attitudes to prostitution, fuelled by military prostitution through R and R and around the big foreign military bases, and by poorer states' search for hard currency in the form of tourist dollars, play on racialised gender stereotypes representing 'Asian' women as passive and exotic. 'Development' and International Monetary Fund aggravated disruptions, wars and state terrorism, impoverish and displace people, and force many of them into 'hospitality' trades. There are international campaigns and trans-national alliances, which some students are involved in, and which help us avoid reproducing 'third world women' as always/already victim.

LEARNING THE DIFFERENCE?

Here, deconstructing (sexualised) difference and the ways it is mobilised in familiar tourist and international airline advertisements, for example, becomes a way of critically engaging with our own images of difference. But here and elsewhere I wonder if my search for women's agency, and our use of third world women's and feminist writing, involves appropriating difference: making it accessible, domesticating it, relating it to our experiences in ways the women themselves might not agree with. There's a problem, too, with academic tourism, selective viewing and retreating back to our own safe places when it gets hard. I try to work against this by encouraging our locating ourselves in relation to those we talk about, in power relations that include power difference between women – while also searching for things that women share as women.

Quite often, especially older women will identify strongly with the women about whom we talk; though again I'm not sure where some of the young men are here. There is also a tendency, running sometimes with and sometimes against identification, of cultural relativism, of suspending judgement (perhaps disavowing white/centre power?). This may be respecting others, or it may be a resistance strategy, a way of not engaging. This becomes especially clear when we are discussing women's rights as human rights, and talk for example about the estimated 90 million women in the world who have experienced female genital mutilation. Again, much care needs to be taken in speaking (and writing) for others. For some, the horror at what is done to women's and girls' bodies becomes a sign of 'their' barbarity, of our comparative humanity, and plays into the hands of received and racialised understandings of the world. Here, we must make clear the grounds for our anger and outrage, as violations of women's bodies and rights. There is a parallel with war rape, long read as shame, as an assault on men's and nations' honour; not as torture. Without care, women's bodies again become sites for other people's politicing, and policing.

Learning about the international, about difference, is learning about the experiences of others, who, on the whole, are not where we are, and often have not written their own accounts, at least not in a language or format accessible to us. But there are now many stories, reports, interviews and other tellings, which can internationalise the account. Connecting these with our own experiences is hard work. Here I totally agree that feminist '[t]eaching, research and supervision . . . are outrageously and absolutely practical, political and intellectual activities' (McRobbie 1982: 54; her italics), far and away from the stereotypical ivory tower of some imaginings of the university.

SOCIABILITY AND POWER

I urge students to learn about the international, to locate themselves in terms of what we're talking about, and encourage them to explore the impact of the international on their own lives. Part of good feminist and experiential learning is creating a safe space, respecting others' knowledges, enabling students to use the course to make sense of their world/s. This can happen in sometimes unexpected ways, as when younger women show relief and delight in being able to talk about sexuality or bodies, and others in discussing their experiences of migration. Soon there is continuous traffic between the personal, the political and the international, with much wondering about how representative or part of a pattern their or other stories are. Caution is sometimes needed here, lest the political be reduced simply to the personal; so we search for ways to move from the personal to the global and back again.

I listen to the ways we talk to each other, and remind myself of an important distinction coming out of feminist research (and there seems to be much less writing on feminist teaching than feminist research: McNeill 1992), between public and private accounts (Ribbens 1987). My giving permission to talk about themselves gives some students practice at making self, investigating and articulating their views of themselves. I'm anxious about pushing for too much self disclosure. Most students did not sign up in this course to do therapy, and some do not wish to talk about their own lives with other students or me. I encourage us all to become careful and respecting – and active – listeners. (What does it mean to listen as woman? (Devault 1990); as a feminist?) Some of the fragments of life stories we are told take us into the realms of oral history, which can be as much self dramatisation as truth telling. Here experience is not something that has already happened, to be pulled out and put on display; nor is the self already made, to be progressively revealed to others – or even to oneself. What is offered may be 'a fictional performance of self' (Hamilton 1990), which doesn't mean it's not real, but that in on-going learnings, it may be being 'tried on'. Does this process favour the braver, more articulate or extrovert students, especially those women's studies women whose own lives may include consciousness raising and much reflection on and practice at self? As mine surely does. How, and who, do I 'perform' here?

The paradoxes of feminist teaching are never-ending, but become especially problematic around my own personal performance and institutional authority. I work very hard at giving up on authority, even while using both expert and referential power – what I've come to know and resources I use in this field. One feminist academic declares (about feminist research) 'No intimacy without reciprocity' (Oakley 1984), and I like the sound of that. But I also have reward power, to pass, fail, to confirm or destroy chances and choices. Another describes the likes of me as 'the bearded mother' (Morgan 1987: 50), expected, and often wanting, to nurture, to be accessible and supportive on personal as well as education terms, asserting an ethic of care. But with assessment and grading 'the mother' becomes more like the stereotypical father, whose approval turns out to be conditional. I call attention to the power relations within which we work, which many are well aware of; inform them as best I can about my expectations and the various tests through which they must pass, and encourage collaborative learning and endless conversations which prompt and cue and give feedback and encouragement. But the bottom line remains as my power, and paid responsibility, to judge.

CONCLUDING

Teaching the international is inevitably and intrinsically about teaching difference, along fault lines of global, national, local and personal power. The boundaries of difference are constructed and defended on the bodies of actual people. Many of my students become adept (though of course some were before) at deconstructing 'difference', and at locating their own identities and experiences in terms of these differences. One recurring observation in evaluations is that the course came to have personal relevance for them, or touched in some ways on their own experiences. While this does raise again the possibility that I/we have 'domesticated' difference, it also reflects the insistence of a pioneer international politics feminist scholar, Cynthia Enloe (1989), that 'the international is personal', impacting on each of us in our everyday lives, and that 'the personal is international', as our own identities, interests and actions become a part of making the world go round.

REFERENCES

Devault, M. (1990) 'Talking and listening from women's standpoint', *Social Problems*, 37, 1, 96–116.

Enloe, C. (1989) *Bananas, Bases and Beaches: Feminism and International Politics*, London, Pandora.

Frankenburg, R. (1993) *White Women/Race Matters*, Minneapolis: Minnesota Press.

Gibson, S. (1993) 'On sex, horror and human rights', *Women: A Cultural Review*, 4, 3, 250–261.

Hamilton, P. (1990) 'Inventing the self: oral history as autobiography', *Hecate*, 16, 1–2, 128–133.

Huggins, J. *et al.* (1991) 'Letter to the editor', *Women's Studies International Forum*, 14, 5.

McIntyre, M. (1993) *Virtuous Women and Violent Men: Salvadoran Women and the Sexual Politics of Machismo*, Canberra: Humanities Research Centre, Australian National University.

McNeill, M. (1992) 'Pedagogical praxis and problems: reflections on teaching about gender relations', in H. Hinds *et al.* (eds) *Working Out: New Directions in Women's Studies*, London: Falmer Press, 18–28.

McRobbie, A. (1982) 'The politics of feminist research: between talk, text and action', *Feminist Review*, 12, 46–58.

Mohanty, C., Russo, A. and Torres, L. (eds) (1992) *Third World Women and the Politics of Feminism*, Bloomington: Indiana University Press.

Morgan, K. (1987) 'The perils and paradoxes of feminist pedagogy', *Resources for Feminist Research*, 16, 3, 49–52.

Oakley, A. (1984) 'Interviewing women: a contradiction in terms?', in *Telling the Truth about Jerusalem*, London: Basil Blackwell.

Pettman, J. (1991) 'Towards a (personal) politics of location', *Studies in Continuing Education*, 13, 2, 153–166.

—— (1992) *Living in the Margins: Racism, Sexism and Feminism in Australia*, Sydney: Allen and Unwin.

—— (1993) 'Gendering International Relations', *Australian Journal of International Affairs*, 47, 1, 181–198.

—— (1996a) *Worlding Women: A Feminist International Politics*, Sydney: Allen and Unwin, London: Routledge.

—— (1996b) 'Boundary politics: women, nationalism and damage', in J. Purvis and M. Maynard (eds) *New Frontiers in Women's Studies,* London: Taylor and Francis.

—— (1996c) 'An international political economy of sex', in E. Kofman and G. Youngs (eds) *Globalisation: Theory and Practice,* London: Pinter.

Ribbens, J. (1987) 'Interviewing: an "unnatural situation"?', *Women's Studies International Forum*, 12, 6, 579–592.

APPENDIX: LECTURE OUTLINE

Week 1

- Gendering international politics
- The international politics of gender

These lectures introduce the course, and ask what is International Politics? what is gender? before reviewing some of the recent feminist writings on International Relations.

Week 2

- Women and the state
- Women and citizenship

The state is a key unit in International Relations, and citizenship of a state is a complex status/identity. Are states and citizens gendered? What are women's experiences of the state? (which state?). What are their experiences of citizenship? In what ways do these experiences differ from those of men?

Week 3

- Women and nationalism
- Women and ethnicity

Nationalism and ethnic conflicts are now key issues in International Politics. How are political identities in international politics constructed and mobilised? How are women and men positioned in relation to national, ethnic and religious categories?

Week 4

- The sexual politics of colonisation
- Black women, white women and the gender of 'race'

'Women' is not a homogeneous category. Race and class position different women differently. White women are ambiguously placed in colonisation and in contemporary settler states like Australia; and indigenous women are placed by their 'race' as much – or more – than by their sex.

Week 5

- Women and migration, women as refugees
- Feminism, racism and cultural difference

Most writing about migration, migrant labour and refugees is ungendered; yet women experience these processes somewhat differently than men. They also experience ethnic minority status and cultural difference in gendered ways. What are the implications of these differences for feminist theory and practice?

Week 6

- Is war a gender/ed issue?
- The sex of violence? masculinity/ies and violence

What causes war? Is man naturally aggressive? Are women naturally peaceful? Women's anti-war action and some feminist readings focus debates on the gender of violence. What happens when we bring these perspectives together with International Relations debates about the causes of war/wars?

Week 7

- Women in the military
- Women and militarisation

Warriors have long been male. Current debates about women in the armed forces provide another perspective on war making. Militarism is a process which affects many women beyond those with direct associations with 'the military'. It is also a global political process, although it affects different women in different states differently.

Week 8

- Women, peace and security
- Women and political action

Many women are involved in the peace movement, and in political action and feminist theory for peace, security and social justice. What do their understandings about politics and power suggest about women as agents for political change? What does taking women's experiences of violence seriously do to strategic debates about security and violence?

Week 9

- Women and national liberation struggles
- Women in the Middle East

Women play crucial roles in nationalist struggles, but many pacifist women and some feminists have difficulties with women as fighters. Women are also used symbolically to mark the borders of difference and nationalism. This is especially evident in contemporary constructions of 'Arab' and 'Muslim' women, whose own identities and roles are often very different from their stereotypes.

Week 10

- Women and the international political economy
- Women and work

The international labour market is segmented along gender lines. Men and women are positioned differently in relation to the global economy, and women's work changes along with the increasing internationalisation of state economies.

Week 11

- Women and development
- Women, aid and non-governmental agencies

'Women in development' (WID) has documented ways in which women are differentially affected by development processes, while feminist analysis and women's organisations have given voice to women's experiences in third world countries. What are women's roles currently as actors within and as acted upon by development policies and international organisations?

Week 12

- Women's rights as human rights
- The international political economy of sex

Human rights are not gender neutral. Women's status as rights claimants is often inferior to (some) men's. What are 'women's issues' in human rights? What do 'new' international issues, e.g. those of AIDS and tourism, have to do with women?

Week 13

- Gender and the environment

- Global feminism?

The politics of globalism now includes environmental issues. What are women in international social movements and in international forums on the environment doing? Is there a global feminist movement? What does the category 'women' mean in cross-cultural and international politics?

8 Using life experience to teach feminist theory

Elizabeth Tisdell

The development of feminist consciousness is an evolutionary process. It is one that incorporates experience as well as reflection on experience. For most, it involves an overtly intellectual pursuit as well, through reading feminist literature or taking courses that incorporate feminist analyses of life experience or theoretical constructs. The purpose of this chapter is to explore the development of feminist consciousness in one particular context, a feminist theory class in a higher education setting. In particular, it considers the use of life experience (as both shared story as well as the provision of experiential learning opportunities) as a way of casting light on various feminist theoretical frames and as a base for learning, developing and revising both feminist theory and one's continued life experience.

Because there are many facets of experience, I have chosen to break the chapter down into three parts. It begins with a discussion of the context in which the learning experience takes place and the implicit assumptions about that learning context that necessarily affect that experience. Second, because my own personal experience and development as a feminist thinker and theorist are important to understanding how I see my role and the kind of experiences I provide in the class, I will discuss aspects of my background and experience which affect the way the class is conducted. Third, the way students discuss and interact with their life experience and each other in light of the course material will be considered.

THE CONTEXT

The context of learning has a profound effect on the way the learning experience is both constructed and construed. The class in question is one in feminist theory offered through the women's studies programme at a major research university in the south-eastern United States. It is cross-listed at both graduate and undergraduate levels. There are many implied assumptions about teaching and learning in such a context. While one may want to create a learning environment where power disparities are done away with, there is no getting around the fact that universities have some power over teachers and teachers always have some power over students. It is impossible to get outside of these particular power relations which are structured into the very life of the university. It is generally expected that a teacher will come to class on the first day with a prepared syllabus of readings and assignments. Various aspects of those assignments may be negotiated with the students, but ultimately how much to negotiate is the choice of the teacher (which is a position of power) who gives a grade at the end of the course.

The university is a place that generally emphasises the development of intellectual capacities and cognitive understanding from a rational perspective. Traditionally, it is not a place where a discussion of one's personal experience is considered relevant. But this is a women's studies class, where different ways of knowing are also discussed and valued, and students' analysis of how theoretical writings fit or define their own experience is considered relevant and important. Nevertheless, much discussion of life experience in any higher education context is considered suspect, and in a recent article, journalist Karen Lehrman (1993) referred to the discussion of personal experience in introductory undergraduate women's studies classes as 'classroom therapy'. She further stated, 'in many classes discussions alternate between the personal and the political, with mere pit stops at the academic' (Lehrman 1993: 46). Lehrman's negative critique reflects a popular assumption that it is not possible to have a rigorous intellectual discussion and examine life experience simultaneously, an assumption with which I strongly disagree. Nevertheless in the context of higher education where grading is required, most teachers (myself included), even of women's studies, grade primarily on how well students analyse and critique or discuss a cognitive understanding of the authors read, not how well they discuss their life experience. Thus, graded written assignments for this class include theoretical papers analysing the similarities and differences among theoretical frames and a final paper relating feminist theory to a topic in their field of study. Ungraded assignments include three one-page personal reflection papers and participation in class experiential activities and discussions.

Course content is also significant to understanding this learning context. The basic purpose of feminist theory is to discuss women's experience, to examine gender as a social construct, to problematise gender relations and to theorise experience. All feminist theories examine women's experience and oppression, and most theoretical constructs have an overt or implied project for social change. Each frame gives a different emphasis to the cause(s) of women's oppression; for example, radical feminists emphasise patriarchy as the root cause while Marxist feminists emphasise the role of capitalism. Writers of black feminist thought deal with the intersections of race with gender and class, while feminist postmodernists discuss how there is no 'Reality' or 'Truth', but that each person's 'reality' or 'truth' is personally constructed amidst multiply intersecting systems of privilege and oppression that one benefits and/or suffers from. Some of these multiply intersecting systems of privilege and oppression include gender, race, class, affectional/sexual orientation, age, ability/disability, citizenship, educational level. All theories problematise 'gender'; thus gender as a social construct, the nature of gender relations, are central to the course. Because 'woman' is not a unitary category, and there are many similarities and differences among women based on race, class, affectional orientation and so on, what 'woman' or group of women the theory seems to be about is examined along with how well the theory addresses similarities and differences among women.

In the US, most who support a feminist agenda are politically left of centre. This is an advanced level women's studies class, so almost all students (both male and female) who take the class already support a feminist political agenda and therefore tend to reflect a left-of-centre political orientation, though there is variation among them on how far left they are. Most are also white and middle class, which is a reflection of the composition of the overall student body at this particular university. Given that the feminist theory literature deals with gender as a social construct and problematises gender relations, the social construction of heterosexuality is also problematised. In light of such problematisation, typically a couple of students will mention being lesbian or bisexual at some point (usually later) in the course. Given that the course content deals with the similarities and differences among women, the similarities and differences among the classroom participants are significant. In the discussion which follows, I refer primarily to two different feminist theory classes. Both had between fifteen and twenty students made up of slightly more graduates than undergraduates, and there was a faculty woman in each class sitting in for her own interest. One class had one male student, the other had one African-American woman student. There was one Taiwanese woman in each class; the rest of the students were white and ranged in age from early twenties to early fifties. In one class, three of the students claimed a lesbian identity, while one defined herself as bisexual. While a cognitive understanding of theory was emphasised, in this learning context the life experiences of myself, the students and women not represented in the class were used to illustrate theoretical constructs through small group activities. In the next two sections I will examine how working with these experiences can facilitate the learning of feminist theory.

MY OWN DEVELOPING FEMINIST CONSCIOUSNESS: SALIENT EXPERIENCES AND THEIR PRESENCE IN THE CLASSROOM

I am hired by the university to teach feminist theory, and to provide a learning context where students can learn and develop theory, which is primarily an intellectual exercise. But theory is only useful if it does indeed reflect the human experiences and practices of a particular constituency. Similarly, practice or experience without any thought to the working theory on which such practice is based might mean that such practice rests on bad theory (Hart 1992). Thus, my purpose in this class is to explore the feminist theory/women's experience dialectic. I want students to understand the feminist frames as discussed by various feminist theorists, but I also want them to understand, critique and reshape the theories by examining their own experience, and the experiences of flesh and blood real women who are oppressed by multiple structures that may forever deny them access to the luxury of taking a feminist theory class in a higher education setting.

So how do I accomplish these goals in the classroom itself? Can I expect students to talk about and theorise their own experience if I am unwilling to provide a model and do it myself? The truth is that my development as a feminist is a complex story, which has to do with both my interaction with structures or systems that privilege or oppress me, and with the totality of male and female individuals that I have interacted with who have had an impact on my understanding or problematising gender relations on both the very personal and social level. So it is to the telling of some of my own personal story that I now turn.

I grew up in the late 1950s, 1960s and early 1970s in a coastal suburban town about fifteen miles north of Boston, Massachusetts, which was nearly all white, mostly middle-class, largely Jewish and ethnic Catholic. I was the fourth of five children from a middle-class home and my family was heavily influenced by the values and mores of my mostly Irish Catholic heritage. My father was a businessman and my mother was a teacher, though my mother did not go back to teaching full-time until my younger brother was well into grade school. Education was emphasised, and it was a given that we would all go to college and that my parents would provide whatever financial and emotional support they could, in order to help all five of us graduate from college. While my family was not overly religious (by Catholic standards), going to Mass on Sunday was a requirement of us all. I was socialised to believe I would grow up, go to college, get married and have children. While I may have a career, it would be secondary to my husband's, and I probably would take 'time out' to raise children.

My first recognised experience of overt sexism was when I was in high school. I was involved with the Catholic Youth Organisation (CYO) and was bothered by the fact that when it came time for elections and one of my girl friends was going to run for president, we were told that the president had to be a boy. We were not happy about that fact, but accepted it without putting up a fight, though we complained about it to each other. It was 1971.

In college I majored in mathematics, and fell in love with my first really serious boyfriend. By the end of my sophomore year, we were discussing the possibility of marriage upon graduation. Such a discussion would have made many young women in 1975 blissfully happy. And it made me blissfully happy too – for about two weeks! The year that followed was a difficult one, a time of deep questioning and soul searching – about marriage in general, about my own relationship and of the assumptions underlying much of my Irish-Catholic background. At the restaurant/ coffee shop where I worked part-time, I remember watching married couples who looked 'settled' but not especially happy interact over dinner or coffee, or overhearing conversations between married women as I would move from one table to another refilling coffee cups. So many looked harried, like their real selves were buried or hidden somewhere deep inside or somewhere else altogether. Their 'look' didn't make the prospect of getting married appealing, and it was a look that I didn't want to see reflected back in the mirror. It was a painful time, and I wondered what was wrong with me. The prospect of marriage seemed so frightening and so 'un-whoever I was becoming'. I didn't think of this particularly in feminist terms, and I remember feeling rather guilty and unhappy that I couldn't make myself want what so many women that were part of the very fabric of my life wanted so desperately for themselves or wanted so desperately for me.

I tried to work out my questions and soul searching about what the 'meaning of life is anyway' by becoming more involved with the Catholic Church. While I saw many inconsistencies in the Church and was pretty sure I disagreed with the Church's official position on many issues, especially those that directly affect women's lives, like contraception and women's role in the Church, it was the only place in my limited life experience that seemed to attempt to deal with issues of meaning and life philosophy. I saw the Church as an institution working for social justice, engaged in social advocacy for economically disadvantaged groups at the grassroots level. That was a part of the Church I liked. And I played the guitar and the piano and it was the era of the 'folk Mass' and I enjoyed singing and playing with a folk group. While I was aware of some bothersome inconsistencies in the Church's social justice agenda, on a personal level I developed a lot of significant and meaningful relationships with both men and women in this context. So much so that with the rise in emphasis on lay ministry in the Church in the late 1970s I did a master's degree in religion and worked as a campus minister for ten years (from 1979 to 1989) after completing it.

By the time I finished graduate school in 1979, I had more of a sense of a feminist consciousness. I remember that my master's thesis had to be written in gender inclusive language, and there was a good bit of discussion of the perils of sexist language in the context of a larger discussion about the second-class citizenship of women in the Church and the world. While I was not very sophisticated in my feminist thinking, I had begun to see as well as to experience the fact that women had less structural power than men in nearly every situation. So for the next ten years, in two different university contexts as a Catholic campus minister, the place of women in the Church and the world formed one among many of my social justice agendas.

During those ten years, amidst a variety of duties, I rubbed shoulders with and heard many young women's stories (stories not unlike my own) of a search for self identity, of struggles in primary relationships, of concerns with sexuality-related issues, of trying to develop a holistic view of life and/or a spirituality that fit who each was becoming. Some were even trying to decide if it was possible to be both a Catholic and a feminist. I too had reckoned and was continuing to reckon with many of these issues in my own life as my own feminist consciousness continued to develop.

In my personal life, I continued to have significant relationships with men and women I loved or with whom I was in love, who taught me a lot about the nature of the social construction of gender and gender relations. I knew I was socialised to believe that only men could meet some of my needs while others were best met through women. Of course these ideas were somewhat based on stereotypes and generalisations of what men and women are like. In the context of these relationships and my developing feminist consciousness, I began to deconstruct some of my socialisation and tried to develop relationships with men and women that were not based on such traditional gender expectations – where some affectional needs could be met from women while some of my needs for a deep personal understanding could be satisfied from men.

It is from both the personal and professional experiences described above that I initially developed my own version of feminist theory. I had begun to see a pattern to women's experience, and to women's oppression in the university, in the Church and in the world. I had begun to develop an understanding of the nature of structural oppression, and also knew that at times in my own life, particularly in my early years of working in campus ministry, I felt some oppression based not only on my gender but on my age as well (I was twenty-four when I began working in the field). I clearly also could see that black women experienced more systems of oppression than I did as a white woman. And I certainly recognised from my personal relationships how much of a hold my socialisation had on my psyche as I continued to try (and still do) to deconstruct my expectations of others based on their gender, or expectations of how I think I 'ought' to behave as a woman on a deeply unconscious level.

So here I write seven years later. I eventually found the discrepancy between my personal beliefs and the official ideology of the Catholic Church too wide even though I had many positive experiences with the individuals with whom or for whom I worked. I dealt with this discrepancy by returning to school and have since finished a doctoral degree in adult education with an emphasis in women's studies. And now I teach feminist theory. How much of this personal story do I tell? How much should I tell in this higher education context in a feminist theory course where I try to use experience to promote the learning and development of feminist theory?

I typically tell a version of the above narrative of my personal story the first day of class. It is easy to tell stories about my interactions with structures and systems that oppress. My experience with the Catholic Church, an extremely patriarchal institution, serves as a good example. Talking about my personal experiences in relationships with people I have loved, or been in love with, is a bit more uncomfortable. I am in class, perhaps the way I have been here. While I refer to the story of my first serious relationship discussed above, I tend to refer to experiences in significant love relationships only in passing to illustrate ways I learned about the social construction of gender and gender relations. Nevertheless, all my experiences, spoken and unspoken, are present with me on the same level as I work with experience to promote the learning of feminist theory in the classroom.

THE STUDENTS' EXPERIENCE IN CONTEXT

Students have their own life experiences to discuss, to begin to learn to theorise, and their own experiences of the class itself. Because it is important to hear at least some of the students' voices, where possible and with their permission, I have included the words of a few of them – either from their papers or from semi-structured interviews.

In order to set the stage for using experience to begin to learn to theorise experience and problematise the notion of gender relations, I tell a good part of my own story – with emphasis on my socialisation, my interactions in the Church – and highlight what I perceived was expected of me as a woman, what I expected of myself and how that changed over time depending on the context. A large part of the first class session (each class is nearly three hours long) is devoted to each of the participants telling key elements of her (or his) story, with regards to developing an understanding of one's own gender, and gender relations in general. Perhaps because I only make general remarks about my own significant love relationships, many of the students at this point will make more or less general remarks about their love relationships, although those who are married or divorced tend to talk about significant aspects of those experiences that taught them something about the nature of gender relations. Those who are single, lesbian, bisexual or not currently 'formally attached' tend to make only general remarks about their intimate relationships and what they have learned from them.

After these introductory stories are told, we examine some of the similarities and differences of our stories, and write on the board elements of our collective story. Some of the things that typically come up here are the significance of gender socialisation, of mothers' primary influence in the home and family, of religion and of a growing awareness in each of our lives over time of the patriarchal nature of most societal institutions that accord greater attention, pay and privilege of all sorts to males in this culture. The one man also talked about these same issues but in somewhat less detail. While most of the women in these classes talk of receiving mixed messages from different people in regards to gender relations, most also tell a story of being told by someone of importance in their lives that they could do or be whatever they want regardless of the fact that they were female. I will ask, after we seem to be finished, what part of each one's individual story is not represented in this collective story in what we have written down. Because most of the students are white and middle-class, they typically do not mention aspects of their racial identity or their class background that affect who they are. In a recent class, it was the African-American woman who brought up at this point in the discussion the importance of race, the Asian woman the issue of national origin and the woman who was from a working-class family background who brought up the significance of class in her own family background. From this discussion came the role of education and its relationship to the challenge or perpetuation of power relations based on race, class and gender, and the interrelationship of all these issues with access to education. At the end of the discussion, I asked the question of what was missing of significance in our analysis – that pertained either to this group or to other groups of women not represented in the class. Sexual orientation, age and ability/disability issues came up at this point, but no one discussed any of these issues from a personal perspective at this time.

Certainly, part of the point of this exercise is group bonding, because we have more invested in our own and others' learning if we know something about each other as participants. But the major point of this exercise is to work with our individual experience, then our collective experience and then to begin to theorise the experience of women and to problematise gender relations. It is also to demystify theory, because as Flax (1993) and others point out, most women have been socialised to see men as more rational, intellectual and therefore more theoretical than they see themselves. I try to make the connection between theory and experience explicit throughout the course by creating an experiential learning activity for each feminist theoretical frame studied. While feminist theory addresses *women's* experience primarily, it does problematise and examine the nature of gender relations. Therefore, it is also relevant to men, and the experiential activities focus either around women's experience *or* the nature of gender relations. While the man in the class did participate in all the activities, he was generally more quiet than the women, and insisted that he also needed to listen to women's theorising of their own experience. Of course a large part of each class was also devoted to digesting and analysing and exploring the ideas in the reading, most of which was quite rationalistic and theoretical, and he was somewhat more vocal in these discussions.

Dealing with the similarities and differences among the students is important in a class like this, both from the perspective of developing a classroom atmosphere where students who have been culturally marginalised can come to voice and move, as Lorde (1984) suggests, from silence to language and action, but also for the experience of developing and theorising the experience of different groups of women. The theme of voice, of needing to verbalise experience as a way of coming to own, analyse and change one's experience of being a woman in the world is a familiar theme both in the feminist literature (cf. hooks 1994, Lewis 1990, Maher and Tetrault 1994, Schniedewind 1987) and of the class itself. Nicole, a Taiwanese woman, alluded to this theme of voice and action throughout the class. The first day she mentioned her need to overcome her fear of speaking in class, since she is not a native English speaker, and later in one of her papers she wrote:

> I believe that there are some women [who], like me, cannot concretely distinguish what [they]/I really want to be from what my own culture wants me to be, because I have grown up under cultural expectations and internalised the cultural values as parts of my self-image. I believe, as hooks and Lewis suggested, sharing personal experience is a good way to radicalise consciousness. Listening to the experience of others, I feel that I am not the only one who suffers [this] anxiety and threat when I am trying to confront myself and reconstruct myself. I spend more time inward-looking in order to figure out [my] real inner voice.
>
> (Chen 1993: 1)

She writes further about the importance of an appreciation of her own standpoint as a Taiwanese woman in a class with Western feminists:

> Also, absorbing the experience of Western women, I have to [be] concerned with my standpoint in order to come to a more appropriate way to educate my people.... The way I want to do it is to encourage and support Chinese women to radicalise their consciousness.... Sharing experience is a good way to understand women's oppression.
>
> (Chen 1993: 1)

Not only does Nicole allude to naming her own experience in order to find her authentic voice in these remarks, she also highlights the issue of her different race and national origin, and her own particular standpoint as a result of it.

While the issue of sexual orientation is mentioned early on in a general discussion along with age and ability/disability issues, it tends to be discussed only in reference to the theoretical literature at the beginning. Feminist theory as a body of literature problematises the whole notion of gender and discusses gender as a social construct. In so doing, all of the theoretical frames, at least implicitly and some very explicitly, also problematise the notion of heterosexuality as a social construct. The radical feminist theoretical literature does this very explicitly, where the socialist feminist and post-modern feminist frames more or less accept as a given the concept of heterosexuality as a social construct. Reading such ideas is new to many of the students, but the lesbian and bisexual students have lived some of these ideas through personal experience. Very often a couple of the lesbian or bisexual students will bring their personal experience in this regard into small group discussion. What usually happens is that it will come up again in discussion in the large group usually well into the second half of the class, only after it has been discussed in a small group context. While most students don't talk in very much detail in large group discussions about their personal experience in general, my sense is that by the time the few students who choose to come to voice and go public in the classroom in regards to these issues, it is neither a surprise nor does it seem to alter the classroom dynamics in a very visible way. However, it does have an effect on the classroom participants in ways I can only know from what students told me after the class was over.

Mary, a woman in her late forties, referred to finding out through her experience in both the small groups and eventually in the large group later in the quarter that a couple of her favourite students were either lesbian or bisexual as an 'eyeopener'. She said:

> It was wonderful for me because some of the people who . . . Nancy was one that just took my fancy . . . I just thought she was funny and fun . . . . The ones in the group that were lesbians . . . they were people out of the group that I particularly liked . . . . It makes me realise all the more, that this is not something that people wear with a scarlet L on their forehead or anything and I just loved it. I loved it! I felt aside from, I guess Helen, and Frieda who was at least relatively close to my age, I just had this feeling . . . it wasn't a feeling that some of us were older and some of us were younger, and some of us were straight, some of us were not. We were just women! And we could all just be together and be who we are and it was great. It just meant so much to me, and that's why I was interested in keeping up that group relationship later. I had never felt that before. I've always enjoyed women, known that I liked being around women and talking to them, but I've never had the feeling before, all these different types of women being together and really truly listening to each other, understanding each other to the best of our ability and enjoying it.

In this discussion, Mary not only addresses the issue of sexual orientation, she also deals with the issue of age and indicated how she was conscious of the fact that she was older than most in the class. The students on the younger end of the scale also discussed the issue of age, but more from the perspective of having less life experience to discuss and draw in with the reading. While these differences are real, many of them discuss how these differences seemed less of an issue later on in the class.

Because many of the students are master's and doctoral students who are at some stage of doing their research, research ethics and the issue of who gets to speak for whom becomes an important feminist question. Together we reckon with our own privilege, at having the luxury of higher education and the luxury to be participating in a feminist theory class theorising the experience not only of ourselves, but also women who are not represented in the class and may not be like us at all. We attempt to deal with the issue of how our privileged position affects what we see, what we experience and how we theorise. Beth, a doctoral student doing research on women with disabilities, writes about both of these issues in her final class paper on an ethic of knowing:

> In attempting to find a way to incorporate this ethic of knowing into my own research socially situated as non-disabled, white, female, and within an economic class that has afforded me the opportunity for full-time university study, I ask myself these questions: Can I as a non-disabled woman ignore the inherent privilege of my 'ableness'? Is it ethically possible to situate myself as a researcher interested in persons with disabilities and ignore this privilege? How can I create a space in which subjects can come to voice and collaborate in the analysis of their stories? In doing so, what power, authority, and claims to that analysis will I give up? As researchers, when we tell the stories of our subjects do we betray trust, do we violate privacy? How much of the telling is our construction/interpretation/interests?
>
> (Ferri 1993: 16)

Perhaps herein lies the question and crux of the difficulty of theorising and even writing about the experience of others in addition to ourselves: how much of the telling and the theorising is really only about ourselves, our experience and our experience of the experience of others? This is a dilemma that all writers, researchers and theorists must face – the inherent systems of privilege that allow us to write, to do research, to be theorists – the very luxury of access to higher education.

AFTERWORD

In this chapter I have tried to explain the context of the class, to examine some of my own personal experiences and dilemmas about how to use experience (my own and the experience of others) that affect the way I try to promote the learning of feminist theory in this higher education situation. I have also tried to discuss my perceptions of the experiences of my students while presenting, as I did in the last section, what is one of the major issues in feminist theory – the issue of power and privilege and who gets to speak for whom. I recognise that as a teacher in a higher education setting, and as a writer of this chapter, I have to one degree exercised power and privilege and have spoken on behalf of and for my students, even though, where possible, I have used their words. But still, in the telling of their stories, in talking about their experience, I have told my own story – my story of how to use experience to promote the learning of feminist theory. I must ask, along with many feminist writers such as Michelle Fine (1992), can I speak on their behalf? Is it ethical to use their experience to support and tell my own story in the enterprise of feminist theorising? Perhaps it is more ethical if I also own that in the telling of this story, in using their stories to facilitate the telling of this one, what I have learned from them. My own understanding of feminist theory has changed and been reshaped as a result of our time together. And in my experience of this telling of our collective story, I am reshaping my understanding of feminist theory as I theorise my own experience with them. Thus as teacher and writer, I am also student, learner and theoriser.

So how successful were we in this classroom venture of trying to learn feminist theory by theorising life experience? The answer depends on how one defines success. Of course we not only attempt to theorise life experience; we also read what feminist theorists from various theoretical perspectives have written. As a teacher, I feel satisfied that students learn the similarities and differences among the various feminist theoretical perspectives. Many of them write excellent papers (one of which was recently accepted for publication in a refereed journal) that convince me they know the theories by their ability to identify what theoretical frames are used in discussions of feminist issues in their various academic disciplines and in political debates. And I believe that the discussion of personal experience, and the attempts at theorising experience, does facilitate the learning of feminist theory and the grasping of theoretical concepts. But I am somewhat aware of the fact that most students discuss theory and experience somewhat separately.

I interviewed a number of the students nearly a year after one of the classes was over in preparation for writing this chapter. Many of them talked about the classroom itself as a learning community, about what they learned about themselves and others, as was noted in some of their quoted remarks in the last section. They mentioned that my story about working for the Church and dealing with my Catholic identity was particularly significant in their examination of what their various religious traditions told them about who they should be as women. They also talked about some of the personal stories they heard from each other in small groups that affected their lives and how they thought about themselves as women in the world. They reported how their experience was changed and reshaped (as mine was also) as a result of our collective experience. But they tended to make specific reference to the theories more when I asked specifically about them. A number of them discussed the fact that they began developing the theoretical framework for their thesis or dissertation in the class. This is clearly useful and serves an important purpose, but more of what they talked about were the stories that were told. While they have a sense of theorising experience, as a teacher I would have liked for them to connect the stories with their understanding of the theories in more explicit ways. Yet it is not for me to decide what should be the *most* significant about students' learning. One of the participants made the following statement, 'Yes, I learned the theories. I can say I now know a lot about feminist theory based on my experience and the reading I did in that class. But what I will always remember are the stories.' Perhaps it is the stories and the context of the experience that promotes learning – at least the most significant learning.

In working with experience to promote learning, one might wonder if I have engaged in what journalist Karen Lehrman (negatively) referred to as 'classroom therapy'? As mentioned earlier, Lehrman does seem to assume that it is not possible to have a serious intellectual discussion about theoretical concepts and analyse one's own and others' life experience simultaneously. I believe that there is a part of good therapy that is and should be educational, and a part of a good educational experience, even in academia, that is and should be therapeutic. So have I have engaged in 'classroom therapy'? I'll leave it to the reader to decide!

REFERENCES

Chen, N. (1993) 'Reflection paper', unpublished manuscript.
Ferri, B. (1993) 'The possibilities of an ethic of knowing', unpublished manuscript.
Fine, M. (1992) *Disruptive Voices: The Possibilities of Feminist Research*, Ann Arbor: The University of Michigan Press.
Flax, J. (1993) 'Women do theory', in A. Jaggar and P. Rothenberg (eds) *Feminist Frameworks*, San Francisco: McGraw-Hill, 80–85.
Hart, M. (1992) *Working and Educating for Life: Feminist and International Perspectives on Adult Education*, New York: Routledge.
hooks, b. (1994) *Teaching to Transgress*, New York: Routledge.
Lehrman, K. (1993) 'Off course', *Mother Jones*, September/October, 45–68.
Lewis, M. (1990) 'Interrupting patriarchy: politics, resistance and transformation in the feminist classroom', *Harvard Educational Review*, 60, 4, 467–488.
Lorde, A. (1984) *Sister Outsider*, Trumansburg, NY: Crossing Press.
Maher, F. and Tetrault, M. (1994) *The Feminist Classroom*, New York: Basic Books.
Schniedewind, N. (1987) 'Teaching feminist process', *Women's Studies Quarterly*, 15, 3–4, 15–31.

Part 4

9   Building on experience
Working with construction workers in Brazil

Timothy Ireland

Writing from experience about experience – our own and others' – is necessarily a messy business. It involves an inside-out approach in which we attempt to make sense of what we do; it involves frequently rather subjective evaluations, the difficult interplay between the individual and the collective and the relation between group practice and the broader social context in which that practice takes place.

This chapter is about a complex chunk of experience in which the central actors are a group of construction workers, living and working in João Pessoa, the capital of the north-eastern state of Paraíba (Brazil). It is also about my own on-going involvement with this particular group which began in 1982 and has continued at different rhythms and with greater or less intensity since then.[1] Despite participating in a variety of other educational experiences over these years, it is this experience which has most assisted me to bridge the gap between intellectual understanding and passion in the sense that Gramsci used it, some sixty or more years ago, when he wrote: 'One cannot make politics-history without this passion, without this sentimental connection between intellectuals and people-nation' (Gramsci 1982: 418).

In order to disentangle the intricate web of this learning experience, I intend to highlight three particular dimensions of our collective social practice: the conceptual framework of popular education, the role of the agent and the dynamic of the educational process.

Popular education is not a particularly meaningful concept in Europe. However, in Latin America its advocates, amongst whom I would include myself, would argue that it provides a dynamic framework for understanding learning processes which seek to advance social change. Conversely, in Brazil the more European concept of experiential learning has gained little acceptance in formal educational circles: even its translation into Portuguese presents difficulties. Could this be because the practice of learning from experience is strongly associated with those segments of society whose educational opportunities are frequently restricted to processes of informal learning which are not the concern of the academy? Hence its absence from formal pedagogical parlance.

Practices of popular education are subject to the specific social, economic, cultural, political and technological context in which they are developed and, therefore, reflect the historical movement of which they are a part. During the period with which we are concerned here, 1982–1994, I suggest that there has been a change of perspective. At the beginning of the period, popular education's educational role was subordinated to its role as an instrument of politicisation, whereas in the present period there is a renewed recognition of the importance of the contents of the educational process. Whilst experience firmly underpins this development, it receives a specific treatment and understanding in each perspective. Clearly my own professional experience is closely woven into this larger movement. The discussion of the role of the agent/facilitator/educator, with particular reference to her/his mediatory role in class terms, will be exemplified by our own practice with the construction workers: the educational process is predominantly mediated by actors whose class situation differs from that of the working classes.[2] Finally, certain elements of the educational dynamic which we, agents and construction workers, have built up together over the years will be analysed together with the way in which this collective learning process has contributed to our own theoretical understanding of working with and building on experience.

To attempt to make sense of this very intense experience I find it necessary to indulge in a little autobiographical archaeology. In 1979, I was appointed to the post of Visiting Lecturer in Adult Education at the Federal University of Paraíba in João Pessoa. The state of Paraíba is one of the poorest states in the north-east region of Brazil which is itself the poorest and least developed region of this vast country.[3] As those conversant with the works of Paulo Freire will know, the north-east is the region where Freire originally lived, worked and developed his understanding of the potential of educational processes for change before being exiled in 1964 by the military – who were equally aware of that potential. At the time of my arrival, the Brazilian military regime still had another six years to run before democratic pressure forced a return to civilian rule.

I arrived in Brazil hot from a Master's degree course in adult education in which discussions of Paulo Freire's work had been a strong influence. This period of study had been preceded by an eye-opening two-year sojourn in General Franco's Spain: I had exchanged English lessons for political discussions with Spanish students. So I considered myself an old hand in military dictatorships.

Working in a university in this setting – an impoverished state in a country in the grips of a repressive military dictatorship – in which our principal theoretical concerns revolved around the possible contributions of education and learning to the advance of the social movements and to social change, it was impossible to ignore, on the one hand, the scale of human misery – social and economic injustice screamed out from every street corner – and, on the other, the courageous attempts of sectors of civil society, albeit in a largely adverse conjuncture, to organise in their struggle to place their demands on the political agenda.

Under the guise of working to promote 'lifelong education', then very much in vogue, our discussions were increasingly centred on the concept of 'popular education' and on attempting to comprehend the purposes of adult and lifelong education within that perspective. In theoretical terms it is dangerous to attempt to formulate a single concept of popular education. However, although there are many different ways of conceptualising practices which fall within the broad category of popular education, it is possible to point to certain basic principles which are common to most. In the 1960s, 1970s and 1980s, when the term popular education gained wide currency, it was closely identified with an explicit political option imbued with a clear class connotation. Popular education was an alternative proposal which sought to place education at the service of social change, whereby sectors of the working class would become both conscious and organised subjects/actors engaged in the pursuit of the structural transformation of society:

> Collective experience was seen as an expression of a collective class cultural identity and as associated with common interests and objectives. This experience – the experience of struggle, of exploitation, of hunger but also of shared common cultural forms, values, resistance and conquests – formed the central content of the learning process.
>
> (Ireland 1994a)

At the same time popular education was seen as expressing a radical critique of the type of education – form and content – offered to the working classes. Public education had become so divorced from the reality, experience and natural learning processes of these classes as to become largely irrelevant to their educational needs as a class.

The occupation of institutional space for progressive activities was also beginning to be raised. Some educators believed that any attempt at emancipatory learning via formal institutions was impossible as the institution automatically contaminated the process: Althusser, Establet, Bourdieu and other members of the French Reproductive School were at the height of their influence. Others expressed their understanding that if the capitalist state was to be undermined this had to be done from within via a war of positions: the influence of Gramsci was already beginning to penetrate socio-political analysis underpinning the basic premises of popular education.

Popular education, then, was largely concerned with the passage in Gramscian terms from 'common sense' to 'good sense' which in Freirean terminology is analogous to the passage from transitive consciousness to critical consciousness. The process was to be a politically progressive liberating education whose purpose was that of assisting the subordinate classes organise autonomously on a democratic participatory basis in the historic struggle to create a new class hegemony. More recently, popular education and, within it, the concept of learning from experience have undergone considerable changes. The disintegration of the socialist block in Eastern Europe and of the Soviet Union, the apparent defeat of the Sandinist government in Nicaragua, the uncertainties surrounding the Castro regime in Cuba, and the ever-deepening economic depression accompanied by growing levels of human degradation, poverty and hunger, have all led to a certain 'loss of innocence', to use Garcia-Huidobro's (1994) expressive phrase, and to a loss of direction. Social liberation is not just around the corner, as it had appeared to be. In Brazil the military have returned to the barracks but despite their replacement by elected governments, the drift into social apartheid and moral disintegration continues. Those who continue to orientate their educational practices by the principles of popular education now face a new and more complex conjuncture.[4]

Concern with education as an instrument for direct politicisation has been replaced in part by a new preoccupation with the contents of education. This is premised upon the conclusion that understanding cannot be limited to direct experience of reality since reality is infinitely more complex and extensive than our capacity to experience it directly. There exists a new concern with quality and with how to respond effectively to the demands of more complex forms of social and productive organisation. Practices of popular education are faced with the challenge of preparing the subaltern classes for a more effective insertion in existing structures without renouncing time-honoured objectives of strengthening democratic grassroots organisation. Without denying the central importance of basing learning processes on the daily life experience of the subjects of the educational process there is an increasing tendency to treat this experience – and particularly that of work – in more formal learning situations in which greater emphasis is given to the political importance of technical-scientific knowledge as a powerful instrument in the struggle for a more just society. Workers require access to scientific and technical knowledge if they are to achieve a broader understanding of society. Literacy programmes premised on the broad principles of popular education have frequently given greater attention to political discussion than to teaching the necessary 'mechanics' of language and communication.

What then has this to do with our educational practice with construction workers? Before answering this question it is clearly necessary to set the scene. If such educational practices are being tailored to meet the needs of those involved, this evidently requires an understanding of the building industry itself and of the characteristics of those who constitute its workforce. The building industry in João Pessoa still functions on the basis of the intensive use of manpower, of which a large part is unqualified. The nature of the product of the industry contributes to its institutionalised instability: when the merchandise (a building, a road, a drainage system, a housing estate, etc.) is terminated, the producer departs from the scene. Clearly this contributes to establish a climate of constant impermanence and 'disposability' amongst the workforce. Here today and gone tomorrow. Decisions to carry out large building projects are frequently dependent on the availability of public finance from federal government departments resulting in the subjection of the industry to politico-electoral manipulative practices. It is not uncommon for a newly elected government to suspend building projects initiated by its predecessor. Brazil is littered with half-finished bridges, roads which disappear into thick jungle and uncompleted sewage systems. Manpower turnover in the industry reaches levels unknown in other sectors of the urban economy. Wages are pitfully low, averaging around US$80 a month, whilst the non-registration of workers is inordinately high. Unofficial estimates put the number of clandestine workers at around 60 percent of the total workforce. Finally, the construction industry is notorious for its poor safety record. Its tally of fatal accidents is one of the worst for any sector of the urban economy.

The workers who make up the bulk of this 'profession' are largely unqualified, male, young (between eighteen and thirty-five years old) and of predominantly rural origin. Whilst some, expelled from the countryside by the growing capitalisation of the rural sector, set up house in the capital, others seek work in the city on a temporary basis, as a result of the lack of land and/or work in the rural areas. In a state which presents a 52.9 percent illiteracy rate, distributed approximately between one third in the urban areas and two thirds in the rural areas, it is evident that a workforce of predominantly rural origin should shelter a large number of illiterates. This illiterate population is particularly concentrated amongst the migrant labourers from the countryside: the temporary or seasonal migrants frequently account for 60 percent or more of the workforce in any one site. Robert Tressell's account of the building industry in Britain in the early 1900s[5] would sound remarkably contemporary to his Brazilian counterparts today.

In 1982, a group of these construction workers decided to mount an opposition slate to contest the elections for their local branch of the Building Workers' Trade Union to be held in 1983. Despite the failure of earlier attempts to organise an opposition movement, the Zé Peão group, as it baptised itself,[6] was convinced that the only way to begin to improve the building workers' situation was by putting an end to the many years of conciliatory and collaborationist union politics practised by the incumbent president. Although the branch was founded in 1934 there exists no record of any union-inspired industrial action in the ensuing fifty years. Despite a defeat in the 1983 elections and the subsequent blacklisting of the majority of its members, the group continued its patient efforts of discussion and persuasion amongst the rank-and-file union members during the succeeding years. This patient effort was rewarded when the group secured a resounding victory in the 1986 branch elections. The group has since been re-elected twice (in 1989 and 1992).

How then did I become involved with the Zé Peão group and what are the implications of this involvement for my understanding of the role of the agent in learning processes of this type? Initially it is important to note that my involvement did not possess an institutional character. I did not represent the university but was present as an educator who also happened to be a university lecturer. During the first four years I worked closely with a colleague, a medical doctor, who was coincidentally a student on the Master's course on which I also taught. This illustrates that particular phase in the development of popular education in which it was considered almost impossible to work through formal institutions.

Initially, we both represented other organisations, for which we worked in a voluntary capacity, on a support committee being organised to assist the incipient Zé Peão group prepare for the ensuing electoral battle. We quickly progressed, on our own insistence, from this auxiliary role to that of direct advisers to the group.

The group's platform was based upon a vision of a new combative trade unionism in which the organised participation of the rank-and-file member was essential for the building of a strong democratic union. In this respect my colleague and I considered our task to be that of assisting the group, as future trade union leaders, to reflect upon its own experience in the industry as a means of developing forms of working with their fellow workers and of establishing the basis for some kind of common identity. In other words, we felt that the content and form of the social practice in which we were engaged should be defined and delimited by the short- and long-term needs to which such activities gave rise. We were convinced that we could not take the place of the workers' legitimate representatives and that our involvement should be a temporary one. In this initial phase of our collaboration, the basic material of the learning process was the experience of the group, experience as building workers – the group consisted of a painter, a carpenter, an electrician-cum-plumber and several bricklayers – and experience gained through the group members' involvement in other types of organisation – Basic Christian Communities,[7] political parties, residents' associations, etc. The learning process took place principally in the regular weekly meetings in which strategy for the campaign and contacts were discussed, the local and national conjunctures were analysed and visits to building sites evaluated. Our constant preoccupation was to assist the group to gain that critical distance from the fact which allows for a more objective assessment. Equally we felt it necessary to provide information for the group, or to put the group in contact with specialists when this was necessary. Knowledge of trade union and electoral legislation soon became essential, as did a more organised approach to campaigning. In the first case, we put the group in contact with lawyers. In the second case we evaluated that a more structured learning process was called for.

The majority feeling in the group was that nobody was better qualified for talking to building workers than building workers. In other words, the fact of being a building worker was a sufficient qualification for the political/educational work involved in the campaign. Our suspicion was that several members of the group were not sufficiently clear about the contents of the programme, that others were talking over the heads of the great majority of workers and that still others would be easily intimidated by workers opposed to the group's proposals. After much insistence it was decided to hold an afternoon workshop in which we organised role play sessions involving tackling a truculent fellow worker and an unco-operative foreman, and practical examples of how to start a conversation with colleagues in the work situation or on the train or bus on the way to or from work. This quickly convinced the majority that their task was not as simple as they had thought and required constant reflection and evalua-tion. A series of other meetings and day workshops were also organised building on the lessons of the first.

Clearly our own credibility was essential to this process. It was evident that our social and economic status was very different from that of the group. We would arrive at meetings by car, they by bus, bicycle or on foot. We both lived in typically middle-class districts; they lived in typically working-class districts which frequently bordered on slums. We clearly lived on different sides of the class divide. And yet here we were wanting to mediate in those learning processes in which they were the central actors. Why should they trust us?

The question of how the agent gains access to the group and by whom he is introduced are important factors for understanding the relationship between the two. In our case we had good credentials. Both of us had been introduced by other groups with many years of proven service to different sectors of the working class. We were also known to some members of the group from involvements with other organisations in which they also participated. Nevertheless, we passed through the age-old testing process which involved being given a number of trivial tasks to complete and being maintained at a certain distance for a period of time. At the same time the frequent meetings provided the opportunity for us to become better acquainted.[8]

Analyses of the many divergent contemporary practices of popular education would suggest that these practices are oriented by politico-pedagogical objectives influenced by a range of philosophical-ideological positions. Although, in theory, the transformation of existing social structures is a basic premise for most practices, the strategies of class mediation underpinning them vary considerably. These can be situated on a continuum stretching from what is frequently called the populist or spontaneous tendency at one end to a vanguardist tendency at the other.

The first, which De Kadt (1970) suggests is a direct descendant of the Russian Populist or Narodnik movement in the second half of the nineteenth century, gives great emphasis to the intellectual/external agent being 'educated' by his contact with the 'common people'. For the populist, education is not something done for the people but with the people and fundamentally by the people. As De Kadt concludes, the populist posture is historically concerned with the intellectual's

> deep-seated horror of the manipulation of the people: their central credo is that solutions to the problems lived by the people must ultimately come from the people themselves, that their own ideas and visions, developed in a wholly different milieu, may at most serve as a sounding board for, but never as sign-posts to the people.
>
> (De Kadt 1970: 98)

At the other extreme, the vanguardist posture clearly attributes a directive or interventionist function to the agent. This evidently restricts the importance of learning processes based upon experience.

Reflections upon our own practice convinced us that we should neither attempt (we neither wished nor should we have been allowed) to direct nor expect divine inspiration to illuminate the Zé Peão group. Our perception was that we should be aiming to contribute to the formation of a new stratum of intellectuals which, in Gramsci's words, 'arise directly out of the masses but remain in contact with them to become, as it were, the whalebone in the corset' (Gramsci 1982: 334). As Gramsci notes:

> A human mass does not distinguish itself, does not become independent in its own right without, in the widest sense, organising itself: and there is no organisation without intellectuals, that is without organisers and leaders, in other words, without the theoretical aspect of the theory-practice nexus being distinguished concretely by the existence of a group of people specialised in conceptual and philosophical elaboration of ideas.
>
> (Gramsci 1982: 334)

In this sense, the intellectual's function involves not only active participation in practical life 'as constructor, organiser, permanent persuader', but also working to raise the intellectual level of, in our specific case, the great mass of construction workers. The Zé Peão group would not only provide moral and intellectual leadership but as such would exercise a vital formative role amongst their fellow workers.

Having taken control of the union branch at the end of 1986, the role of the now executive committee evidently changed. The overall preoccupation with the construction of a collective professional identity remained as the necessary basis for a strong democratic organisation premised upon the participation of the rank-and-file membership in the running of the branch. The new directors retained their concern with the need for constant contact with the workforce through regular visits to the sites where they both listened to the workers' complaints, suggestions and problems and also discussed new proposals and the difficulties facing the branch. The first strikes within the industry, which were carefully prepared and, when over, evaluated at all levels, also proved to be powerful learning experiences for leadership and membership. The strike offered one of the few chances for the workforce to assume and live its collective identity. It proved a moment in which the imposed divisive hierarchical barriers were forgotten and the weight of those elements which united the category – the exploitation, the long hours, the appalling working and living conditions, the lack of security, etc. – predominated.

These new concerns clearly contributed to a redefinition of our roles as external agents/union advisers. For union directors and agents alike it was a period of intense learning. For the directors, the majority of whom had at most two or three years of precarious formal primary schooling, the responsibility for learning to administer a complex bureaucracy such as that imposed on the union movement was accepted as a challenge. The branch, for example, had a clerical staff of six and a medical department which employed nine doctors. Thus, on the one hand, the directors had to learn to face up to engineers and owners of building firms whilst, on the other, coming to terms with the fact of themselves being 'employers'. For the agents it signified initially a much greater involvement in helping to solve questions related to the union machinery without losing sight of the more general question of leadership formation. For this end we frequently mediated between the expressed needs of the directors and those 'specialists' whom we deemed capable of assisting without wanting to create links of dependency. At the same time all training opportunities offered by other organisations (trade union, church and independent groups) were taken up. The weekly meetings of the branch executive continued to provide one of the most important spaces in which to reflect upon the relationship with the rank-and-file membership and that with the employers' organisation.

Within a year in office the union leadership had won the grudging respect of the employers for their legitimate authority amongst building workers in general – unionised or not. Clearly the first strikes were a test of the directorate's capacity not only to mobilise what is traditionally supposed to be a difficult group of workers to stir into action but also to plan a strike strategy and to know when and how to negotiate with the employers. The strikes were equally important for workers and union leaders alike to understand firstly the strength of a united membership and secondly the necessity of making a critical analysis of the economic and political context before embarking on industrial action. For the leadership the strike gave greater support to its belief in the need to forge strong links between leaders and rank-and-file membership and to identify and encourage intermediate leaders whose standing amongst their fellow workers on the site was based upon a certain natural leadership.

During this initial period, although some attempts were made to contribute to the formation of the rank-and-file membership, there was a tendency, imposed by the urgency of the situation, to concentrate on the learning needs of the union directorate. As its domination of the bureaucratic and administrative machinery grew so also did its recognition of the importance of some more systematic educational process involving particularly those migrant workers from the rural areas amongst whom levels of formal schooling were minimal. Literacy came to be seen as essential for strengthening processes of organisation and informed participation in union matters, and as a prerequisite for professional qualification. Contradictorily, several semi-literate members of the directorate, whilst defending the essential nature of literacy, attempted to explain their own resistance to participating in such programmes by using such time-honoured explanations as 'You can't teach an old dog new tricks', and Brazilian variations on the same theme.

Thus, from 1990 onwards, our involvement as external agents was more closely related to the question of systematised learning via literacy and post-literacy programmes. At the same time, the relationship between union branch and university became more overt and institutionalised. The consequences of this process of institutionalisation tended to be more positive than negative. University premises and resources were made available to the educational project and members of staff involved were able to include their activities within their departmental work plans. Literacy teachers were recruited amongst undergraduate and postgraduate students. Whilst the learning process took on a more formal guise, its content continued to be based upon the workers' experience. The classrooms in which the educational process took place were situated within the building sites themselves. The role of the Zé Peão School, as it became known, was both that of socialising systematised knowledge in a critical form and of exploring the question of work as an educative principle, taking as its central concern the specificity of the world of the construction worker. In operational terms, literacy became the central axis around and through which other areas of knowledge were to be explored. The reality of the building industry constituted the focal point for reflection, for the re-elaboration of knowledge and for the acquisition of new forms of social language. In this way the school became another of the learning strategies developed by us, agents and union directors, as a means of satisfying the learning needs of this socially and economically discriminated segment of the working class.[9] Others included the circulation of information via a news sheet; regular and well-attended assemblies (in 1994, the average attendance at union assemblies was over 250); frequent visits to building sites; courses and talks organised by the branch or other entities (on topics ranging from work security and labour legislation to AIDS and the crisis of

Cuban socialism); and participation in other regional and national trade union organisations and events.

There is no doubt in my mind that both partners in this joint venture have undergone profound learning experiences. I would point to three fundamental lessons which I have distilled from this longstanding relationship. Firstly, over the years it has become increasingly apparent that bonds of friendship and shared political ideals are both necessary ingredients of the learning process. Such relations are constructed over a period of time and form the basis for mutual trust and confidence. And it is their strength which creates a space in which learning is possible, and where both failures and successes can be analysed and discussed rather than summarily judged. That is, a climate of trust and confidence promotes learning. Continuity is beneficial so long as it is not accompanied by comfortable complicity. Coupled with this, I consider that the experience has taught me both the importance of learning to listen and the need to be patient or 'patiently impatient', to use Paulo Freire's expression.

On a second level, the accumulated evidence from this experience reinforced our comprehension of the educational process as a long-term one which is also profoundly affected by the conjuncture in which it takes place and one in which the needs of the learner and facilitator evolve and alter. The union directorate today has less need for the advice or mediation of its former advisers in the day-to-day running of the branch and more in specialised areas such as labour law, work safety and security, literacy and educational processes. This movement reflects not only a change in the needs of the branch directorate but a change in the social, economic and political conjuncture. The Brazil of 1994 is very different from the Brazil of 1982. On a slightly more pessimistic note, we have witnessed a general diminution of the learning spaces traditionally associated with popular education during this time. The dynamic of the social movements over the last decade has altered and the thrusting force of the trade union movement been tempered. This cannot be dissociated from changes of direction within the Roman Catholic Church where the strong social preoccupations of the 1970s and early 1980s have been replaced by a return to more traditional 'spiritual' concerns. Those movements which provided such rich learning opportunities for many workers have not been replaced. In our specific case, all the original members of the Zé Peão group came to the trade union movement with experience in a variety of other popular organisations. In recent years the formation of new leadership has become more problematic due to this lack of previous organisational experience.

Thirdly, the experience of the past twelve years would suggest that the permanent interplay between experiential learning and more systematised learning processes within the perspective of popular education is particularly pertinent for workers with low levels of formal schooling. This is not only true for those involved in the trade union movement but also for those competing for employment in an increasingly demanding job market. From this analysis, it can be seen that experience is an invaluable dimension of informal and formal learning processes in the same way as theory and practice are two sides of the same coin. Politicisation and systematised content are neither mutually exclusive nor antagonistic but necessarily complementary parts of the process of learning for change.

In retrospect, when reviewing the past eight years, members of the union directorate have often been surprised by their accomplishments. Within three months in office several directors had passed their driving tests and within a year had come to grips with the intricacies of union management and accountancy. Since then they have developed still further their organising skills and their understanding of the complex technical-ities of the industry sufficiently to out-argue highly qualified professionals. Members of the group give press and television interviews in the most natural and mature fashion and there is little doubt of the respect in which they are held by the rank-and-file membership, by other trade unions and by the employers' association. Union directors are frequently invited to take part in seminars and debates at the university where they have won the respect of staff and students alike. One director confided to me recently that he used to quake in his shoes when he first visited the university. Years of contact have served to demystify the mantle of superiority which formerly enveloped the university in his eyes and to demonstrate that his reflected experience was every bit as valuable as the products of the academy.

In conclusion, the question remains as to the pertinence of Gramsci to contemporary Brazil and to the practice of popular education. What has Gramsci to contribute to discussions about helping others to learn from experience? Firstly, Gramsci stressed the potential educational dimension of working-class movements (political party, trade union, factory council, etc.) to those engaged in them and the role of the organic intellectual capable of exercising the function of the whalebone in the old anti-ecological corset. He was both perspicacious about the function of the intellectual as constructor, organiser and permanent persuader and equally certain, on the basis of his own long experience as educator and intellectual, that 'Intellectuals develop slowly, far more slowly than any other social group, by their very nature and historical function...The proletariat, as a class, is poor in organising elements. It does not have its own stratum of intellectuals, and can only create one very slowly, very painfully' (Gramsci 1978: 462). Educational processes are slow and only prove efficacious when associated with other changes. And, secondly, Gramsci stressed the significance of the experience of work as a means by which a person gains consciousness of himself or herself. The task of contributing to the process whereby workers become not only conscious of the form of their insertion in the natural and social world but also of their capacity to transform the nature of that insertion through a clear under-standing of it, is both a profoundly educational and a political one (Ireland

1987). There is little doubt that many contemporary forms of education ignore to their cost the fundamental contribution of experience as a basis for the learning process. Finally, Gramsci demonstrated, by his own example, that we can only hope to facilitate the learning of others if we ourselves are open to new learning. The ability to learn from experience, and to assist others to do the same, remains a decisive characteristic of the Zé Peão group.

NOTES

1 Although writing from my own point of view, during this period I have worked both on my own and with a number of partners and teams. I have learnt much from discussions with all those with whom I have worked and particularly with Dr Everaldo Ferreira Soares Júnior, my longest-standing partner.
2 In order to facilitate the comprehension of the reader not familiar with the socio-cultural reality of Latin America, I have chosen to translate what in Portuguese would be *classes populares* by 'working class/subaltern classes', despite being fully aware of the difference which exists between the two concepts.
3 In the latest United Nations *Report on Human Development* (1994), in which countries are ranked according to social indicators, Brazil is second only to Botswana in unequal distribution of income. In a separate chapter on the Northeastern Region, the UN data show that those living in this area earn, on average, 40 percent less than those living in other regions of the country. Expectation of life is also seventeen years less in the Northeast than in the remainder of Brazil.
4 A much-used term in the Spanish and Portuguese languages which is equally useful in English: 'a combination of situations, usually producing difficulties' according to Longman's *Dictionary of English Language and Culture*, 1993 (3rd impression).
5 Robert Tressell, *The Ragged Trousered Philanthropist*, London: Grafton Books, 1987. Robert Tressell (born Robert Noonan) was a painter and decorator who died of tuberculosis in 1911 when he was forty. In his Introduction to the Grafton edition, Alan Sillitoe comments that 'Robert Tressell's workmen either had no class feeling, or they regarded themselves as totally inferior. Because they saw no way of getting out of their predicament, they could only say "It's not for the likes of us"' (p. 9). The story of the Zé Peão group in João Pessoa is about a group of building workers who, like Tressell himself, refused to believe that there was no way out.
6 The term peão is a general description applied to all workers in the construction industry. The name Zé is a contracted form of José (Joseph), one of the commonest males names in Catholic Brazil. By bringing together the two names the group hoped, on the one side, to instigate the formation of a collective identity – by identifying himself with the programme being put forward by the group the worker would identify himself with all the other Zé Peãos in the construction industry – and, on the other, that the forthcoming struggle would invest the name with a new dignity. In this way it was hoped that Zé Peão would become a collective expression of pride and a recognition of the need for collective action.
7 The Basic Christian Communities or CEBs (Comunidades Eclesiais de Base), as one of the most important expressions of the Liberation Theology movement,

played an important role in the re-democratisation of the country as well as providing a privileged space for practices of popular education.
8 Initially the group held a Sunday meeting once a month, to which a larger group was invited, in addition to a regular weekly meeting. In the period prior to the elections in 1983 (August–October), the rhythm of these meetings increased dramatically to four or five a week. We, as the group's advisers, attended all meetings.
9 For a more detailed account of the Zé Peão School see Ireland 1994b.

REFERENCES

De Kadt, E. (1970) *Catholic Radicals in Brazil*, Oxford: Oxford University Press.
Garcia-Huidobro, J. E. (1994) 'Mudanças nas concepções atuais de educação de adultos', in *Anais do encontro latino-americano sobre educação de jovens e adultos trabalhadores*, Brasília: Instituto Nacional de Estudos e Pesquisas Educacionais.
Gramsci, A. (1978) *Selection from Political Writings 1921–1926*, London: Lawrence and Wishart.
—— (1982) *Selection from Prison Notebooks*, London: Lawrence and Wishart.
Ireland, T. (1987) *Antonio Gramsci and Adult Education: Reflections on the Brazilian Experience*, Manchester: University of Manchester.
—— (1994a) 'From politicization to pragmatism: popular education and experiential learning in Latin America', in M. T. Keeton (ed.) *Perspectives on Experiential Learning: Prelude to a Global Conversation about Learning*, Chicago: Council for Adult and Experiential Learning, 67–69.
—— (1994b) 'Literacy skills as building bricks for trade union democracy: the experience of the Construction Workers' Trade Union in João Pessoa, Brazil', *Adult Education and Development*, DVV, 42, 81–88.

10 Community empowerment
What happens when a community decides to do things differently

Jim Brown

When I agreed to contribute a chapter to this book I was persuaded by Nod Miller to use it as an opportunity to explore an aspect of my work which I found problematic. I have always found it difficult to describe my work; it is continually shifting between job titles such as consultant, trainer, adult educator and facilitator. This was particularly true of one project I was engaged in during the late 1980s on a housing estate I shall call Fernhouse. It was a difficult project, about which I had many unresolved feelings, not least of which was the nature of my own role.

Through writing this chapter and reading the other contributions to the book in draft form, I have at least resolved one matter – that my work might be best described by the job title of animator. I shall attempt to contribute to the central discourse about the role of the animator in working with experience.

Inevitably, this chapter has changed form several times in the course of writing and reading the contributions of others. Midway through the process I decided to use Paulo Freire's work *Pedagogy of the Oppressed* as a device to explore my own work practices. Freire's writings were formative in my education some twenty years ago. I therefore chose to use the first edition of *Pedagogy of the Oppressed*, published in Britain in 1972, as my main reference source, although I acknowledge that Freire has subsequently written a second edition which contains major revisions to his original work.

Having reached the end stage of this process, with Nod pursuing me for my final version of the chapter, I found myself wanting to start again. Many of my feelings about the Fernhouse project remained unresolved. I felt slightly cheated that the process of writing had failed to produce a reconciliation. I thought about scrapping the homage to Freire's work – if the truth be known I found him difficult to read – but I cannot deny his lasting influence on my work. In the end I have settled for a major reworking of the postscript. This may have done the trick.

MY WORK

During the 1980s I was involved in a number of projects concerned with the development of community businesses. Such initiatives are driven by a powerful vision of how community owned and controlled businesses can be vehicles for local economic development, based on participative and democratic principles. Business activities are established to meet local needs; jobs are created for local people; social and commercial objectives are intertwined; profits are reinvested in the community.

My involvement with community businesses came about as an adjunct to my main field of activity, as a freelance consultant and trainer to the workers' co-operative movement. The contemporary workers' co-operative movement in the UK sprang from the alternative movements of the late 1960s. In its early days it was a predominantly white, middle-class initiative, driven by well-educated young people seeking a self-sufficient alternative to the hegemony of advanced capitalism. I had lived in a housing co-operative in the early 1970s, and studied industrial democracy at graduate level in the mid-1970s. By the late 1970s I was involved in establishing a residential training and conference centre for workers' co-operatives, which was itself a workers' co-operative.

Whilst workers' co-operatives and community businesses share a similar philosophy, in practice they have developed in very different ways. The reason for this, I believe, has to do with the contrasting pedagogy of the two movements. The workers' co-operative movement is a civil initiative. It has learnt the best ways of achieving its goals through its own experience. Practices have steadily evolved over the last fifteen years, informed by the experiences of earlier activists.

In contrast, community business is largely a state-led initiative. It was a model imported by local government in England and Wales during the 1980s, from the earlier experiments in the USA, Ireland and the Highlands and Islands of Scotland, to solve the problems faced by impoverished communities. Nearly all community businesses in England and Wales have been heavily dependent on state funding.

Very few community businesses have lived up to the expectations of local government. The number of jobs created has been very low and few initiatives have achieved economic independence from the state. The failure to achieve commercial viability has been variously explained, but most frequently put down to the lack of business expertise within the host communities.

It is my contention that this perceived failure of community business stems from the pedagogy surrounding its development. To substantiate this claim I want to reflect on my experiences in Fernhouse. This case study also illustrates some of the central concerns of this book about animation and learning from experience.

FERNHOUSE – A CASE STUDY

Fernhouse is typical of many council owned housing estates in Britain today: high levels of poverty and unemployment, poor housing and few local facilities. It was built in the 1930s to house the families of workers in nearby factories, and for the first thirty-five years it was a thriving and settled community. But as the housing stock aged, there was insufficient investment in maintenance and renovation. In the 1970s unemployment rates began to accelerate. By the 1980s Fernhouse had become somewhere people definitely didn't want to live. It was the last resort for people on the council housing waiting list. Fernhouse had a bad reputation.

The first contract

I first got involved with Fernhouse in the autumn of 1989 when I was invited by the Economic Development Unit of the local council to conduct a review of a community business known as Fernhouse Enterprises Ltd (FEL). It had been established in 1985 by the chair of the local community association, a young junior manager who had recently been made redundant. He was inspired by similar initiatives in Scotland, and with the backing of the local council had set about creating a number of community business initiatives.

Within the first four years he had managed to set up two sister companies – Fernhouse Training Ltd and Fernhouse Building Ltd – and a credit union. He secured funding from the local authority to convert two derelict buildings, one into a training and resource centre, the other into a block of fifteen enterprise workshop units.

But by 1989 things were starting to go wrong. The manager had resigned following a dispute with the chair of FEL. Two government funded schemes, the Community Programme and the Voluntary Projects Programme, had come to an end, resulting in the loss of over thirty trainee-ships and the closure of Fernhouse Training Ltd. A community cafe and gardening business were on the verge of bankruptcy, and work on the renovation of the two buildings was behind schedule and over budget.

The local council was worried about the problems facing FEL. This was their flagship project, which was supposed to demonstrate how disadvantaged communities could be regenerated. Their analysis of the situation was that most of the problems stemmed from a weak, inexpert management committee which repeatedly ignored their advice. They were seeking a solution which would improve managerial control and focus the organisation on commercial viability.

I started my fieldwork by meeting John, the chair of FEL. His first question to me was about how much I was getting paid by the council. It turned out that my daily rate was roughly the same as his monthly welfare cheque. We had both already guessed this, but it was his way of

establishing a common understanding about the nature of our relationship. He saw me as yet another professional, earning good money on the
back of other people's poverty. He wanted to know more about my motives
and philosophy before agreeing to co-operate with me.

John dismissed conventional ideas about how community business
should work, favouring instead a political model based on the struggle for
social justice. He believed that local people had a right to jobs. In helping to
create FEL the local council had accepted responsibility for this; it was now
their duty to find the money to keep FEL employees in work. He rejected
the notion that FEL should be run like a commercial business – it was not on
his agenda – instead his aim was to create as many jobs as possible. Such
attitudes and beliefs were not popular amongst the council officers. John
was thought to be a troublemaker, who had engineered himself into a
position of power and influence within the project.

Using Freire's framework of analysis, the situation can be described as a
confrontation in which the oppressors – represented in this case by the
local council – were engaged in a campaign of antidialogical action against
FEL. Freire points out that a tactic of oppressors is to demonise the
oppressed, presenting them as the source of the problem. Freire goes on to
list four central characteristics of antidialogical action: conquest, divide
and rule, manipulation and cultural invasion. All these characteristics
were present within this project.

The local council had set out on a mission of conquest, to eliminate 'the
difficulties' encountered on the estate. This reinforced the codification of
Fernhouse as a problem estate, already well established by the local media.
The strategy of divide and rule was well in place. The local community was
not happy when FEL laid off the Community Programme funded workers.
Other local community groups weren't happy that FEL received more than
their fair share of local government resources and attention. Divisions and
resentment were growing on the estate. In commissioning the review of
FEL, the local council can be described as practising manipulation, seeking
to pressurise FEL into conforming with their prescription, presented as
objective and independent advice. Finally, the process of cultural invasion
was embodied within the thesis of community business, which describes
the initiative as being community owned and controlled, yet is demon-
strably subject to funding and regulation by the local council.

However, at the time I was conducting this review, I had only the
vaguest conceptualisation of these issues. My position, as a consultant to
the local authority, not to FEL or the people of Fernhouse, severely
compromised my perspective. I was being employed as an instrument of
oppression, a fact that I was reluctant to come to terms with. I lacked the
courage and conviction to explore these feelings and diverted my
attentions towards devising a professional and mechanistic solution to
the problem.

I proposed that a new body should be created on the estate, that brought together all the local community groups under the single umbrella of a Community Development Trust. Such structures were being promoted by central government as a mechanism for community regeneration, building a partnership between local communities, local government and the local private sector. The partnership arrangement would introduce more experienced and professional management to the community businesses, as well as opening up new business opportunities with other local, larger and more established businesses.

The rationale behind this proposal was twofold. Firstly, it dealt with my mixed feelings about John and his influence over FEL. Whilst I had a great deal of sympathy for John's position I felt that his major weakness was that he did not have the widespread support of the community he claimed to be representing. I argued that the aim of FEL was far more than just job creation – it was committed to raising the quality of life on the estate, an aim that was embraced by the whole community. Therefore, a key task was to unite the community in a single strategic initiative to secure this broader aim.

The second reason for recommending the creation of a Community Development Trust was connected with central government policy towards urban regeneration. The Department of the Environment controlled the major source of funds available to the local council for work on estates like Fernhouse. They had recently published a good practice guide promoting the concept of Community Development Trusts. It seemed likely that future government funding would be dependent upon adopting this model. At the time it felt like the most pragmatic course of action to take.

With the benefit of hindsight I am now much less sure. There were two conflicting explanations of why the community business was failing. The council officers believed in the model but doubted the capability and expertise of local people to make it work. The solution was to import expertise. Early attempts to educate and train local people had not worked, so the alternative was to bring in expertise from outside, either directly in the form of consultants like myself, or indirectly by changing the model to promote the concept of partnership, which would bring in managers from the public and private sectors.

An alternative explanation was that the host communities were being prevented from developing a consciousness of their experiences. Given the high level of poverty, discrimination and disadvantage experienced on a day-to-day level by people living on such estates, it is hardly surprising that a political, oppositional culture should emerge from community organisation. This political consciousness was actively thwarted by the community business model. Instead the model reinforced the discrimination local people experienced. For instance the failure of community business only reinforced the stereotype amongst council officers of local people being incapable, lacking the expertise to manage their own affairs.

The second contract

In February 1990 I was invited by the local council to implement my recommendations. I was reluctant to accept the job, because by then the doubts expressed above were starting to surface in my mind. I had had time to reflect on my experiences on the estate and felt increasing sympathy for the position taken by John, that this was a political struggle, not a business problem.

I was uneasy about promoting a partnership model of organisation, when it was clear from the start that the community would never be equal partners in the relationship. At the same time I was worried about the utility of the local community pursuing political confrontation with the council. Without the support of the council, I felt they would be unable to access funding or support for any initiative. The main dilemma was who would be my clients in such a situation, the local council who were paying me, or the local community who were supposed to be the beneficiaries?

Underpinning this dilemma was the question of my role. Was I meant to be a consultant offering expert advice, a trainer and educator developing skills, or a facilitator bringing the community together? In the end I put my doubts to one side and accepted the job. My terms of reference with the local council envisaged a 250 hour project over six months, at the end of which the trust would be up and running. It turned out to be a gross under-estimation of the task ahead.

I started by meeting local community groups on an individual basis, to talk about the problems on the estate and to introduce them to the idea of a Community Development Trust. It was a very slow business. I listened to hours of gripes and complaints, suspicion and cynicism. They didn't have much faith in new ideas. They showed no interest in the Community Development Trust concept. Besides this, they were busy with their own groups and activities and didn't have much energy left for yet another initiative. With the exception of the tenants association, none of the other groups shared the political consciousness of John and FEL.

The contract changes

I was now three months into the project and I was worried that I had made little progress. I continued to meet informally with many groups on the estate, discussing their problems and trying to help out. But there wasn't much enthusiasm for the Community Development Trust idea. Meanwhile, the local council were pressing me for progress.

Paradoxically, this lack of progress was actually helping me move forward. I was slowly abandoning my prescription for the estate – the Community Development Trust idea – and entering into genuine dialogue with the local community. I was being introduced to the realities of life on the estate, what Freire calls generative themes. With the benefit of hindsight, I can now see that my position was slowly shifting from the role of consultant to animator.

One of the main concerns on the estate was the local pub, the Hayfield. A cathedral sized building, it dominated the centre of the estate, dwarfing all the surrounding houses. Years ago, it had been the centre of community life. But over the last decade it had become a safe haven for drug dealers. The police seemed to be operating a policy of containment. They knew where the problem was and from a safe distance could keep an eye on it. Most local people didn't use the Hayfield any longer. Most of the dealers and buyers were outsiders. Some younger people on the estate were drawn towards it; the lure of easy money and superficial glamour were greater than anything else on offer. It upset their parents, but what could they do about it?

According to Freire, this can be described as a 'limit-situation', whereby a generative theme is conscientised as a limitation on freedom. The more I talked to people about the Hayfield, the more it became clear how the local community were treated with total disregard. It highlighted how power-less the community was to affect its own future. Local people felt some-thing had to be done about the Hayfield and at the same time became more aware of the difficulties of organising action on the estate.

The growing feeling that the community had to act, made a link to my talk of a Community Development Trust. Something had to happen. Members of FEL and the tenants association suggested I should arrange a meeting of local community groups to talk about life on the estate and what could be done to improve it.

The meeting was held on a balmy summer evening in July 1990. Most of the local groups attended. They listened to me talk about Community Development Trusts; they talked about the problems facing the estate, especially the drug dealing at the Hayfield. Gradually the mood of the meeting soured. Talking about the problems they all faced had a depres-sing effect which turned into anger. John, the chair of FEL, tore the concept of a Community Development Trust to shreds. 'No way are we going to be told how to run our lives by the council.' He was supported by the chair of the tenants association. This attack turned into a long-winded tirade against the council, consultants and the other community groups repre-sented at the meeting.

Then a remarkable thing happened. The chair of the local credit union erupted. A molten stream of invective poured from his mouth, concluding with a masterful challenge, 'Why don't we create our own bloody council – forget about this partnership crap – we'll form our own partnership on this estate.' A stunned silence was followed by an even more direct challenge, addressed to me, 'and who the hell are you working for – us or the council?' The Community Development Trust died that night, to be reincarnated as the Community Development Organisation.

Freire's description of dialogic action is helpful in understanding what had happened that night. The thematic investigation of the Hayfield issue had helped to focus attention on limit-acts and at the same time unveiled the objective limitations of the Community Development Trust proposal. The first problem with that proposal was that it assumed the existence of a community consciousness on the estate, that there was unity and co-operation between different groups when this was clearly not the case. Secondly, the Community Development Trust proposed a partnership with external bodies who were in fact seen as the oppressors by most people living on the estate.

In proposing to create the Community Development Organisation the meeting had achieved praxis, transforming their reality. This new project contained all the elements of Freire's dialogical theory of action: co-operation, unity for liberation, organisation and cultural synthesis. In the coming months, these elements were to display themselves as we set about constructing the Community Development Organisation.

Furthermore, the meeting transformed my role into that of animator. They wanted me to work for them, to help them to develop their ideas, to contribute my expertise to solving their problems. They did not want to be taught; they wanted me to work with their experiences.

Co-operation

In describing co-operation, Freire says, 'The dialogical theory of action does not involve a Subject, who dominates by virtue of conquest, and a dominated object. Instead there are Subjects who meet to name the world in order to transform it' (Freire 1972: 135). By challenging who I was working for, and in turn inviting me to work for them, the meeting had transformed the relationships in the project. No longer was I the Subject, with a mission to conquer the estate. Instead we shared a joint project, in which I was to have a specific role, determined by my co-Subjects.

As the project progressed this was most clearly demonstrated by my contractual arrangements. When the original contract ran out after six months, the community pressed the local authority for a three-month extension. When this too came to an end, I continued to work with the group on a voluntary basis for a further five months until a new contract was secured with a new funding body (not the local authority).

Throughout this time I had major doubts about the efficacy of what I was doing. The sense of solidarity I felt with people on the estate was permanently tinged by the difference between our material lifestyles; something which they now had a direct hand in funding. I knew that there would be an end to the project for me – but not for them; John pointed out that professionals like me come and go, but that for most people living on the estate, this would be their lives forever.

It got to the point where I could hardly bear to go to Fernhouse. The prospect of each meeting filled me with dread, counterbalanced invariably by a sense of mild euphoria following the achievements of each successive meeting. We were making progress, but I never felt in control of the situation. The consultant inside me found this very scary.

Unity for liberation

Freire describes unity for liberation thus: 'In the dialogical theory the leaders must dedicate themselves to an untiring effort for unity amongst the oppressed – and unity of the leaders with the oppressed – in order to achieve liberation' (Freire 1972: 140). Probably the single most important function I served within this project was to act as a broker between the different groups of people living on the estate. From the start, I tried to involve every organised group on the estate in the project. This included not only groups with a direct interest in community development, such as the community association, the tenants association and FEL itself, but also other groups which are traditionally seen as having little to contribute to community development. This included the local football club, a Caribbean domino team and a martial arts group. The rationale behind this was that the community could be most effectively reached through pre-existing organisations on the estate and that there should be no discrimination shown towards these groups.

The meetings developed a familiar pattern. Agendas were constructed at the beginning of meetings, but quickly reverted to free-for-alls, based on who had turned up and the primacy of issues. Discussions were noisy, rowdy and frequently bad tempered. My role changed into being the independent chair of the meetings, acting as a peacemaker between the warring factions. I also took lots of notes. Chairing consisted largely of not letting anyone walk out of the meeting with an issue unresolved. Meetings always ran over time, often not finishing until ten or eleven at night. The meetings usually ended peaceably, either through resolution or exhaustion.

The notes I took at meetings formed the basis of a newsletter, which I wrote after each meeting and delivered to every person who had ever attended one of the meetings. I used this delivery round as an opportunity to persuade non-attenders to come to the next meeting and to discuss issues and events. I encouraged people to speak their mind.

When the community meetings first began, I fully expected that after two or three meetings local enthusiasm would wane, leaving a hard core of committed activists. But instead, the meetings grew in size. Upwards of forty or fifty people were regularly attending the fortnightly meetings. It became a venue for all sorts of concerns: a local business that was being forced to close because it did not have planning permission to use its yard for storage, the football club which could not get its junior team accepted for membership by the local league.

Organisation

According to Freire:

> In the theory of dialogical action, organisation requires authority, so it cannot be authoritarian; it requires freedom, so it cannot be licentious. Organisation is, rather, a highly educative process in which leaders and people together experience true authority and freedom, which they then seek to establish in society by transforming the reality which mediates them.
>
> (Freire 1972: 146)

In defining the central task of the project as the creation of the Community Development Organisation, rather than more direct forms of action, such as campaigning for the closure of the Hayfield pub, the people of Fernhouse displayed considerable discipline. Whilst the pub was the generative theme, its closure was not the praxis; instead it was the recognition of the need to organise the community so that it could act on such issues.

At least ten community meetings were devoted to the process of designing and developing the structure of the Community Development Organisation. Much of this time was spent identifying and resolving outstanding issues of power relationships between the different interest groups on the estate. The most contentious issue was negotiating that the assets and resources of FEL should be transferred to the new organisation. Had the local council been involved in these discussions, it would have been impossible to achieve this outcome.

The purpose of the new organisation, christened Fernhouse Community Council, was to develop policies to guide the future development of life on the estate. Individual community groups would retain their autonomy and continue to run their own affairs. Any new projects initiated by the community council would be handed over to a new group set up specially to run it. This way the community council could concentrate on policy, not the day-to-day maintenance of individual initiatives.

In choosing to name the new organisation a council, the community challenged the local government council's own authority over the estate. This had a symbolic potency which revealed the true nature of relationships between the local authority and the estate. At first the council refused to accept the name and threatened to withdraw funding unless it was changed. But the council's opposition to the name only hardened the resolve of the local community to call themselves a council. It summed up the growing sense of empowerment experienced by the community. They didn't have to do what they were told.

Cultural synthesis

Freire states that, 'In cultural synthesis, the actors who come from "another world" to the world of the people do so not as invaders. They do not come to teach or to transmit or to give anything, but rather to learn, with the people, about the people's world' (Freire 1972: 147). I have already mentioned my ambivalent feelings about working with Fernhouse; that I came to dread visiting the estate, yet experienced a sense of euphoria after each visit. This roller coaster of emotions had much to do with entering 'another world', to witness a deeply rooted oppression of the human spirit and at the same time to share in the experience of liberation from that oppression. The poverty of existence of life on Fernhouse had a grinding effect on my confidence, optimism and belief in the possibility of change. Whilst I had worked with many such communities before, this time I felt myself being sucked into the frustration, anger and powerlessness produced by poverty.

The source of euphoria came from being part of a learning process that progressively managed to transform thematic investigations into programmes of action. The issue of the pub was a good example. It was eventually closed down by the brewery. The community council immediately sought to re-open it as a community business. The local authority was reluctant to get involved. This was partly to do with cost – over £200,000 was needed – but also because it did not want to be seen to be encouraging the drinking of alcohol in an impoverished community.

Such remarks, made in all innocence, cloaked a deep disregard for the liberty of people living on the estate. However, none of this deterred the community council from announcing its intention to re-open the pub, an objective it eventually achieved twelve months later, having negotiated a loan from the private sector.

POSTSCRIPT

Earlier drafts of this chapter ended on a very gloomy note, questioning the utility of my work in Fernhouse and Freire's ideas. I doubted the value of enabling people to be acutely aware of the discrimination and disadvantage they encountered, especially when the causes of this oppression stemmed from societal change, which meant that there was little that could be done at a community level to make a real difference.

But with the passage of time I begin to feel more certain about the value of my work and that of other animators who work with communities to effect change, even if the only tangible result of that process is the unbearable knowledge of oppression. Of course I would like to report a happy ending to the story of Fernhouse – that full employment had returned, poverty eradicated, violence and exploitation banished forever – but that is the stuff of fairy tales.

Britain is becoming an ever more iniquitous society. Change will only come about if enough people become acutely aware of the problems we face as a society and feel passionate enough to take action.

I firmly believe such change requires civil action; the state is incapable of transforming its oppressive relationship with civil society. In the case study the local council were committed to the objectives of equality, democracy and fairness, but this was not sufficient to transform its relationship with the local community. Community empowerment only occurs when the community actively seeks to take control, pursuing an agenda it has written for itself.

In our desire to build a better world there is a strong temptation to take short-cuts. The motives of the state in promoting concepts such as community business or Community Development Trusts may be entirely honourable. But such efforts to reproduce models of regeneration have a tendency to fail because they do not achieve the transformation of consciousness necessary to make principles such as democracy, equality and fairness work.

The role of the animator is to enable conscientisation to take place. Strategies for action, such as community businesses, Community Development Trusts or community councils should stem from this conscientisation. This process cannot be achieved in reverse; strategies for action will not result in conscientisation. Furthermore, there is no formula available to guide the work of the animator. Working with experience means just that; preformulated abstract conceptualisations will merely reproduce what already exists. This might be why Freire is so difficult to read. It lacks easy prescriptions to the problems we face.

REFERENCE

Freire, P. (1972) *Pedagogy of the Oppressed*, Harmondsworth: Penguin.

Part 5

11 Animating learning in teams
A Gestalt approach

John Bernard Harris

I am sitting in a room with eighteen people who call themselves a 'team'. They are chatting together animatedly in twos and threes. I look round, taking in the atmosphere, trying to get a 'flavour' of this team. I notice who talks to whom, who sits quietly, who looks excited or scared by the prospect of spending two 'away days' with colleagues.

Soon it is 9.30am, and the agreed starting time. Some people cast expectant glances at their watches and then at me, and when they see me patiently waiting for the hubbub to cease they finish their conversations. The room quietens. Now I have their attention, and we are ready to begin.

So began a two-day team-building session which I facilitated.[1] I will continue the story in a little while, but first I would like to introduce myself and my contribution to this book.

INTRODUCTION: ME AND GESTALT THERAPY

Who I am, what I do

Like everyone, I have a background of life and work experiences which has profoundly influenced me. I have been involved in finding out what makes people 'tick' for as long as I can remember. Coming from a family in which I had many confusing experiences, I acquired a practical interest in individual and group psychology from a very early age. I learned that in this area knowledge is often power, and that the better I understood people and situations, the easier my life would become.

After leaving school I was a student and then teacher of philosophy for ten years, before moving to work in the 'helping professions' for nearly twenty years as a generic social worker and then social work manager in the field of mental health. For the past few years I have been working independently as a trainer, organisational consultant and group therapist.

I have, over more than thirty years, studied what others have written about individual and social learning, finding some of it useful and much irrelevant to my career as a learner and teacher. I am still trying to find out what makes people tick, and it is this excitement and curiosity that provides energy and enthusiasm for my work helping others to learn in different settings. I see myself and the people whose learning I am trying to facilitate as partners in learning.

In this chapter I offer a description of my practice in promoting learning in the form of an account of a team-building event, combined with an account of the theoretical ideas which inform my practice, many of which are strongly influenced by Gestalt therapy.[2] I would like to set the scene by stating some of the 'first principles' of my approach to the animation of learning.

On learning from experience

I believe that human beings are, by their very nature, highly skilled experiential learners. But as part of our socialisation and education myriad blocks and inhibitions to learning are erected by 'the system'. If these can be brought into awareness and removed, people will regain their natural ability to function in a healthy manner and learn what they need to learn.

Let me explain these statements further. It is an obvious (but neglected) fact that human beings are 'the learning species' (Kolb 1984). We *must* learn from experience if we are to survive, and we have highly developed capacities to do this. Consider, in this regard, the human infant: from birth she is fascinated by her surroundings, and continually explores and experiments in order to learn more about it. Babies are the ultimate experiential learners, and they set about their task with gusto from day one. No one teaches them how to do this; they know how to do it innately.

As we get older and need to learn more and more complex concepts and skills, our innate capacity to learn (and to learn *how* to learn) becomes developed and modified by experience. Our desire to learn, the subject matter of our learning and the ways in which we learn are all affected by socialisation and education processes. Such processes are necessary for social beings, but they always have a normative element and are often designed to channel our behaviour in certain directions, depending on our family and cultural background. The end result is often that we come to believe that we know little or nothing about certain areas of our lives, compared to 'experts'.

Often this belief is mistaken. Take, for instance, human psychology. 'Interpersonal relations' is an important topic for all of us, yet most people would say they knew little about it. But *all* human beings have taken the best practical course in interpersonal relations around and were *very* highly motivated when they did it (Enright 1980). We know how to size someone up almost instantaneously: to know what's important about them in regard to themselves, and much, much more. But we may not realise just how well-developed our skills in this area are, and we probably lack a way of drawing out and talking about them.

So part of what I try to convey in my work is that living and learning are inseparable.[3] We *know* how to learn from experience; we've been doing it all our lives and have acquired in the process a massive amount of knowledge about subjects which are of vital importance to us.

If, indeed, people know how to learn from their experiences, then it follows that they don't really need me to tell them how to do it. I therefore see my role as a facilitator as primarily involving two tasks. The first is *to help people to recognise, access and use their life experiences and the knowledge and skills they have gained through them.* And the second is *to help them make full use of all their faculties in the present task.* If they are aware of their surroundings and themselves – what they perceive, think, feel and want – they will find creative ways to solve their current problems.

Having clarified my starting point as an animator of learning, I now move on to describe my practice in one area of my work in more detail.

INTEGRATING PRACTICE AND THEORY IN TEAM-BUILDING

Background to the event

I will begin by sketching the background to the team-building event I am describing. It is 1992, and we are in England. The team is a multi-disciplinary group of eighteen people, who deliver services to local people from a community mental health centre. There are social workers, administrative staff, a consultant psychiatrist, community nurses, group workers and a psychologist. Eight are men. A mixed bunch, then, with different backgrounds, trainings and line-management, who face the challenge of working together to deliver the best possible service to their clients.

The two 'away days' (as they are called locally) were set up in discussions between the centre manager and myself. In team meetings, dissatisfaction had been expressed for some time about what was felt to be poor functioning and low morale, and team-building identified as the way forward. I was recommended as a facilitator and after speaking to the centre manager on the telephone, I arranged to visit a team meeting.

Most of the team attended – I got a look at them and they at me. We discussed possible methods of working and I talked about how I like to work. In particular I told them a little about how Gestalt ideas influenced my work as a facilitator, saying that I believed that teams demonstrate a fundamental Gestalt axiom: that the whole is greater than the sum of the parts. Teams can achieve by working together what individuals cannot possibly achieve on their own. Most teams are aware of this – at least as a unrealised possibility – and this is what they are striving towards.

At the end of this meeting, we were all satisfied enough to want to proceed. I arranged to send team members a simple confidential questionnaire, to be returned to me before the event. This asked for details of their work at the centre, what they like and don't like about what they do, individual or team issues they felt should be put on the agenda, and finally asked them for their hopes and fears about the two days. Almost all of these were returned, and I had a good deal of useful information to help me plan the two days. At this stage, the individual and team learning goals are very general. Put simply, they wish to function better as a team, and that means developing more efficient working practices. At this stage, that is enough.

In planning team-building programmes, I have in mind a particular model of experiential learning, the Gestalt contact–withdrawal cycle. This is an important part of my thinking on 'experiential learning', and I would now like to explain it before starting my account of the two days.

The Gestalt contact–withdrawal cycle

The fundamental starting point of the Gestalt approach is this: human beings are living organisms with on-going wants and needs that they seek to satisfy by interacting with their environment on a moment-to-moment basis. If at any given moment there is something I want (and nothing else I currently want more) I will 'organ-ise' myself and take action in order to meet it. This organisation affects my whole self, and my energies are directed towards achieving it. It influences what I perceive, feel, think and do. While this particular desire is 'foreground', the focus of my current attention, other things around me fade into the background. For example, earlier while writing this chapter I was struggling to find exactly the right sentence to express my meaning. All my attention was on the computer screen, and I failed to notice that it had started to rain heavily on the washing I put out on the line earlier.

In Gestalt therapy theory, this sequence of organism–environment interaction is represented as a cyclical process, with a number of distinct stages (Zinker 1977). The first is the *sensation* stage, in which I begin to take in sensory information from my environment. To use my earlier example, as I sit at my computer I might suddenly hear pattering sounds and see drops on the window. The second is the *awareness* stage, in which I become aware of the meaning that this information has for me: in this case, I realise that it is raining and the clothes are getting wet. Next is the *mobilisation* stage, in which I begin to plan and energise in order to deal with the situation. In this example, I decide to get up immediately and bring the washing in. The fourth stage is the *action* stage, where I experiment with different ways in which I can meet my current need. Here, I look for the washing basket. Next I dash out and bring in the washing, noticing that it is still largely dry; this is the *contact* stage. Finally I fold up the washing, put it in the airing cupboard and return to my writing; this is the *completion* (sometimes called *satisfaction*) stage. Figure 11.1 shows the stages.

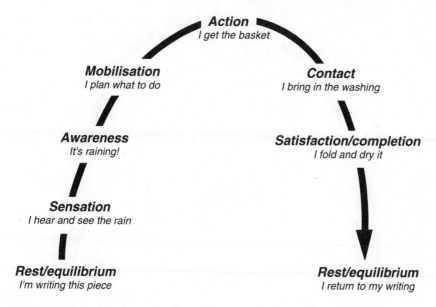

Figure 11.1 The contact–withdrawal cycle

According to this model, I start from a state of rest or relative equilibrium with the environment, and in response to the stimulus of the rain progress through the stages of sensation, awareness, etc. through to satisfaction. When this cycle is finished, I am ready for the next challenge that presents itself. The process is thus one of moving out to and engaging with the environment to get my current dominant need or want met, and then withdrawing again, before moving on to the next important interaction. All our human needs – physical, psychological, social and spiritual – are met in this way and throughout our lives we are engaged in such cycles continuously. Some last only a second or two – as when my eyes fleetingly meet yours across a crowded room; others last minutes, hours, days or even years. We can view our lives as a series of cycles 'nested' within cycles, with many different ones going on simultaneously.

The cycle as a model of team development and process

I have introduced the Gestalt contact–withdrawal cycle as a model of individual human functioning. But I also use it to describe the interactions within groups and teams (Philippson and Harris 1992). On this view, I imagine the team as an (even more complex) organism in its own right. The team, just as individuals do, engages with itself and its external environment in a cyclical fashion, in the stages shown in Figure 11.2.

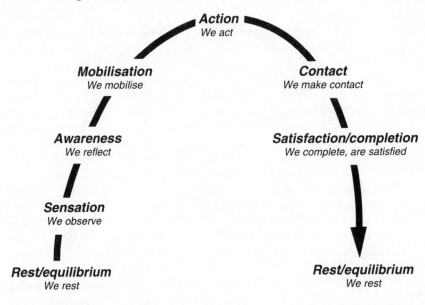

Figure 11.2 The team contact–withdrawal cycle

The model illustrates the stages the team goes through in dealing with any situation; and we can envisage each stage as having a particular set of tasks associated with it. For example, at the sensation stage, the task is gathering as much relevant information and data as possible; at the completion stage, the task is doing whatever is necessary to 'finish off' the interaction for now.

How does this model help to plan the team-building event as it unfolds? First, I use it as a simple model of team development, with the stages in the cycle representing the stages and tasks that I hope the team will move through over the two days. To help this process I plan to offer a wide range of activities and tasks over the two days, each kind of activity being associated with one of the stages.

But second, and just as important, I use it as a model of team 'pathology' and also a way of noticing when the team is stuck. For the moment I will merely indicate this diagnostic use of the cycle, and return to discuss it in more detail later.

From rest to observation: the cycle begins

I now return to my description of the team-building. My initial aim is to provide opportunities for team members to begin to gather information about the training room, themselves and each other. I know that what helps them to start the cycle of learning are the natural, childlike qualities mentioned earlier: an interest in people and situations, a willingness to 'keep their eyes and ears open' and to notice what is happening around them and to them, and feelings of excitement and curiosity which drive them onwards.

So now, as I sit in the room with them, I am excited at the unfolding possibilities. I wonder how *they* are feeling. I am aware that many will not have experienced anything like this experiential event before, and are likely to be nervous. So we start simply by saying 'hello'. At my suggestion they walk round the large group room, at first exploring it, and then greeting each other (and me) in whatever way feels appropriate. The greetings range from hugs to handshakes, and much excitement and laughter is generated. Encouraged by this energy, I decide to move straight into a group 'sculpt' called 'the swimming pool'.

I set out four chairs to mark the corners of the 'pool', and designate 'deep' and 'shallow' ends. I tell them that the 'swimming pool' thus created is a metaphor for the two days, and they should place themselves in and around it in relation to how they are feeling about their participation in the event. Some are tentative and want to dip their toes in at the shallow end. Others 'dive' straight in at the deep end. Still others move to the 'spectators' seats' at the side, where they can watch without getting wet. Once placed, I ask anyone who wishes to say as much or as little as they choose about their position and what it says about how they are feeling. Almost everyone says something. This exercise provides us with a snapshot of where the group are at; and also a base-line for measuring progress, because we can always recreate the swimming pool later in the event to see how their feelings have changed.

The 'swimming pool' has provided team members with a way of discovering how they and their colleagues feel about the event; and now the question in the air is, 'What's going to happen next?'

At this point, I want to hear something from each individual team member, so we have a round of introductions, during which they say whatever they feel like saying by way of introducing themselves to me. I also say something about myself and my background. After this, I feel it appropriate to talk to the team for ten minutes about team-building, and how I see it. During this input I also introduce some important distinctions, such as that between task and socio-emotional issues in team functioning, and generally describe how I intend to work.

Before we get on to the important task of agenda setting, I want to find out more about members of the team as individual workers. So I suggest an exercise on 'triumphs and disasters' over the past year, which allows them to talk in pairs about what has gone well and less well for them at work recently. After they have done this, I offer a chance for those who want to to share something on this theme with the whole group.

The team are starting to enjoy this rare chance to listen to each other and now appear more relaxed. It is important that I take stock of how the group process is developing, and I mentally use the contact–withdrawal cycle to help me reflect briefly on this. In terms of the two days, we have barely begun: we are still at the 'observation' stage of the cycle. This means that the opening exercises have begun to provide information about individuals and how they function which is available to all. Some of the initial fears have been dissipated, as the team observe my relaxed manner, and begin to believe my opening statements that they will not have to do anything that they do not want to.

Moving from observation to awareness

The team need now to move from the initial observation and 'settling in' stage to the awareness stage. This is the point at which, having used their senses to obtain data from the environment (and ourselves), they are beginning to get a sense of the fresh and exciting demands it is making upon them. This in turn leads naturally to thinking how they want to respond, and what they need or want to learn to be able to respond properly. In short: team members need to start to form an idea of what their learning goals are, and what strategies they might use in this situation.

One way of doing this is to ask people to pair up again (talking to just one other person is relatively unthreatening at this stage), and for each person in turn to help their partner to draw up a list of issues that they feel are important; both issues for them as individuals, and for the team as a whole. The resulting lists are then shared, and collated on a flip-chart by me during the coffee break. I know from past experience that this will produce common themes and issues, and we can then prioritise them and agree on a starting place.

During the break I look at the material produced, to gain a sense of what the important issues are. After the break, and before we begin to prioritise, I offer the team a suggestion and a warning. The suggestion is that they look at some of their 'process' issues before moving on to look at task issues; they are unlikely to make much progress on dealing with the latter until they sort out some of the former, and it is in helping people to look at these matters of 'personal relationships' that external and 'neutral' facilitation is invaluable. The warning is that we will not manage to deal with *all* their agenda items in two days; which means that planning how to deal with left-over team business will be an important second-day task.

On this occasion, it is clear both from the written information people have sent me and from the previous exercise, that there is an issue here in the foreground which I call 'old team–new team'. Just as individuals may prevent themselves from functioning fully in the present because of past 'unfinished business', teams often also have an analogous problem. Teams which, like this one, have been in existence for some time often seem to divide into 'old' and 'new' sub-groupings, and these will often have different norms and goals. This can be – and, as the teams list of issues shows plainly, is in this case – a considerable source of tension and bad feeling. The team and myself agree that this is a good place to start.

From awareness to mobilisation

Having agreed a starting place, the contact cycle suggests to me that the team are now ready to move to the stage of mobilising, where, having some idea of what we want to do, we prepare and 'energise' ourselves for doing it. My Gestalt therapy background offers some pointers for an exercise which will help the team to explore these issues. Where there exist differences and conflicts of this kind, both sides must be given a voice: we need to *separate* before we can *integrate*. I also imagine that both the old and new teams have well-developed fantasies and stereotypes about each other, and that we need to examine some of these projections.

So I suggest first of all that team members line up according to how long they have been on the team – longest-serving to the right, and newest members on the left. In order to get in their correct places on the 'continuum', they have to share information, and this continues for over ten minutes before they settle down. There are some surprises: not everyone knows how long some people have been in the team. Team awareness around this issue is beginning to be raised.

I then suggest to them that there is a natural split in the line, with old team members on one side, and new team members on the other. After some discussion ('When did things really start to change?'), they manage to divide into two groups. I then ask them to sit opposite each other, and to tell each other, in turn, what it is like to be a member of their sub-grouping. This leads to a dialogue between the two teams, in which mutual fantasies and differences are explored.

They realise after a while, with little prompting from me, that there is much more to unite them than divide them, and the integration phase begins. The old team members are ready to leave the past behind them and consider how they can welcome the newcomers; the newcomers, while now appreciating the importance of team history to team identity, are eager to commit themselves to a fresh start. Shared goals and ways of diminishing the 'split' are identified, and the exercise ends quite spontaneously with them standing up and moving more closely together; this graphically symbolises how they would like things to be in future. The exercise finishes with the team in high spirits, and with a reminder from me that healing this division in the team will take on-going work on everyone's part. Wishing does not make it so.

Using the cycle to diagnose team problems

The 'old team–new team' exercise shows the team at work, and graphically illustrates some of the problems they have been creating for themselves.

How does this fit with the contact cycle? I now pause in my account of the two days to look at the contact cycle as a model of team 'pathology'.

The examples given in my earlier account showed what a fully completed contact–withdrawal cycle might look like. In this sense, the cycle offers a model of healthy functioning for both individuals and teams; we are 'healthy' when we can pass through each stage of the cycle, doing the necessary work of each stage, responding both to our own needs and wants and the pressures and resources of the environment.

Failures to complete the cycle arise in two basic ways: either the environment is unable to provide what we want, or – and for present purposes this is the most interesting possibility – we prevent ourselves from meeting our goals. To understand how this happens, I encourage the team members to look closely at how they manage aspects of their contact with each other from moment to moment: for instance, how they communicate with regard to both personal and work matters. And this is the focus of working with teams. If the team is working well together, they will move through the stages of the cycle easily both here and in their normal working life; if not, we need to diagnose where the sticking points are. The question is always: 'How do we, collectively and individually, prevent ourselves from achieving our full potential?' In trying to answer the team begin to understand how they frustrate themselves in their drive towards healthier functioning.

Moving from mobilisation to action

After lunch, I decide to introduce the team explicitly to the notion of the contact–withdrawal cycle as a model of team functioning, using the 'here and now' material generated by the previous exercise as an illustration of the ways in which the team block their learning about themselves. They then begin, with my encouragement, to offer other examples of team misfunctioning which seem to fit the model. They decide that as a team they have a tendency to talk and moan a lot, but find positive action more difficult, thus identifying 'avoiding action' as an area they need to work on in the future.

The afternoon finishes with an exercise which clarifies and explores the different roles in the team. The different occupational groups get together, and draw up posters which advertise what they do (and equally importantly *don't* do) in their work roles. These are then presented to the whole group, and lively discussion takes place. It is clear that not everyone understands fully what other team members do, and that this process of role-clarification and boundary setting is much needed.

Other issues emerge: for the centre manager, who is now in a group of one, the exercise highlights her feelings of isolation, and at one point she starts to cry. I move to support her. Other people's feelings about their work – what they like and what they dislike about their jobs – emerge. One person feels unappreciated; another describes how boring her job is. I decide to gently encourage this emotional expression, and opportunities are thus created for team members to publicly listen to and support each other. The team is learning that strong feelings can be expressed, and that they can be dealt with. My role in 'giving permission' for this expression, and 'holding the boundaries' while they do it is important.

The session finishes with the team identifying further process issues about enhancing support levels, and task ones about how the different groups need to co-ordinate their activities better, being flagged for future work. The mood, as we finish for the day, is thoughtful, and a little subdued. There is much to reflect upon.

Day two: moving towards contact

Overnight, team members will have begun to chew over the meaning and implications of the day's events. They have begun to become clearer about what they want and to take on board each other's perspectives. In consequence they are readier to meet one another in a more authentic way and, hopefully, they will start to move towards more profound learning which affects deeper levels of their individual and collective being.

Anticipating that there will be feelings and issues left over from the previous day's work, I decide as I arrive the next morning not to rush the team into a 'business' agenda. My experience is that it is the social process issues that teams find it hardest to deal with, and it is important to convey several messages to them on this subject. The first is that this work is crucially important to their development: I often say to teams, 'If you look after the process, the task will take care of itself.' The second is that they can fully explore emotions such as anger, fear and sadness, and still survive intact. The third is that they themselves have the skills within the team to do what they need to do – such as explore feelings more – but that to do this they need to recognise and value those team members who have skills in appropriate areas, such as 'socio-emotional leadership'.

So, at my suggestion, we begin with a 'check-in' – a chance for team members to talk in turn about anything left over from yesterday; express how they are feeling about today, and make any specific requests for today's programme. This starts slowly – it's an unfamiliar exercise – but quickly generates a quite heated discussion in which some members of the administrative staff (all women) express angry feelings about how they are treated by some other team members. I encourage them to speak their minds: they are offering exactly the kind of emotional leadership I have in mind in taking the risk to share angry feelings in public. I act as facilitator of the exchanges which follow, actively supporting both sides and suggesting and modelling constructive ways of giving feedback. I know as well that administrative staff, because they have an overview of the workings of the team, are in a unique position to observe the team process and are often very shrewd in their judgements: the problem is, nobody listens to them!

After coffee the circle of chairs reforms and I muse aloud on the best way to proceed. I share my sense that there are still things people need to say to one another, but some people may feel inhibited by talking in the large group. We need to find other, more flexible ways for people to make contact with others. So I suggest a 'street' (Philippson and Harris 1992). In this we agree spatial and time boundaries and within them the team can do as they please. The boundary is the main group room and a large landing outside, and the time boundary one hour, with an additional half hour for review. The team are hesitant about such a relatively unstructured exercise but trust me sufficiently by this stage to give it a go.

Immediately the street begins, the centre manager and the head of administration find a quiet corner and start up an earnest conversation. Others gather in small groups, some talking about team issues, others not sure what to do. Feeling playful, I canvass a group whose goal is to get round the street territory without touching the ground on the way. This starts slowly, but soon about eight people join in, laughing and enjoying themselves. Once people get used to the idea of the street, the general atmosphere is lively and energetic for the rest of the hour.

The review is also lively, with most people sharing their feelings openly. Several announce that they have had important conversations about work arrangements, and share the decisions that have been reached. Others say that they enjoyed having fun, and there is a discussion about how serious the team has become recently, and what can be done about it. I throw in the thought that 'teams that can play together, stay together'.

From contact to completion ... and satisfaction

After lunch, the team get down to business in a different way, and several important team business issues are discussed, each being dealt with briskly and competently. I take time before the tea break to remind them of the contact cycle, and how they seem to have broken through their 'block' to action, and to be functioning well. We identify more precisely some of the ways in which the team are doing this, for future reference.

The two days are now drawing to a close. Using the contact cycle model, I know that the team need to be finishing off the 'contact' stage and moving towards the 'satisfaction and completion' stage, where they review what they have learned, and note what remains to be done. We may also be drawing out further learning; about how we went about things, and how this might be done better in future. It is also important here that the team make time to reflect on and – if appropriate – congratulate themselves on what they have achieved.

I encourage them to spend most of the afternoon identifying issues for future action, and getting them to be as specific as possible about how they will be tackled. In this, I particularly want them to consider basic aspects of team 'infrastructure' such as communication – a real problem in a team as diverse as this – and regular team meetings. If they never meet together, they are not likely to make progress. I also ask them to consider how they are going to continue the process of team review and development they have begun, and they suggest a follow-up day in six months time. I am invited.

At the end, team members get together again in pairs to talk about what they have learned from the two days, and then come back to the large group to share this. There is a general sense, which I encourage, of much good work having been done; the foundations, I point out, for lots more that needs to be done if they are to progress. Team-building is not an easy option, but my hope, as we part, is that they have glimpsed enough of the potential rewards of this approach to want to continue it.

CONCLUSION

I believe that team-building offers a wonderful opportunity for individuals and groups to mobilise their (sometimes hidden) capacities in the service of better functioning. The experiences generated in the event can, if processed properly, provide a rich source of learning, as I hope the case study illustrates.

I use the Gestalt contact–withdrawal cycle not only as a useful model in team-building work, but also as a general guide to the planning of experiential learning in any social or group setting. At any point in the cycle there are both *personal* (internal) and *group* (external) factors relevant to the learning process which may either *promote* or *inhibit* an individual's (or team's) learning in that situation. Identifying and working creatively with these is, for me, at the heart of animating learning experientially.

I would like to conclude with some brief cautionary remarks. The Gestalt contact–withdrawal cycle is for me a useful model of individual and group functioning but it is a rather simplistic one. As in any developmental model, the stages are not in reality demarcated as clearly as my account implies, and the sequence in which they occur not so regular. If this is borne in mind, though, I have found that it is an important piece of 'practical theory' which most people can understand and relate to their own experience.

The skills of working with 'blocks' either in individuals or teams in the 'here and now' are considerable, and must be thoroughly learned. As a team-builder, I have considerable knowledge in a number of areas, without which I could not function effectively. I am well read in a number of areas – therapy, groupwork, organisational theory. More important, I have learned a little from my own experiences. I know a fair bit about myself; my strengths and weaknesses as a person. I know about groups and group dynamics from years as a practitioner; and in particular I know about teams and how they function, from long personal experience as team member and manager. Because of all this, I know the limits of models when they confront the infinite complexities of human nature, and use them accordingly. In terms of promoting learning, in team-building or any setting, practice makes ... better.

NOTES

1 An earlier description of this event appeared in Harris 1993.
2 For a more detailed discussion of Gestalt therapy, see Harris 1989. For an account of the origins of Gestalt therapy, see Clarkson and Mackewn 1993: Chapter 2.
3 For an excellent and readable development of this theme, see Claxton 1984.

REFERENCES

Clarkson, P. and Mackewn, J. (1993) *Fritz Perls*, London: Sage Publications.

Claxton, G. (1984) *Live and Learn*, Buckingham: Open University Press.

Enright, J. (1980) *Enlightening Gestalt*, Mill Valley, California: Pro Telos.

Harris, J. (1989) *Gestalt: An Idiosyncratic Introduction*, 2nd edition, Manchester: Manchester Gestalt Centre.

—— (1993) 'Team building, Gestalt-style', *Topics in Gestalt Therapy* (Manchester Gestalt Centre), 1, 3, 12–21.

Kolb, D. A. (1984) *Experiential Learning*, Englewood Cliffs, New Jersey: Prentice-Hall.

Philippson, P. and Harris, J. (1992) *Gestalt: Working with Groups*, 2nd edition, Manchester: Manchester Gestalt Centre.

Zinker, J. (1977) *Creative Process in Gestalt Therapy*, New York: Random House.

12 Writing and power
Influence and engagement in adult literacies

Jane Mace

THE FEAR OF THE READER

> The thought of writing an essay makes me want to put my head under
> the pillow. I see the question and I think I haven't a clue how to do it,
> even though, in reality, I might know quite a bit about it.
>
> (Undergraduate student, October 1993)

What you are about to read is an essay. It is not a letter; not a report; not a
poem; and not an autobiography. Yet it has elements of all these. My
intention in writing it has been to attempt to disentangle and re-thread the
various issues that face newcomers to the activity of essay writing, and
connect them to those which face students of what is usually known as
'literacy'. Like the student essay writer, I began with a topic proposed to me.

From then on our paths began to diverge. The student writer is writing
under different constraints than I. Before her is the prospect of formal
assessment; her work, in the average academic course, is only likely to be
read by her course tutors and/or examiners – one or two readers, at most.
The critics I face are also formidable: but they do not have the power to
close the gates and 'fail' me in quite as direct a manner. And, as protection, I
have editors who, between first draft and public performance, have an
investment in helping me produce readable, and even coherent writing.

In this chapter I want to restate the value of such editorial support and
collaboration in the process of academic student writing, and I want to
argue that if we are to be effective in enabling our students to develop as
writers, we need to be acutely conscious of the conditions of work that
make that possible for us, too. Hidden from you, as you read this page (or
any other page), is the working and re-working that came before, the
intervals of time between one draft and the next, and the comments offered
on earlier stages by other readers. Hidden from you, and, by now, history to
me. But three features of this process, I suggest, would improve the
optimism of the academic student writer – features which have long been
important to adult literacy education.

First, while the student setting out to write an essay may have pauses
and feedback at outline and draft stages of their writing, the practice of

lecturers giving feedback, and other students acting as peer readers, appears to be a rare experience. (Even when the academic concerned has the will to ensure such feedback, this work is labour intensive; and as Griff Foley, in an interesting essay on the matter (Foley 1995), suggests, the increased pressures on higher education make such labour-intensive work increasingly difficult to sustain.)

Secondly, the issue of timing. Students commonly have to move between choosing (or being given) an essay topic and arriving at a finished text within a matter of weeks. In the case of this chapter, the timespan was nearly two years (between January 1993 and November 1995). (This, of course, has some disadvantages, as well as advantages – not least, the sheer effort of reviving the original 'muse' or framework of thinking in which an earlier version was being written maybe six months before.)

And finally, the student's readers are in a different power relationship to her than are the readers of a published book to its authors. Critics, yes; but not, quite, arbiters of their fate.

To adult literacy students, this image of a reader as a judging and judgemental figure is all too familiar. In a literal sense, these students have no real examiner waiting to assess and grade their work, but their idea of the reader is no less intimidating to them. Spelling, punctuation, grammar and choice of words all loom like impossible tests, too. Their imagination is peopled with others who are more competent and clever than they are:

> 'Through all them years that they've been going along, not being able to read and write, they think that everybody round them has this sort of magic standard, this sort of invisible pass mark, and they never reach that pass mark.'[1]

In contrast, there are those adult literacy students who, having participated in a process of community publishing of their writing, address their readers as equals:

> Nobody realises how much time and work you have to put in to publish a book. It takes about a year to write, publish and distribute one book. It is nerve-racking because your ideas, personality and life are exposed to so many people. It is exciting to do things together with a group of women that we know. I have never been into a bookshop or library, because I can't read most of the books and I can't find the ones I can read. Libraries don't often have our books here.[2]

The potential value of a practice of community publishing in adult literacy education has often been in an extraordinary transformation: the writer, however much the process has been 'nerve-racking', is finally writing with the knowledge of another kind of audience, and she grows bold (Mace 1995). Unlike the university student, who has experience of the world of other books, this woman had none of this experience; yet she had herself become an author appearing in a book. This time, the imagined readership that she had to deal with is plural: they are spectators, more than judges: watching her expose her 'ideas, personality and life'. In the company of 'a group of women' that she knew, she has put herself, not in the dock, but on stage. The 'invisible pass mark', at least on this one occasion, had been surpassed.

A MEETING OF MINDS

While it is true that I have a lot of practice in this kind of writing, and equally true that I have taught writing to many groups of students over a long period, I still found myself, on each occasion when I resumed this particular project, facing great waves of inner resistance: and putting my head under the pillow seemed like a very attractive idea. The usual procrastinating went on: other, optional activities became imperatives. In the end, like the student essay writer and the student author, I had to remind myself that this was a voluntary activity. I had chosen to accept the task; its attractions were the opportunities it offered me to crystallise half-formed ideas and to discover the shape of others, as yet unformed. Such a reminder may still not be enough: any writer still needs some means to release the energy with which to tease out the connections between one idea and other, and the language to express them.

The single most useful strategy to which I turn at such a moment is to revive this sense of a *relationship* between me writing and someone else reading. And if I am effectively to work against any fears I have of her/his indifference to or even contempt for the ideas I am trying to express, I have to imagine that such a listener-reader feels a sympathy and an interest in what I am trying to say. To do this, I have to create the idea of a reader as if he or she were here in the room, nodding as I speak, disagreeing with what I say, asking me questions and prompting me to say more. It is this sympathetic listener-reader who needs also to be conjured up for the paralysed essay writer as much as the newly literate student, writing in the classroom, the library, or the kitchen: writing, as they both are, with the reader-as-judge still competing for space with the reader-as-peer.

Writing for publication is a performance, and any writer is justified in feeling an attack of stage fright from time to time. Meanwhile, for her part, the reader (or audience) may actually be experiencing something quite other than either the sympathy that the writer hopes for or contempt that she fears. Students in both university and adult basic education settings speak frequently of being intimidated by the authority of the published text (and hence of its author). Enormous pedagogic effort – again in both settings – is given to the business of persuading such readers that they have not only the *right* but also, in some sense, the *responsibility* to shed such deference – and the hostility, as well as the fear, that may go with it. In order for fully 'critical' and 'active' reading to take place, both study skills teachers and literacy educators exhort our student readers to move position, and enter into a different relationship with the writer. We invite them to move out of passive silence into active voice: so that they can begin to treat the writer if not on equal terms, at least as someone they can challenge.

This, for example, is the text of a book review generated from such a moment by a student called Jacqueline, handwritten, and filed in the classroom 'book review file'. Its composition was a major achievement for her, and entailed much reworking of vocabulary and spelling. Such errors of punctuation as remain are the surface evidence of this creative effort:

> this book is an autobiography of Louis Shore. this is Her Life story she was born in Jamaica. She tell us about her school work and what Her ambitions was. and coming to England. I like some of it because it reminds me of Home and lot of things that Happened to Her Happened to me it depressing Because she is no better off in the End. I like the part in Jamaica best. and I dislike what happened to her over the House. she should have stood up for Herself more. its sad But interesting it make you feel you're not the only one in the world suffering.[3]

The autobiographical writing in adult literacy work which has been published has provided texts for others to read in which they recognise moments of their own experience; and literacy educators use such moments to encourage a student towards their own writing.

The potentially fruitful dynamic between a writer and a reader which this review suggests has preoccupied me for a number of years, and there are two different kinds of power released by this dynamic that I want to discuss: the first is the *power to influence*, and the second what I shall call the *power to engage*. The examples (and research literature) to which I shall refer are taken from a time of significant change in my own life as a writer and teacher of writing (between 1989 and 1994) when I was in transition from being a 'practitioner' in adult basic education to becoming an academic and researcher.

Re-examining a number of my own published writing efforts of the time, they now seem to me to represent a central paradox. On the one hand, as exercises in a particular kind of academic literacy, they offered me a certain empowerment. On the other, as efforts to construct particular arguments, they sprang from a kind of rebellion against an enormous sense of powerlessness. I was living through an experience of being both the agent for and victim of a structural change in funding, precisely targeted at cutting off support to the kind of education to which I had been committed for nearly twenty years.

THE POWER TO INFLUENCE

By 1989 I had been working for nine years as head of a community education centre, funded as part of a higher education institution. That year, a policy decision was taken to close the centre eighteen months later. In the event the centre remained open for a year longer than that decision had intended. For the eight months from December 1990 until July 1991, I was responsible for the complex work of closing it down, finding alternative places where the five hundred or more current users and students could go instead, writing references for the twenty-six part-time staff whose jobs were to end, organising the distribution of the furniture and resources in the building and completing an archive of the eighteen years of the centre's life.

At the same time, with a kind of irony, I was becoming increasingly involved in research and policy work in the field of adult literacy education. The year before the centre closed, 1990, was also the year I won a research grant designed to fund the study of participatory education in literacy work;[4] it was also International Literacy Year, a time when I was invited to travel to Geneva to contribute to an international symposium on literacy and the university; and it was the year when, with Wendy Moss, I began teaching a postgraduate Diploma in Literacy and Adult Learning. After the 'Goodbye Festival' we held at the centre that summer, I moved office into the main building of its parent college, and my transition from the role of adult education practitioner to academic teacher was complete.

For over a year dozens of the women and men who used the centre as students, or who worked there as tutors, crèche workers and staff, wrote letters, signed petitions and completed reports with the aim of reversing the decision to close the centre. The following is the text of just one of these letters, handwritten in March 1989 and addressed to the then principal of the college, written by a young man called Simon:

Dear Sir
   I am writing because I hear that the future is bleak for the Lee community Education Centre which is part of Goldsmiths College. I cant read or write But the centre come to my Help in teaching me to write a bit and to read some words [you] can read and write and take it for granted It has taken me seven years to do what I can do now What will happen to me and people like me if the Lee centre is closed can you put a price on being able to read and write This letter has taken me several hours to write and then only with a lot of help. I hope to be able to write a letter on my own some day. But only with a lot more help from the Lee Centre.[5]

This letter, along with others (written beneath a variety of letter-headings, including that of the House of Commons), achieved the one-year reprieve on the closure of the centre. It did not, ultimately, prevent it. But like much other writing from the women and men who at the time were using classes at the centre for their particular literacy purposes, it remains an expression of power, born out of a specific moment of powerlessness – and anger. Far from being the letter of a humble supplicant, it is the outcry of a man wronged. It has an authority, deriving from the writer's knowledge that his reader, albeit with more institutional power than he has, cannot know what he knows ('[you] can read and write and take it for granted').

That writer did not succeed in persuading its reader to alter the balance of the power relationship between them. The significance of the writing, however, is in its capacity to disturb that reader's view of the world – and of what it is that he is reading. As the reader of countless other texts, he had no reason to question a usual (but usually unconscious) assumption in reading this one that the labour of this writing would have taken any longer than his labour in reading it. Suddenly, nearly at the end of the letter, he reads this: 'This letter has taken me several hours to write' – and no other writing will look the same to him again.

Writings such as Simon's letter have been a profound influence on my own ever since I first became a literacy tutor in 1969, and witnessed, time after time, the eloquence and effort of many groups and individuals working, like him, at expressing their ideas and experience in writing. The contradiction that I lived with during those last two years of the Lee Centre's life was that I, like the college principal, was a member of the literate elite with the institutional power to oppress others.

Nothing I wrote myself at that time had the power to change the decision to end that particular centre. Everything I wrote, in that period, was influenced by the expressive power of adult students like Simon, there and beyond. Between 1990 and 1992 I published four articles and a book, all of them, in different ways, attempting to grapple with a sense of my own failure to prevent the ending of the same centre.[6] Two of the articles dealt with the relationship between universities and basic education centres; two others, written with colleagues, dealt respectively with the problems and purpose of bureaucratic and academic literacies and issues of identity, authorship and status in adult literacy practice. In the book, I was working on the principles at work in democratic adult literacy education. All this writing used illustrations from my own and others' experiences as students and educators at the Lee Centre.

THE POWER TO ENGAGE

Criticisms of 'poor English' and laments about declining literacy standards are routine in political, popular and educational discourse. 'Good English' is defined by its absence; and to some extent, the 'good essay' is in the same boat. Since 1993, I have had a responsibility for my college's effort to improve the quality of the support for undergraduate and postgraduate students in carrying out the coursework required of them. As part of this, I have taught study skills and approaches to academic writing to many groups of students, studying in different departments of the college.

The two questions I frequently discuss with these students are: What is it that makes a 'good' essay? And what, for them, is the purpose or value of writing one? The usual answer has something to do with coherence, making an argument, showing your understanding, being clear; and the various (and often useful) guides on writing essays allow them to elaborate on this (among others, Clanchy and Ballard 1981, Fairbairn and Winch 1991, Northedge 1990). The concept that I would like to develop is that of the essay writer as having the *power to 'engage'*, precisely because it can encapsulate two, simultaneous meanings:

- the power of the writer to *engage with their subject*, and with other sources that they have researched to explore it; and
- the power to *engage their reader* with this thinking and reflection.

For students of academic literacy, the barriers to this engagement include not only their fear of the reader, but also a lack of explicitness as to the nature of the task itself.

Among studies on the source of the problems facing academic students, I want here to refer to two. The first, by Brigid Ballard and John Clanchy (1988) using examples of essays and lecturers' comments on them from courses in anthropology, social psychology, English, economics and the law, argue for a clearer understanding of the 'fundamental relationship between the culture of knowledge and the language by which it is expressed' (p. 7) There is, they contend, a specific literacy required of student writers which expects them to perform 'those functions required by the culture in ways and at a level judged acceptable by the reader'. Literacy, they point out, varies significantly within different cultural contexts; 'illiteracy' in this context (as it is in all others) is a relative matter, related to those of the disciplinary 'dialect', the specific mode of analysis expected in that discipline and the scope of the subject itself. For many academics, they found, errors of language are of less importance than a concern for the structure and development of an argument; and it is here, they suggest, that the 'rules of the culture' lie deepest (p. 14). The university student, as they put it, has to

> master the alphabet of linguistic and cognitive behaviour. The letter 'A', for example, introduces key elements in the academic culture, as well as standing for 'Excellent' at the end of an essay. 'A', the new student learns, stands for *Analysis* ('I want analysis – not mere description'). 'A' also stands for *Argument* ('I want an argument, not a polemic. This is mere opinion – where is your argument?') 'A' stands for *Assertion* ('What is the evidence for this claim? You can't just assert something...').

> (Ballard and Clanchy 1988: 11)

The issue of when and how to include the personal and explicitly autobiographical is deeply mixed up with ideas of position and authority in academic writing. Like Ballard and Clanchy, researchers of academic literacy in Lancaster found mystification at work, from an examination of their own experience as students and tutors in dealing with the writing demands of three different subject studies (Benson *et al.* 1994). One result, they reported, was an overwhelming sense of separation which students felt 'between study and life': academic writing, they found, 'is often viewed as being entirely separate from any other writing that people may do in their day to day lives' (Benson *et al.* 1994: 70).

Studies such as these suggest not only the need for some explicit articulation of the expectations of student writers in different disciplines, but also the need for an integration between one kind of literacy experience and others: between writing the kitchen note and drafting the report, and between writing for a judge (whether an examiner or a potential employer) and writing for a relative (Mace 1994). Until recently, when the 'new vocationalism' imposed its particular stamp on the adult basic education (ABE) curriculum, ABE teachers had in one respect a greater freedom than their colleagues in higher education, since they had been free of the pressure to ensure that their students fulfil the standards expected for the achievement of certain qualifications. This may be one reason why, as Sue Gardener suggested in her study of writing development in adult education 'Fresh Start' and 'Return to Learning' courses, 'tutors with basic education experience will be used to seeing unfulfilled potential, while tutors with more experience of externally validated work may be used to seeing students failing to meet criteria' (Gardener 1992: 8).

Of all the writing genres familiar to adult students such as those in Sue Gardener's study, the essay, as she put it, is the 'Everest of the range' (p. 48). Crushed with the sense of authority of other writers published in textbooks, student writers need not only to learn strategies for taking notes, brainstorming, drafting and so on, but also to hear two important messages:

- *all* you are writing is an essay (it is not your last word on the subject; nor is it the only way you could write about it); and
- *only you* could write this essay (it is not the total and definitive solution to the problem, or answer to the question that your reader is looking for; it's *your understanding* of it).

The mountain looms; and on either side of it loom two others – on the one hand, that of *plagiarism* ('the ultimate crime') and on the other, that of *originality*. To plagiarise, they are told, is to cheat: a plagiarist is a thief. At the same time, to be original is to have arrived at the summit: the ultimate requirement of the doctoral thesis. And these two ideas are also those by which the academic teacher is haunted: if we fail to negotiate a path between them in our own writing, the penalties are menacing.

Both originality and plagiarism assume the writing endeavour as an entirely individual and solitary journey. If, instead, it is understood as being about positions and relationships, then teaching a group of academic students is not that different from teaching those in adult literacy classes:

for what we are teaching them is to share their reading, compare their draft writing and include their own life experience and reflections in the work. In their quoting, referencing or paraphrasing of other authors, they learn that they need also to include their own commentary, reflection and argument, in order to place their own reflections on a subject in an active relationship with these others.

My own search for studies to answer Ballard and Clanchy's call for more analysis of the expectations for academic writing has revealed critiques from the disciplines of linguistics (such as Ivanic 1993 and Cameron 1989), sociology (Norton 1990 and Torrance *et al.* 1994) and women's studies (Kirsch 1993) – not to mention the considerable array of analyses published in periodicals like *College English* and *English Journal* (notably Anson 1988 and Brodkey 1994). There is the impression that in North America, the debate pre-dates the work now emerging elsewhere, going back to the influential work of the Basic Writing Program in City College New York developed by Mina Shaughnessy in the early 1970s (Shaughnessy 1977). Adrienne Rich, paying tribute to Shaughnessy, remains an eloquent writer about the role of academic writing:

> I think of myself as a teacher of language: that is, as someone for whom language has implied freedom, who is trying to aid others to free themselves through the written word ... I have always assumed, and I do still assume, that people come into the freedom of language through reading, before writing; that the differences of tone, rhythm, vocabulary, intention, encountered over years of reading are, whatever else they may be, suggestive of many different possible modes of being.
>
> (Rich 1980: 63)

It is *engagement* of this kind which teachers of both academic and adult literacy students seek to encourage. Rich's words towards the end of the same piece speak of a context only too familiar twenty years on:

> What fascinates and gives hope in a time of slashed budgets, enlarging class size and national depression is the possibility that many of these young men and women may be gaining the kind of critical perspective on their lives and the skill to bear witness that they have never before had in our country's history.
>
> (Rich 1980: 67)

Bridges between access and entrance, between the world outside and that inside academia, need continually to be rebuilt. The people who choose to engage in an educational enterprise as students, either in the literacy classroom (in an adult education setting) or the lecture hall (in an academic one) bring to the enterprise of freeing and extending their powers as writers, their own luggage of life experiences, of hopes and fears, and of literacy histories. As I said at the beginning, an essay contains elements of other kinds of writing – including reports, poems and letters, of which they already have experience. Here are three of the activities I use with students in higher education to discover what those experiences of writing might be, and to help them use their reflections on these to foster a fresh approach to that which now confronts them. One is for me to read students a poem and then ask them to write for five minutes on the same subject as the poem. When the exercise is over, I do not ask anyone to read out their writing: instead, I ask them to share *the experience* of the writing. What had happened? What got in the way of the writing? In the same way, I ask students to work in pairs to collect and write down ideas for an essay, which they then stick up as posters to share with the group. Again, when they share the results of their collaborations, we talk about, not so much the written result, but on the experience of working together: What were the surprises? What interest did they find that their partner had in their ideas, and vice versa?

A third, and important, exercise is for us all to introduce ourselves to the group as writers. For this, I always insist on two things: that they think of all the kinds of writing that they do (not only the essay(s) pressing down on them that week); and that they think of one positive thing that they can say about this writing – some kind of writing that they enjoy, or are good at. Mature students on both undergraduate and postgraduate programmes bring several years of other writing experience to their work in academia. Such is the status of academic literacy, however, that this experience is difficult to call to mind, or to recognise as valuable and relevant. The initial self-portraits offered to the group in response to my invitation are therefore often framed in negative terms, such as 'I lack confidence in putting down what I want to say,' or 'If it comes to longer words, I stop thinking for myself and start relying on the writers themselves, what they have to say.' The task of the teacher is to move students beyond these preoccupations to a point where they can use the experience they have of other genres of writing to provide the basis of their approach to 'the essay'.

SOME CONCLUSIONS

Writing often makes people feel ill. The purpose of literacy education of any kind is to enable student writers to learn to associate writing for different purposes and in different contexts with a feeling of well-being. Instead of a sense of powerlessness, they are encouraged to develop a sense of themselves as potentially powerful. For it is in the perception of the relative power that reader and writer each perceive to be in the possession of the other that, as I have argued, lies the key to the full exercise of literacy in any discourse, whether it be poetic, political, bureaucratic, academic or any other kind. In order for there to be an interconnection between the general life experience of writer and reader and the specific experience of writing or reading, we need a parallel interconnection between reading and writing, in which readers and writers are engaged in social relationships with each other. The best phrase I can offer to summarise the conditions necessary to achieve this, and the approaches indicated in this chapter, is that of a *democratic learning environment*.

Meanwhile, I continue to try and invent you, the reader, as being present with me in the same room. Reading other texts, I continue to work myself at making present the author hidden behind the printed words. In the context of this persistent effort between writer and reader, the moments when authors and their readers are, literally, in the same room come as a special pleasure. In 1994 I was present at two such events. The first was the celebration of a community publication of writings by students in a local adult literacy scheme. The second was a public performance of poetry in a concert hall. At the first event, there were some thirty people present, plates of crisps and nuts on the table, plastic cups of juice or wine being passed round. Eventually, with some persuasion, some of the authors in the room consented to read for us: holding copies of the newly printed books in their hand, they stood and read aloud poems, short stories. One author, Steve Junor, stood to read his: but before he began reading, he introduced us to the poem's subject, sitting next to him. We listened and watched as he began:

> I love my grandmother with all my heart
> I like her West Indian meals.
> She cooks rice and chicken, and I lick
> my fingers too.
> She is a genuine Jamaican woman.
> Her experience to me, educates;
> she makes me think.
> She makes me see.

(Anon. 1994: 61)

It is hard to convey the emotion in the room at that moment; and it would be easy to sound trite. Later, Steve's grandmother herself took the floor to explain to us one of her 'sayings' quoted in the poem. The event took place in the back room of a bookshop.

A few months later, I sat in a darkened hall with several hundred others and watched Adrienne Rich. Listening to her then, and reading back one of the poems later on the page, I recalled her wish expressed over twenty years before, as a teacher, to introduce college students to another 'mode of being'. Having heard the cadences of her voice that evening, they re-echo for me each time I re-read it:

> I know you are reading this poem,
> late, before leaving your office
> of the one intense yellow lamp-spot and the darkening window
> in the lassitude of a building faded to quiet
> long after rush-hour...

I know you are reading this poem as you pace beside the stove
warming milk, a crying child on your shoulder, a book in your hand
because life is short and you too are thirsty...

(Rich 1991: 25–26)

In this chapter, I have suggested that it is reading of all kinds, poetry as
well as prose, theoretical as well as autobiographical texts, which allow us
to picture both one reader and many. In order to enable our students to
develop their powers as writers, we who are teachers of writing have to
overcome our own fear of the reader, and find a mode of address, as well as
a mode of being, which allows reader and writer to go beyond 'magic pass
marks' or power games, and engage in a process of mutual influence and
reflection.

NOTES

1 These are the words of a man called John, who, when I interviewed him, had just
   'moved on' from a literacy class to a writing workshop, near where he lived in
   Liverpool. He speaks of 'they' from first-hand experience. Quoted in Mace 1979:
   59.
2 Joan is the author of this piece, introducing a publication called *Our Lives:
   Working Women*, published and distributed by the group of which she was a
   member, the Eden Grove Women's Literacy Project, in 1984.
3 Jacqueline was reviewing Louise Shore's book, *Pure Running*, published in 1982
   by Centerprise Publishing Project.
4 The study was funded by a grant from the Leverhume Trust, and carried out by
   Rebecca O'Rourke with me. Our report, *Versions and Variety: Student Publishing in
   Adult Literacy Education* (1992) is available from: Jane Mace, Goldsmiths' College,
   New Cross, London SE14 6NW.
5 Simon's letter is in the Lee Centre archive, which is lodged in the library, at
   Goldsmiths' College, University of London.
6 The articles were: Mace 1990, Mace and Wolfe 1990, Mace 1991, Mace and Lesirge
   1991; the book, Mace 1992.

REFERENCES

Anon. (ed.) (1994) *Looking Backward, Moving Forward*, London: Deptford Bookshop
   and Literacy Centre.
Anson, C. (1988) 'Book lists, cultural literacy, and the stagnation of discourse',
   English Journal, 77, 2, 14–18.
Ballard, B. and Clanchy, J. (1988) 'Literacy in the university: an "anthropological"
   approach', in G. Taylor *et al.*, *Literacy by Degrees*, Buckingham: Open University
   Press and the Society for Research into Higher Education, 9–23.
Barton, D. and Ivanic, R. (1991) *Writing in the Community*, London: Sage.
Benson, N., Gurney, S., Harrison, J. and Rimmershaw, R. (1994) 'The place of
   academic writing in whole life writing', in M. Hamilton, D. Barton and R. Ivanic
   (eds) *Worlds of Literacy*, Clevedon, UK: Multilingual Matters, 52–73.
Brodkey, L. (1994) 'Writing on the bias', *College English*, 56, 5, 527–547.
Cameron, D. (1989) '"Released into language": the study of language outside and
   inside academic institutions', in A. Thompson and H. Wilcox (eds) *Teaching*

Women: Feminism and English Studies, Manchester: Manchester University Press, 4–14.

Fairbairn, G. and Winch, C. (1991) *Reading, Writing and Reasoning: A Guide for Students*, Buckingham: Open University Press and the Society for Research into Higher Education.

Foley, G. (1995) 'Coming to grips with complexity in the formation of adult educators', *Canadian Journal for the Study of Adult Education*, 9, 2.

Gardener, S. (1992) *The Long Word Club*, 2nd edition, Bradford: Research and Practice in Adult Literacy.

Ivanic, R. (1992) 'I is for Interpersonal: the discoursal construction of writer identities and the teaching of writing', *Working Paper Series No. 42*, Lancaster: Centre for Language in Social Life, University of Lancaster.

—— (1993) 'The discoursal construction of writer identity: an investigation with eight mature students', PhD thesis, Lancaster University.

Kirsch, G. (1993) *Women Writing in the Academy: Audience, Authority and Transformation*, Carbondale and Edwardsville: Southern Illinois University Press.

Mace, J. (1979) *Working With Words: Literacy Beyond School*, London: Readers and Writers.

—— (1990) 'Adult literacy and mutual improvement: the challenge to higher education', in I. Haffenden *et al.* (eds) *Towards 1992: Education of Adults in the new Europe: Proceedings of the 20th Annual Conference*, Sheffield: Standing Conference on University Teaching and Research in the Teaching of Adults, 84–93.

—— (1991) 'Trust grew, and so did we: reflections from the United Kingdom', in L. Limage (ed.) *Literacy and the Role of the University*, Paris: UNESCO, 62–70.

—— (1992) *Talking about Literacy: Principles and Practice of Adult Literacy Education*, London: Routledge.

—— (1994) '"The swift course of my life": the CV and community life story writing', in M. Lea *et al.* (eds) *Life Histories and Learning: Language, the Self and Education: Papers from an Interdisciplinary Conference at the Universities of Sussex and Kent*, Falmer, Sussex: University of Sussex, 97–101.

—— (ed.) (1995) *Literacy, Language and Community Publishing: Essays in Adult Education*, Clevedon, UK: Multilingual Matters.

Mace, J. and Lesirge, R. (1991) 'Read this and pass it on: writing, academics and managers', *Adults Learning*, 2, 6, 236–237.

Mace, J. and Wolfe, M. (1990) 'Identity, authorship and status: issues for the UK in International Literacy Year', *Adults Learning*, 1, 10, 264–266.

Northedge, A. (1990) *The Good Study Guide*, Buckingham: Open University Press.

Norton, L. (1990) 'Essay writing: what really counts?', *Higher Education*, 20, 411–442.

Pratley, R. (1988) *Spelling it Out*, London: BBC Books.

Rich, A. (1980) *On Lies, Secrets and Silence: Selected Proses, 1966–78*, London: Virago.

—— (1991) *An Atlas of a Difficult World: Poems, 1988–91*, New York: W. W. Norton.

Sellars, S. (1985) *Grammar Rules OK*, Milton Keynes: Chalkface Project.

Shaughnessy, M. (1977) *Errors and Expectations: A Guide for Teachers of Basic Writing*, New York: Oxford.

Torrance, M., Thomas, G. V. and Robinson, E. J. (1994) 'The writing strategies of graduate research students in the social sciences', *Higher Education*, 27, 379–392.

13 Feeling the fear

Bob Johnson

FEAR IN ACTION

'Jonnie H is the laziest of all. He sits on his butt all day, drinking tea by the quart.' He accounted for 400 tea bags a month. His capacity for work, in any sense recognisable to the outside world, would register negative on all reasonable scales. His cheerful strategy, should he ever be released from prison – which he never seriously believed – would be to find a woman right away to look after him, get her to cook and clean for him and settle down to the only life he ever knew, one in which work and he were incompatible. 'I don't work,' he stated, not so much as a challenge, nor yet a boast, merely a simple statement of fact.

When he wasn't asleep, he would spend his time gossiping, or hatching some plot or other to wangle more drugs out of the doctor. Since I was then the new doctor on the wing, most of his considerable pharmaceutical mischief found its way in my direction. Most prison officers told me that such behaviour was only to be expected from an 'old lag', now in his middle forties, who had spent almost his whole life behind bars.

If Jonnie H turned up in front of you, how would you set about tackling him? What sort of challenge does he represent? And in particular what are the barriers, the hidden reefs upon which the best intentions can so easily founder? If I said that, three years later, he has changed, you would be entitled to be sceptical. Nevertheless he is now off all major drugs, he hoovers the staff quarters, including my office, with a ferocity and vigour which is quite tiring to watch. He builds toy garages, which he paints lurid colours for his newly rediscovered grandson. He actually gave back to the dispensary a Valium tablet – considered gold in prison currency – because it was in excess of his 'withdrawal' regime. He vows never to touch the stuff again, breaking a habit of consuming 30 mg a day for twenty-seven years.

If this sounds quasi-miraculous, then that is partly because it is. It would be easy to dismiss it as a fluke, an aberration, to say that we do not need to modify our penal policy, because such things are not really feasible. What actually happened has a wider significance. What changed was Jonnie's thinking. And the stream of human consciousness is a miracle whichever way you look at it.

Sitting on your butt all day must be about the most boring thing you can think of doing – but it was all Jonnie's consciousness would deliver for him to do. 'Fun' in Jonnie H's world was teasing the doctor, provoking the officers and standing by to batter all and sundry just in case they were standing by to batter him – preferably he striking the first blow.

Now he has a wider horizon. He has a future. He thinks about his extended family, having recently renewed contact with his estranged daughter. He philosophises that we are put on this earth to have grand-children – and lo and behold he now has one. I can relate to this philosophical benignity, since I too recently joined the grandparental ranks. But the point is, he is now thinking for himself. He now conjures up into his own stream of consciousness things to do, ideas to have, philosophical notions to propound, as grandfathers clearly have a biblically anointed right so to do.

My claim to credit in this transformation is a strictly limited one. I facilitated it. I am not responsible for his manifestly civilised and mature behaviour, I do not prompt new and healthier ideas into his cranium, there was no way I could have compelled him to yield up his excess Valium tablet. But what I did do was tap into his emotions, I unblocked an emotional dam, unfroze his major emotional plumbing and facilitated his renaissance.

The fact that I was repaid a thousandfold by his entertaining wit and mind-diverting conversation is merely par for the course with any successful educator anywhere. So what had changed? What is this emotional glacier I managed to persuade him to melt? And how widely does it afflict other learners?

And here we come to the major deficit in twentieth-century psychology – where is the sensible framework for emotion? Four decades ago, my psychology professor advised ignoring them; they were too diffuse to be measurable, so were best avoided altogether. This is a recipe exactly akin to Jonnie H's – sitting on your butt for want of something better to do.

My present position, arrived at over a number of years, is that the one emotion that matters above all others is fear. All the rest seem happily capable of taking care of themselves, often in new and delightful ways. But the one you need to watch out for, since it regularly gives rise to all the trouble, is fear. Fear controls our thinking and our actions, fear distorts our perceptions of the world and fear dominates our other emotions. It concerns me not a jot that I cannot define fear, nor indeed that I am making a massively value-laden judgement in awarding it the status of master emotion.[1] What does concern me greatly is the damage it does to all manifestations of human consciousness, and the overwhelming signifi-cance it has in impeding human growth and development, not least in our ability to learn.

For whatever situation we may find ourselves in, whatever problem we currently face, if we cannot learn from our past experience and in due course from our present predicament, then our outlook is bleaker than was Jonnie H's. Learning is clearly the key to so much that is important to us as human beings, that if it is disabled in some way, then we all suffer. This is to take learning not so much in the narrow sense of education, though this is important enough in its own right, but in the broadest possible meaning of expanding human consciousness, for without that we face a dismal future.

But even having identified it as the chief toxin for learning, which I am convinced beyond doubt that it is, fear has a further savage surprise for an unsuspecting humanity. Fear can be hidden. With the best will in the world, the most serious victim of it can be totally ignorant of its presence.

Well, if emotions in general caused the objective scientific psychologist to quail, the possibility of a fear that is not only subjective, intangible and diffuse but also hidden, unseen and unavailable for comment as well would cause them to drop off their perch altogether. And of course there are a myriad ways of misunderstanding the notion, indeed of abusing it in most uncivilised, unethical, even barbaric ways. Nevertheless it remains a fact, in my experience, that fears can be utterly hidden from their possessor. They control us by obscuring our very awareness of their presence. Indeed if they were not thus distorted but obvious and available for correction, then so many (one is tempted to say all) of life's activities would proceed in a far smoother, more rational fashion than is presently the case.

These hidden fears need to be seen in action, preferably inside your own sensorium, to be believed, let alone understood. Here a simple illustration must suffice. We all suppose that we are sensible civilised people. We behave politely to strangers even when they are sometimes a trifle uncouth with us. But place yourself for a fleeting moment in a position of some disaster – imagine your helicopter has lost its blades and is falling rapidly into the sea, or your cabin on the ocean liner is filling rapidly with excess sea water – what happens next?

What happens is that you cease to think straight. Your mind goes into emergency mode. In a word you panic. Some gallant souls, of course, keep their cool and may be able to rescue the situation for the rest of us. But when the threat is overwhelming, we panic. We think only of saving our skin. In a state of panic, we are no longer seeing ourselves or our surroundings clearly – everything becomes distorted. The priority is survival, and details, indeed sadly enough reality itself, become secondary and discardable.

There are some events in childhood which induce a particular sort of panic – a panic from which there is no obvious or immediate escape. Human infants are totally dependent on adults for their survival, so the opportunity for disaster scenarios are rather more frequent than occur to helicopter flyers. When these panic situations are too severe, they leave a lasting scar in the mind. They set up a ferment which prevents that particular event being brought up for further consideration. In particular, the fact that the panic is now over, and has been for some decades, this simple and healthy fact is kept from everyday reality, and continues to exert its baleful influence. The fear in this case, as with Jonnie H, is hidden – he didn't know he had it, so it was not a problem for him to solve.

Some may suppose that because fear is such an important emotion, it is therefore the last one to remain hidden. In fact it works rather the other way. People become too fearful to see straight, or to think straight – and one of the things that become distorted in this way is the fear itself which is doing the distorting. Again, this is easier to display in practice than it is merely to describe.

CAN I TRUST YOU?

Although this chapter is ostensibly about fear, it is really about trust. For though it may not be immediately obvious, the converse, indeed the antidote for fear is trust. Trust may be fleeting, as may fear itself – but without it, learning is slow, tortuous and usually tedious for all concerned. How different from the Victorian classroom, where the cane was used to fix the facts into so-called recalcitrant young heads. Another vignette from the special prison wing where I work shows how the 'student' will assuredly test both the boundaries of fear, and by the same token, though in more positive terms, those of trust.

Eddie is a big lad, heavily built, in his early twenties. He has an approach to life which seems to involve jutting out his jaw and grinding sullenly forward, expecting to be hit or worse, but damned if that is going to stop him. His social skills were negative if anything, in that he would ask for what he didn't want, and not ask for what he did. To be friendly, he would normally radiate hostility, a social strategy in which his earlier experiences had eminently trained him. In his medical record, his IQ was rated at 88, which is easy to achieve if you are trying to fail. In my estimation, he would make an excellent PhD student, he has application, admirable attention span and a sharp mind when so disposed.

On the day in question, he accosted me in the middle of a mêlée of other prisoners and officers, as I was making my way to my office. He had carefully chosen the scene for maximum impact. What I am about to describe will be echoed in many a deprived institution where 'informal' access allows the students to express themselves spontaneously. What may be different is the language, for which I apologise to the more sensitive reader. It is a curious feature of prison life that four-letter Anglo-Saxon words become the norm, even seeping unconsciously into one's own everyday usage. Intriguingly, when seeking a worse term than part of the female anatomy, they will often come out with 'dog', as in 'Eddie's a dog.' With his shallow social finesse, you can see why they might think so.

'Why did you tell me to fuck off yesterday?' Eddie is bristling up to me in the crowd. He says it with almost a sneer, but with calm deliberation. He is not prepared to accept any throwaway or trivial answer. It is clearly a challenge, and a frisson runs through the by-standers – how will this new doctor react? What is Eddie really after? Surely he is not going to hit him? Some of the more sober inmates begin to back away ever so slightly; while some of the officers tend in the reverse direction, bracing themselves for possible rescue action.

I had no time to think things through. I couldn't really make out what he had in mind. He had largely avoided me previously, so I didn't really know him as well as I knew some of the others. Indeed of the original thirteen on the wing, he was one of only two who refused point blank to be interviewed by me in my first week. Needless to say, his accusation was unfounded, but I did not fancy I would succeed by couching my response in such delicate phraseology. I reacted by deploying my full personality, something that has been my policy in my work for some time.

'I did not tell you to fuck off yesterday, Eddie. I never tell anybody to fuck off. I have taken considerable time and trouble trying to establish a relationship with you, so there is no way I am going to tell you to fuck off.' I considered this a direct response, to the point, bringing the 'conversation' back to the reality as I saw it. I found myself using his terminology to add a certain forcefulness to my reply, and to show him that whatever he was about, I was prepared to join him on his own ground, yet not concede the major point.

I may say I was mildly surprised by the impact this declaration had. He relaxed, as did the assembly, and we all went about our business. It was over as soon as it began. But what was he really doing? What was he up to? What did he really want to know? One thing was clear, he was putting out feelers in my direction, unpleasant ones since he knew no others, but nevertheless he wanted to know more about me and my boundaries or, as you might say, my limitations.

On looking back, always a safer viewpoint, it is clear that he was exploring what I was made of, and in particular how I felt about him. His social vocabulary had always been pitiably small; he had been carefully trained to expect rejection at every turn; so he was merely using the nearest verbal phrase that came to hand to see if I would react violently to him, as had always been his due. In other words, despite his crass verbiage, he had a serious intent, a highly significant message to which he desperately wanted a reply.

I was able to react straight, to respond off the cuff as it were, because I was confident of my position. There was no hidden agenda in me which said this man is scum, he needs taking down a peg or two. To suppose that he needed teaching a lesson was right on the mark, but to suppose that he need teaching manners by disciplinary action or the exercise of my power or authority would have been entirely counterproductive.

Eddie needed to know if I was afraid of him. Happily on this occasion I was not. I freely admit that on other occasions with other individuals, and indeed on other occasions with him, I have been afraid. So since fear is the master emotion, when it rears its ugly head all manner of problems can erupt – in this case the most likely would have been anger. 'How dare you!' and similar outraged reactions would quite have obliterated the delicate social negotiations he was attempting.

This can only be an abbreviated account, so it may sound rather *ex-cathedra* – it is really an attempt to describe what I do, and what I find to work. The expression of anger is clearly a loud noise designed to defend you from some perceived threat. You can't be angry unless you are also a little afraid. There is nothing unhealthy about being afraid – if you are not afraid of walking across busy highways, you will soon have nothing to fear ever again.

The ideal response to someone saying 'I'm angry with you' is to persuade them to trust you. For, since fear is the master emotion, and the antidote for fear is trust, then by dispensing the latter, you allay the former, and the anger evaporates. At least that's the model. Again, this is something that can only be acquired with practice – it is far easier to say than to do. It's a bit like saying 'be beautiful' – beauty and trust are in the eye of the beholder, so it is sensible to have a care when dispensing same. Nevertheless this is the key question in any human relationship – do you trust me? Just because it is so often devalued, and frequently sabotaged by people's hidden fears, this detracts nothing from the fact that too many negative answers jeopardise our very civilisation.

We first learn the status of trustworthiness when we are very small. Large mysterious adults around us have to be trusted to feed, clothe and comfort us. If they fail, so do we. The difficulty from a learner's point of view is that there is a tendency to imagine themselves back in the cradle again, when in reality they are lusty lads and lasses, quite capable of looking after themselves.

Infants develop an ingenious range of parent string-pulling skills. Why should they not? They are vastly more observant, intelligent and aware, even in the first few days of life, than ever they are given credit for. What else is there for them to do? They try out their limited range of motor abilities – the squeak, the squeal and then later, of course, the smile – and watch closely to see what happens. Often quite predictable things happen, so they can always try it again later, when things are slack.

But owing to the vicissitudes of human development, these parent-controlling skills are retained long after the other goos and gurgles of infancy have sensibly been consigned to the past. In other words, adults placed in authority above them are still seen as fair game for manipulation, even though the parent–child relationship is so unrealistic as to be poisonous.

Don't be deceived. These string-pulling techniques can descend upon you as light as thistle down. The real problem is that you are betrayed from within – you find it rather flattering to be so elevated, to have significance beyond your current office bestowed upon you – remember, these wiles can stitch you up before you have had time to say hello.

A moment's thought will show how hazardous this false parent–child milieu can be. Independent young adults (or old adults for that matter) do not need to manipulate other adults as parent-figures. It is only the non-independent who are still running on unreconstructed child-strategies. And they, of course, are the ones whose real parents gave them least sense of independence and responsibility for themselves.

So my fervent advice to all who are responsible for learners, whether the latter are old or young, is to avoid being a parent at all costs. Be friendly, be authoritative, be expert, yes. But if you find yourself tempted, or being asked, to wipe their noses, brush their hair or the emotional equivalent of changing their nappies – then back off. The sort of parent they are asking you to be is exactly the worst sort of parent you would ever want to be. Such parent-figure, child-figure entanglements may seem to make life sweeter, even neater, but beware, it is no longer real, and where things are unreal, that is precisely where the dreaded hidden fears flourish.

HUNTING HIDDEN FEARS

Driving down the hill to work just before crossing the railway bridge, I would glance nervously at my watch – five past nine, oh-mi-god! I had been working as a family doctor in that neighbourhood for fifteen years. I owned the surgery, I was entirely self-employed, I had no 'boss' in that sense. I knew for a fact that though appointments began at 9, if I didn't see the first patient until 11 not a single complaint would be heard. The reason for this was simple – though I couldn't have expressed it in such terms at the time: the patients trusted me.

So what on earth was going on inside my skull to start fretting in this ridiculous way because I was a couple of minutes late? The point to stress is that there was simply no conceivable penalty in the offing – nobody cared less. Yet the feeling in my head was real – I was suffering from a hidden fear. Note that these fears do not simply go away because they are hidden – they are hidden from sight, and merely seep out to poison whatever it is you happen to be doing at the time.

This is a long story, but suffice it to say that because the patients trusted me for so long, after fifteen years of such support I was able to examine where this particular fear came from. It came from my schoolmasterly father who used to insist on being punctual. Slowly, oh so slowly, I managed to drag this hidden admonisher out from the back of my mind, and so discard it. It sounds simple, but it is not.

These hidden fears are the very devil. Take Jonnie H again: his hidden fear was vastly bigger than mine. It derived from being inexplicably deserted by his mother at a tender age. This fear had paralysed him at the eight-year-old stage. He was behaving in adulthood exactly as he was doing when calamity struck. He simply ceased to grow. He stopped learning about the world around him, and how he could cope better with it. His emotional stagnation or freezing came from the fear hidden since childhood.

Asked now how he got rid of it, he describes how I chipped away at his protective coat of chain mail, link by link, until it all fell away and he was able to get on with his life. Now I do not suggest that such a process is as easy to do as it is to describe – remember, these hidden emotions have a ferocity tied in with life or death situations. They remain hidden because the individual feels that even to expose them to today's reality will precipitate the panic and disaster from yesterday, from which they originally arose.

I, for example, would have taken a great deal of umbrage if you had had the temerity to suggest that the true origin of my fretting was my past. I should take great care never to divulge such intimate, humiliating details to such an abrasive nosy individual like you, ever again. So have a care when approaching hidden fears, your own or other people's. The forces needed to deflect a sensible human being into paths of irrationality are potent, usually overwhelming.

Eddie too had been well trained to expect no for an answer. He had encountered very little trust in his entire life – sadly not an uncommon situation. So his uncouth question had a deeper component – is it possible to establish relationships of trust in this cruel world? Is there a future in trying to establish trusting relationships? Note that having been liberally endowed with negative social skills, he phrases the question in the worst possible terms. Nevertheless, that is what underlay it. Trust really is the key to fears, whether hidden or not – though it is often fiendishly difficult to deliver.

In essence the topic under discussion is the learning process from neonate to adulthood. We, everyone of us, learn what kind of world we have been born into. We usually learn it is a lousy place, full of crabby old people who have a hard time making a go of things. The problem is it is hard to learn anything different. Fears are toxic to learning, and hidden fears are most toxic of all. There are remedies, as I have suggested, but they are not always easy to apply. If you are in the process of educating, or facilitating other human beings, it should not be long before you see that fear acts like a lethal mist, wiping out all traces of what was supposed to have been learnt yesterday, and heavily impeding progress today.

But why be negative? There are ways of expediting learning. There are means of overcoming suspicion, paranoia, lack of trust and deeply hidden fears. When you do get it right, as I did with Jonnie H (and later even with Eddie), the mutual confirmation that that is the right way to proceed is quite delightful, to all concerned.

EXORCISING FEARS

In a film I watched as a schoolboy, the good guys are being threatened with annihilation by a stampeding herd of cows. How innocent this all seems now compared with the terrors dreamed up in today's video nasties – all of which come from and evoke common hidden fears – but that's another story. So up steps our hero to save the day – the trick is, apparently, to deflect the stampede by standing in the way. The story goes that panicking cows have only ever seen men on horseback rather like at bull fights, so a solitary human being standing there on her own two pins freaks them out, and they obligingly go off and trample all over somewhere else.

I have no way of knowing the truth of this handy manoeuvre – my knowledge of cowherding is patchy to say the least – but it provides a graphic metaphor for what is demanded by human beings when learning. And here we are moving from learning by the students, whoever they may be, to learning by the facilitators themselves. For clearly if a trustful atmosphere is indispensable for any learning to take place, then the person standing on their own two pins out at the front is primarily responsible for generating that condition *ab initio*.

Now clearly some bovine stampeders are safer than others. Though trust is entirely virtuous, in a crucial sense it has also to be earned, on both sides. An injured facilitator, like a broken cowhand, is of little future value. Foolhardy is subtly different from courageous. Even so, trust is the indispensable ingredient for all human comity, and, since this is our current topic, for learning.

So you need to know how to generate trust, how to trust others and indeed yourself. Now since the only source of trust is a more confident human being, then those are they to whom you must turn. Any learning you are trying to promote is done largely with your own influence, by the way you automatically respond. Conversely if you don't achieve as much as you could, perhaps hidden fears are blocking your soaring ambitions, as they did mine.

So whichever way you look at it, honing up your abilities to relate as best you may is precisely what you need, both for yourself as much as for your work. Sociable human beings spend a lifetime learning to be more so – only perhaps ceasing at the end. Clearly the best way to learn is from a group of peers, dedicated to addressing fears, both hidden and otherwise, namely a support group.

Sadly enough, to be brutally frank, many of our colleagues are just as crabby and cantankerous as were those adults from whom so many of us first learnt our social ABCs – and they are often precisely the ones who are so like us it's embarrassing. So the answer, as with any new skill or knowledge area, is to find someone who knows more, who can facilitate *your* learning. It's no good saying that you can't work in a support group because there are too many personality clashes – that's like saying all your students fail because they just aren't being educated well enough.

Personality and other emotional clashes are a sure sign that communications are going awry. If a group of sensible human beings sit down for a rational co-operative session and end up scratchy and negative, you can be sure something fundamental has gone wrong. Worse, you can be sure that something fundamentally hidden has come into play. Why come to the table, if you don't intend to eat? The problem is that you make all the right protestations – of course I want to learn, of course I want to eat – but underneath, your hidden fears are saying, clam up.

Again space is limited. On the other hand, recipes can be very brief, though difficult to fulfil none the less. Working directly with personalities in the way described has worked well in a most hostile institution, where expressions of discontent or even dismay are generally brutal rather than verbal. A *prima facie* case can therefore be made to say that if it can work in a maximum security prison, surely it can work anywhere. What you need, as I am most fortunate to have, is an ethos which allows these questions to be raised, an atmosphere where they are not immediately proscribed. I am happy to pay tribute to the officers who work with me on this special wing. If they were as negative as some of their colleagues, my tentative ventures into 'trust therapy' would be stillborn.

What is essential is a confident facilitator, one who is not fearful of giving this a go, one who is setting out his or her stall so that you can come to trust not only him or her, but yourself and all those other curmudgeonly personalities like you, who make your life and your work so unnecessarily difficult.

If you haven't got a confident facilitator, why not find one? If you wanted to speak Mandarin Chinese, you would not rest until you found a Mandarin speaker. If you want to learn more about sitting down and gaining support from a group of your fellow human beings, find someone who knows how to do it, and learn from them. What? Don't you trust me? Or worse, perhaps deep deep down you secretly believe learning is something that only other people do.

ACKNOWLEDGEMENT

Thanks to Dr Geraldine Finn for her tightening the converse of fear and trust.

NOTE

1 I have chosen this term in full consciousness of its gendered nature. Fear dominates in an oppressive masculine manner.

Epilogue

14 Ending with ourselves
Reflections on animation and learning

Nod Miller and David Boud

The common injunction in learning from experience is, echoing David Hunt's (1987) well-known phrase, to 'begin with ourselves'. Our original conception of the book was to do this in the introductory chapter and to use our own experience as a way of framing what was to follow. As we edited and reworked the introduction, it seemed less and less appropriate to include a substantial element of autobiographical material there. However, we were convinced that it would not be true to our values to deny our locatedness. The solution was to end with ourselves.

While this strategy appears to reverse the conventional wisdom of learning, it does point to the importance of a major sub-theme of the book – the significant role of reflection in learning. In this final chapter, we explore some themes relating to working with experience which have emerged in our editorial process. Questions we address here include: Where did our interest in working with experience come from? How did the book come about? What have we learned from our experience of creating the book?

In the course of our meetings and conversations about this book, we spent a good deal of time in systematic reflection on aspects of our professional practice and personal experience, in an attempt to work out where our current preoccupations had come from. Here we were putting into practice something about which we have theorised a good deal. David has over the last decade been involved in conceptualising reflection and its importance in learning from experience (see, for example, Boud, Keogh and Walker 1985, Boud, Cohen and Walker 1993). He has focused on the importance of processing and making sense of experience (Boud and Walker 1990) and on how some of the barriers to learning from experience can be overcome (Boud and Walker 1993). Nod has designed, described and analysed dozens of experiential learning events, and reflective autobiography has been a theme in much of her recent research and writing (see, for example, Miller 1993a, Miller 1993b, Miller 1993c).

Despite the fact that reflection in theory and practice has been such a central feature of our professional lives, we did not find the exercise of making sense of the experiences which have led us to where we are now an easy task. Our repertoire of displacement routines to delay getting down to work was extended and elaborated in the course of carrying out the tasks which have fed into the production of this chapter. There is perhaps a lesson to be learned here about the ease with which animators sometimes suggest that learners engage in reflection, as if it were a simple, automatic or stress-free process. Looking back may require dealing with painful, distressing or embarrassing events in the past, and for the two of us, like many other learners, this was something in which we were rather reluctant to engage.

Nevertheless, we could hardly ask the other contributors to 'write themselves into their chapters' if we were not prepared to reciprocate. In keeping, then, with the approach we have tried to foster in earlier chapters, we present here autobiographical accounts in which we have tried to highlight experiences, some quite distant in time, which we see as having shaped and influenced our current preoccupations.

Preparing this book has developed our thinking, reinforced some concerns and challenged some assumptions. We end this chapter with some reflections on the insights which we have derived from our work in compiling and editing this book, drawing out some of the thoughts which have been provoked by the accounts of animation provided by the other contributors, and some directions for our own further development.

SOME FEATURES OF OUR AUTOBIOGRAPHICAL EXPERIENCE

David Boud's story

I suspect that my interest in learning from experience started to emerge during my time in secondary school, as it dawned on me that the traditional classroom lesson was a pretty poor way of learning. I have a clear recollection, during a lesson in a science room when my fellow pupils were messing around and distracting the teacher, of thinking that learning didn't have to be like this; schooling was a vast waste of effort and it didn't allow for people either to develop their interests or to engage in activities which they thought were meaningful. Teaching neither connected with me or my peers, nor was it being conducted well on its own terms.

At around the same time I recall having a new temporary physics teacher – an African as it happens – who declared that he was in the process of obtaining the teaching experience he required to qualify as an educational psychologist. Not only was he an excellent teacher, even though he clearly didn't want to spend his career teaching, but he also began to demystify for me the process of learning. Subjects like physics weren't just arbitrary collections of odd facts to be memorised, they had a shape and elegance of their own, they helped us make sense of apparently baffling phenomena and the ideas themselves ended up making an impact on the world. And, most importantly, some of that understanding was actually available to us, right now. In his friendly and straightforward way he was shifting my conception of learning.

I grew up in a working-class family in inner London. At primary school everyone appeared to have a similar background to myself, so difference was not a big issue – wasn't everyone like us? There were others, of course, but they inhabited the world of newspapers, books or the radio. My first inkling that something was amiss came when I tried to gain entry into grammar school. I had passed the selective test – then the 11-plus – and applied, along with a group of my peers, to the local grammar school. They all gained entry, even those who did less well in class than I did. I did not. I tried another school, but again I was barred. This was hurtful and puzzling. Was I not good enough? My parents tried to reassure me by shouldering the blame themselves. But this was even more of a puzzle. They talked about the school judging them, and them not speaking well enough. They clearly spoke quite normally to my ear; what could it mean?

Later, as I began to mix with a wider range of people, many of whom spoke differently (posher, I would have said then) from myself, what my parents had known all along began to dawn on me. The only explanation could be that I had been discriminated against by reasons of social class. I was very shocked by the notion that someone should be treated differently not because of what they could do but because of an identity over which they could exert no control. Later, I realised how commonplace this was, and much later still I realised to my intense discomfort that I was perpetuating those practices which I knew were wrong and hurtful.

One of my earliest memories of primary school is that of being told that I couldn't write and had nothing to say. In the junior school we had a daily task of writing a diary about what we did at home. I had a literal mind and duly recorded the repetitious round of events. The task seemed full of traps. I knew that I could only list those things of which the teacher approved. When asked to write a story I brought the same expectations to the assignment, and found myself frozen out of fluency.

This difficulty stayed with me. Later, when I was confronted with my first set of external examinations ('O levels'), I found myself able to deal well with the technical and factually based subjects, but I had real problems dealing with English. After two miserable failures I finally scraped through in English Language. English Literature was given up for lost. This was my first experience of a so-called 'objective' failure and it was one that had a continuing effect. Confidence in my ability to succeed was undermined and I limped along with the burden of believing that I couldn't write. The residues of that are still with me, but luckily I managed to escape the worst of this limitation by concentrating on the content and task dimensions of the academic work I was doing and avoiding thinking of it as an act of writing!

While the incidents described above sowed the seeds of the development of my subsequent views about learning, a stronger base of positive experience was required as well as the stimulus of new ideas and concepts. Study for a physics degree added to my confidence, but it reinforced my sense that there was a lot more to learning than I had imagined, and teaching was often a very wasteful enterprise. I flourished in the liberating role of research student – I could be self-directed both in my immediate studies and in a broader sphere. Then a great opportunity presented itself. I became involved with the Human Potential Research Project (HPRP) at the University of Surrey and came under the striking influence of John Heron. Through the personal and intellectual impact of his work and associated activities in personal growth groups I began to discover in practice what I already knew intuitively: that there was much more to learning than the intellect, that significant personal issues could be just as much a focus of study and exploration as the physical world and that the conventions of the classroom were often part of a tacit conspiracy between teacher and taught to avoid learning.

Through participation in, and some first steps in leadership of, human relations groups ranging through encounter and Gestalt to co-counselling, I started to form the views I presently hold on learning from experience. I found that such learning involved risk-taking, self-disclosure, acknowledgement of past problematic experience, trust and the caring (and at times confrontational) support of others engaged in a similar quest. It was possible to make sense of messy and confusing experience. This was not the same sense that is made by the physicist, but an understanding no less significant and certainly more powerful at a personal level.

Following this, I began to see the public and private worlds of learning as no longer being distinct and separate. Learning was seamless and the insights I had in institutional study and in personal exploration were not bound to the domains of formal education. My work in staff development, which has occupied a large part of my career to date, was strongly influenced by my experiences with the HPRP, although translations to different groups such as university staff and adult educators, and to different countries – Scotland and then Australia – added to my understanding.

For much of this time the influence of broader contexts was beyond my immediate awareness. In working within the university I could pretend that many social issues did not impinge on me. I knew the force of class oppression from my past, and had heard some of the arguments of the women's movement, but it took ten years of professional practice before I could acknowledge that classism and sexism exerted their malign influence through me also. It was some time before I could face the difficult task of confronting the limitations of my own practice.

Through reflection and further reading and talking I began to extend my awareness into critical social science, sexism, racism, including the outrageous treatment of Aboriginal people, and class prejudice. The insidious nature of how oppression works in society and the way in which we shield ourselves through our taken-for-granted assumptions about the world took a long time to surface in my consciousness. I realised that I had been oppressed both by individual people and by social structures which operated beyond individual action. Eventually it dawned on me that I acted in ways which were oppressive to others and that I did so despite some level of awareness of the issues. This was profoundly disturbing.

My personal history started to have a more direct effect on my research and writing. I became preoccupied with processes of learning from experience, dealing with difficult events, ways of reflecting on experience and how to make sense of one's own learning. I did much of this with others, as I found that the best way I could externalise many of these issues was through personal dialogue, only later transforming this into the written conventions of papers and books.

All this formed part of the background leading up to the creation of this book. I had come to the following realisations about experience and learning:

- A psychological or individual perspective on learning is not enough.
- The social and cultural context is more powerful and pervasive than I ever imagined. It can easily inhibit and undermine the development of self-confidence and frame one's thinking to disguise its influence.
- Learning is everywhere and we can often learn more from non-formal and unconventional settings than we can from the classroom.
- The role of the person who helps others learn from their experience is extremely important. Teachers and facilitators do make a difference, but unfortunately not always for the better.

Nod Miller's story

My interest in working with experience was aroused initially by my negative experiences of being taught. During lessons at school my personal experience was largely ignored, but that was what I had been socialised into regarding as normal. At grammar school, I learned to manage the tension between the working-class culture of my home and family and the middle-class culture of the school, and given the negation of my home culture as well as the emphasis on hierarchy and authority in the culture of the school, I should have been surprised if my teachers had placed much value on my personal experience as a resource for learning. However, I had higher hopes of higher education.

I chose an undergraduate course in social science. I had very little knowledge of what sociology was about, but I expected that it would help me to understand people and groups better, and perhaps to make sense of the tensions between the working-class culture of my family and the world of the grammar school (although I probably could not have expressed my expectations in that way at that time).

I soon discovered that sociology was taught consistently as if the experience of students and staff – those actually present in the classroom – was almost completely irrelevant. On a very small number of occasions a seminar discussion would take off into the realm of 'real life', and I can recall a couple of occasions when a lecturer on a course in the sociology of religion encouraged us to do some undercover fieldwork by going out to visit church services organised by unfamiliar religious groups. Otherwise my undergraduate studies were undisturbed by the need or the opportunity to reflect on my own direct experience. For the most part, I became alienated from formal study, and concentrated my time and attention on gaining life experience through various youth subcultural activities and complex heterosexual entanglements, at the same time maintaining a minimal presence in classes in order to complete the three years with an undistinguished degree.

Given the nature of my early experience of higher education, I am rather surprised to find myself, two and a half decades later, in a relatively senior university post. When I finished my time as an undergraduate I was convinced that higher education had little to offer me. And I had always asserted that I didn't want to be a teacher. However, after some months spent selling bathroom equipment I happened (by accident, it seemed) into a temporary part-time lecturing job in a college of further education. The possibility of spending time engaged in fulfilling activity (at least by comparison with my work in the plumbers' merchants) in an educational environment considerably different from the grammar school or university was sufficiently enticing to propel me into a postgraduate teaching course, and ultimately into a career as a professional educator.

Over the last twenty years I have worked with learners from all over the world and of all ages in the context of courses in liberal studies, communication and media studies, adult learning, interpersonal behaviour, sociology, psychology, group dynamics, community development and research methods, and organising conferences, workshops and symposia across several continents. Through this work run threads of concern with the processes by which people learn (gain knowledge, acquire skills and form attitudes), and of preoccupation with the design of learning spaces and events. It seems that the energy I have put into these activities has been generated out of my alienation from much of conventional formal education, and my conviction that there must be a better way.

At about the same time as my uncomfortable experience as a working-class child in the middle-class environment of the grammar school led me to reflect consciously on the significance and unfairness of class divisions and discrimination, I became aware of the sexual double standards which operated in my peer group, and observed with indignation the imbalance of the gendered division of labour which was lived out in my home. A few years later, when I first encountered the writings of the contemporary feminist movement and became active in women's liberation groups, I developed a theoretical framework which helped me to make sense of my earlier experience.

This framework, most simply summarised in the early feminist slogan 'the personal is political', has informed my professional activity and the way I attempt to live my personal life ever since. Gender and social class are central organising principles in the way I see and interpret the world, and I am committed to working with others to raise awareness of inequality and oppression and to devise strategies for social change.

I was brought up in a white, small-town community where racial and ethnic conflict and oppression were largely invisible (although not, of course, absent); it was not until my twenties that I began to gain direct experience of dealing with people from other cultures and nationalities. More recently, I have built up substantial experience of working in different countries, including those of the third world, and much of my professional life has been conducted in multi-national, multi-ethnic groups. Colleagues and students who are very different from me in terms of culture and appearance have helped to shape my consciousness of the often subtle operation of racial oppression and discrimination, and I have become increasingly concerned to take into account the complex interplay of gender, ethnicity and social class in the learning contexts within which I operate.

In 1973 I took part in my first experiential group. I was both intrigued and repelled. I was moved to experiment with new approaches to teaching, making use of role-play and drama in the teaching of sociology and general studies in the college where I then worked. At the same time I was uneasy with the individualistic focus, elitism and detachment from the social world which seemed to me to characterise the approach taken by the group leaders.

Ten years later, I attended my first T-group laboratory, an event organised by the Group Relations Training Association (GRTA). I had relatively low expectations of the event, and was not prepared for the effect it turned out to have on my professional practice and personal life. I found that the T-group provided a powerful microcosm in which to explore social structures and processes, and my understanding of the minutiae of gender and class relations was greatly enhanced by the laboratory experience (described in detail in Miller 1993b).

Over the course of the last decade, much of my work has involved research, teaching and training in the field of group relations. I became active in the organisation of GRTA, and served as its chairperson for three years. While convinced of the value of T-group methodology as a medium for personal and social development, I remained critical of much group-work practice, which often focused on individual behaviour and was styled 'apolitical'. In the course of researching the social and educational history of the T-group I discovered its origins in the work of Kurt Lewin, and this renewed my belief that laboratory training had great potential as a vehicle for social change.

My central interest has become how to use personal experience in order to understand social and economic structures and political processes. This may involve the modelling of learning spaces using the methodology of the T-group in order to create microcosmic worlds where features of social and political reality may perhaps be more readily captured and understood, or it may mean engagement in systematic reflection on past experience through writing and group discussion. Influences on my thinking and practice include the work of Lewin, already mentioned, as well as C. Wright Mills' idea of the sociological imagination as having the quality 'to understand the larger historical scene in terms of its meaning for the inner life and the external career of a variety of individuals . . . to grasp history and biography and the relations between the two within society' (Mills 1970: 11–12). Another important influence is the work of contemporary feminist scholars, particularly some who are known to me through personal acquaintance as friends as well as through their writing (Stanley and Wise 1993, Stanley 1992).

SIMILARITIES AND DIFFERENCES

Some common themes emerge from our stories. Both of us were strongly affected by negative experiences of being taught. Both of us experienced inequality and discrimination at first hand early on in our lives. We have a shared concern with learning from experience and how it can be promoted and some common experience as university teachers, researchers, adult educators and human relations practitioners. We have both been influenced by personal acquaintance with educators whose methods, approaches and values we share and admire. Our present practice is influenced by our past experience in ways which it is practically impossible to articulate.

Although it may not be immediately apparent from the accounts given above, we are of the same generation. We are both white and British by birth, although we now live on different continents. We are also different in terms of our background disciplines. Despite Nod's exasperation with the way in which sociology was taught during her undergraduate course, she still defines herself as a sociologist, and her concerns with social structures and political economy provide the theoretical framework for her teaching and research in media and cultural studies. By contrast, David's undergraduate studies were in the physical sciences, and his work in adult education has spanned humanistic psychology and professional practice. He no longer identifies as a scientist although he retains, sentimentally, his membership of the Institute of Physics. In attempting to bring together socio-economic and political analysis with psychological and philosophical approaches, we hope that we have achieved a fruitful synthesis.

THE ORIGINS OF THIS BOOK IN OUR COMMON PERSONAL EXPERIENCE

The discussions which led to this book began when Nod was on study leave in the University of Technology, Sydney, where David was then Head of the School of Adult and Language Education. They grew out of conversations about interviews he had undertaken with experiential educators in order to draw out essential features of their practice. We debated the implications of that earlier work, and out of that process grew the present project.

We began by talking about our interests in facilitation, and our ideas about what had not been said on this subject that needed to be said. We brainstormed topics and sets of headings, and compiled lists of people who might contribute to a book. Some of those we included in our lists were close friends and colleagues, while others were people we had never met, but with whose work we were familiar through their writing. Eventually we arrived at a set of contributors with which we were happy, and began to work out a detailed timetable for the completion of the work. In the event, the timetable was considerably extended. Everything seemed to take much longer than we had anticipated.

After Nod returned to the UK at the beginning of 1993, most of the work on this book was carried out with the two of us on different continents. There were spurts of progress when David was visiting London, but much of the time has been characterised by long spaces of silence interspersed with frantic bursts of e-mail activity.

After completing the detailed work on the rest of the book, we were faced with the challenge of ending it. The conventional approach to this problem is to have a final chapter which pulls together the threads of the book in an authoritative way and points to future directions. While we were tempted by this solution, and urged by some of the contributors to adopt it, we decided that this would not be appropriate, for several reasons. Firstly, in a book which argues for the centrality of learning from experience, it would be contradictory to presume to tell readers what they should take from the book. Secondly, even if we thought this desirable, it would not be very effective. There is no formula or set of principles which animators *should* adopt. To imply that there is such a formula is to mistake the nature of the role and the process. In the light of their own experience, and that of others which they read or hear about, animators need to find a way of operating which is consistent with their own values and ethical positions. Animators need to debate and argue these views with others to test their commitment to them and the implications which arise from them. But they do not need to be told what to do.

While one solution to our dilemma was to avoid any final statements, this seemed to us to deny our own experience as producers of this volume. We end therefore with our own, necessarily personal, reflections on the chapters. These illustrate our continuing process of making sense and attempting to relate the experiences of others to our own practice.

THE IMPACT OF *WORKING WITH EXPERIENCE*

As we read through each chapter yet again during the final editing process, we had the experience of seeing things which we had missed previously and reflecting on what the book now meant to us. We realised the significance of the idea which has been argued most recently by theorists of the post-modern (for example, Usher and Edwards 1994): we take what we want from texts. Our readings of the text of each chapter of this book say more about ourselves than perhaps about what the author is saying. We interpret the ideas of others according to what we bring to those ideas, and according to our preoccupations and our proclivities, and we understand these ideas through the dominant discourses within which we are constructed. Other readers will necessarily bring quite different sets of concerns to the text.

Nevertheless, to end our own process of constructing this text, each of us offers here some reflections on earlier chapters in order to complete the story of the book as a whole.

David Boud's reflections

I could identify with Joyce Stalker's story of how she shifted her major perspectives over time. I don't see the world now in the same way as I once did and I can't expect my students to see it in the same way as myself. As I become more conscious of my own changes and see my own perspectives shifting, the question arises, 'What do I stand for now?' As I ponder that question further I realise that while I may have become more skilful in some ways, I may also be less useful as an animator for some learners because I do not hold a position which allows them to get what they need from me. My view of the world no longer fits with theirs, and while this can provide a stimulus for new learning, it also means that some common points of identification are absent. This can result in our not starting in the same place and forever avoiding the contact that can lead to mutual exploration of perspectives. Learning to be an animator is not a simple progression to more and more skilful practice. Some kind of match between animator and learner is also required.

Joyce Stalker also demonstrates that ideas of animation are appropriate in a formal teaching context, even one that is traditionally conceived of as lecturing and explaining. It is important to equip learners with conceptual tools to help them reflect on and make sense of their experience and to question what they are told. The demystification of perspectives, or the process of naming the world, are not just intellectual exercises. They build confidence and can enable learners to go beyond what is given. This analysis complements Stephen Brookfield's strategy of getting professionals to eschew experts in the search for solutions to the problems they face. He illustrates how we are socialised into learning not to trust ourselves and our peers, despite the fact that the only way we can learn is through such trust.

I found it impossible to read John Heron's chapter without images of my earlier contacts with him constantly intervening. I wondered how the chapter would be read by those who do not have this shared experience. Will it be seen as too esoteric, not grounded in the 'real' world – whatever *that* may represent? His chapter is, for me, an important one because, amongst many other things, it speaks of an aspect of human experience which is unrecognised in most writing about professional practice and which I rarely allow myself to acknowledge on a day-to-day basis. It is an aspect which is, however, undeniably present. To talk of the spiritual or the transpersonal is to risk being dismissed as irrelevant in the pragmatic world of work, but Heron talks about them as part of the normal range of events which occur in groups mainly comprised of busy professionals. He makes possible discourse about such dimensions alongside the political, the technical and the personal. If I were asked to pick which of the many themes will need to be developed much further in years to come, I should say that it would be this one.

My connection with Bob Johnson is personal rather than professional. I have heard him recount his experiences on the Special Wing of Parkhurst Prison many times and been impressed with his insight into the way emotions lead us into acting in the most extraordinary ways. Although the people with whom he worked were 'hardened criminals', they were, behind this screen, vulnerable individuals who had coped in the most extreme ways with the emotional pain that had been visited upon them in their early lives. Both I and others I know well were just like these people. We may have suffered less, but we were no more able to cope with the residue of emotional trauma and we inadvertently express this in ways which undermine the learning we need to engage for our present day tasks. I saw vividly that whenever we fail to act with confidence and respond rationally to the demands of a new situation we are experiencing our previous hurts inhibiting our present behaviour.

But what can I do about it when I am in the role of animator? To break through these affective barriers I believe an animator is needed who does not get sucked in to the fears and fantasies of our internal world. This person needs to be someone in whom I have reason to trust and someone whom I am able to trust. This trust helps me trust myself and so quiet the voices which tell me what I cannot do or should always avoid doing. The theme of trust and the barriers – both internal and external – to trusting reappears once more.

In discussing personal experience and ideas such as trust, it is easy to slip into the discourse of the individual, to pretend for the sake of convenience that we do not operate in a social context or that many individual acts are not a result of influences wider than the persons who appear to be responsible. This book for me was a way of shifting the balance between the individual and the collective to give greater recognition in my own practice to the social and political. I find it easy to acknowledge in principle the importance of both, even discuss both aspects separately. The challenge for my own practice is in putting these dimensions together so that many sets of considerations are present and available for me to draw upon at any one time. I notice that many other people have the same problem. They either focus on the individual or the social explanation and struggle to synthesise the two.

The most helpful bridges I have found are through stories and, in particular, from accounts which have come from a broadly feminist perspective. The slogan that Nod refers to above, 'the personal is political', is exemplified many times, not least by two examples here. Both Jan Pettman and Elizabeth Tisdell write about their own experiences in university teaching (my own field of practice) and how they work with personal experience in the context of much greater forces – the international in Jan's case and patriarchy in Elizabeth's. Through their reflections on their teaching it is possible to see ways of operating which both respect the individual and their own experience, which may at times seem quite distorted, and the socio-political influences which help create the worlds in which they operate.

John Smyth also focuses on socio-political influences. His chapter, albeit in quite a different style to the two others, confronts us with how easy it is for socio-economic metaphors to dominate discussions about learning and education. I am dismayed about how readily I can slip into such language and how I have used it to promote educational ideas which have other much more substantial reasons for being developed. It has become the new language of power and influence. It is used against those who hold unfashionable views about what is important and who may use a discourse of learning rather than economics. Smyth helps us to see how we can be reflective and resist, and help others to resist, such discourse by focusing on whose interests are being served by our own practices and what is worth fighting for.

Nod Miller's reflections

Jane Mace's chapter speaks powerfully about the importance of acknowledging the fear and feelings of inadequacy which can affect both animators and learners. The context with which she is concerned is adult literacy, but her observations have application to other settings. In some of my earlier writing, I have referred to my experience as a novice university teacher in terms of my anxieties about being an impostor, and my worries about being found out (Miller 1993a: 44). This thought is often quoted back to me, and it seems to strike a chord with others. More recently, I have come across references to fears and insecurities of this kind in the work of other writers. For example, Stephen Brookfield, who argues persuasively in his chapter in this book for the importance of learners developing self-confidence and belief in the value of their own knowledge, has also focused on 'the impostor syndrome' (Brookfield 1990). Animators have fears of inadequacy to contend with; they can suffer from stage fright about their 'performance'. Learners are subject to fear about their ability to 'perform', too; I find that I am still often fearful and anxious about taking part as a learner in activities which involve me in 'performing' or revealing something about myself in groups of strangers. In dealing with issues of 'success' as an animator, I take the view that animation is partly about rendering oneself invisible; the less visible the act of animation, the more successful it is. Of course, the activity is by no means all under the control of the animator. Since it is largely to do with getting learners to set their own agenda, it is inevitable that it will be hard to judge 'success'. The issue of fear of failure as an animator is one also raised by Jim Brown in his chapter.

David makes an observation above about being personally acquainted with several of the other contributors, and refers to his curiosity about how their chapters will be read by those who do not have the benefit of direct knowledge of the writers. This is an issue for me as well. Seven of the contributors are in varying degrees known to me personally. They range from people with whom I have collaborated closely over a number of years to people with whom I have spent time at international conferences. There are four contributors whom I have never met face to face. My editorial reaction to what the people I know have written is inevitably mediated through the extent of my knowledge of and involvement with their work as animators – and with them as colleagues and friends. For example, I have worked very closely with Jim Brown at various times since 1983, and the points that he raises about the limited power of animators to determine outcomes and effect change resonate strongly with me; they relate to concerns with which Jim and I have frequently grappled in the course of our collaborative endeavours.

I have also worked with John Harris over many years in numerous experiential groups. Although I have been full of admiration for his skill as an animator, which he exercises with great humour and lightness of touch, I realise in re-reading his chapter that I have remained largely in ignorance of the detail of the theoretical insights, derived from Gestalt psychology, which he brings to his practice as an animator. Furthermore, I recognise that my view of humanistic psychology has been coloured by prejudice against practices which I have dismissed as 'individualistic', 'self-indulgent' or 'touchy-feely'. In the course of editing this book, I have been pushed to confront my own intolerance and contradictions, and to recognise the need to draw upon psychological as well as sociological insights in developing theoretical frameworks to analyse learning from experience. I have also been brought to the recognition that principles of psychotherapeutic practice, as well as regard for spiritual and transpersonal dimensions of learning (to which David has already drawn attention), have a good deal to offer to the activity of animation. The synthesis of educational and social scientific traditions which is a central theme of Chapter 2 of this book provides the single most important element of personal development which has resulted for me from this editorial task.

Tim Ireland is someone I have come to know in recent times, in the context of an collaborative research programme linking universities in Britain and Brazil. His chapter prompts me to recognise the importance of viewing learning and animation in an international context, and the value of the insights derived from the struggle to communicate across divisions of culture and class. In my autobiographical account earlier in this chapter, I acknowledged the importance of the experience of the tensions and discomfort of upward social mobility. This uncomfortable experience has, I believe, been important in my practice as an animator, particularly in informing my concerns with social justice and social change. My practice and values as an experiential educator have been immeasurably affected by my work with adult educators from Africa, Asia and Latin America. I have found that communicating across cultural boundaries can be fraught with frustration but hugely satisfying.

My work with people from other cultures has forced me to interrogate the assumptions and world view which I bring to the process of animation, and to be respectful in the face of wisdom derived from worlds I cannot know. The language of 'development' is full of the legacy of cultural imperialism, and of implications that learning across cultures amounts to a one-way transmission from 'first' to 'third' world countries. Tim Ireland's chapter provides an important reminder of the rich tradition of theory about learning from experience which has developed outside Europe and North America, but which is frequently overlooked by those in the 'developed' world.

ANIMATION INVOLVES LEARNING TOO

We were surprised to discover how great the links have been between the issues which appear in the book and our own personal experience. Although the chapters were written by others, they, and the issues they were invited to address, were of course chosen by us in the light of our own concerns about learning and animation. This discovery made us realise that the book can probably only hope to speak meaningfully to those whose experience and aspirations have something in common with our own – to those who wish to work with others to assist them to learn in terms which are meaningful for them. Animators, as we have described them here, hold their own educational values, are committed to working in ways which respect the integrity of learners and care about the need to avoid oppression no matter what form it might take.

Perhaps all animators can do is make personal sense of animation and recognise the shared ideas and concepts which have influenced and are influencing their thinking and practice. That making sense may lead to change in their practice. That subsequent change is the most important. As our autobiographies reveal, we were both adversely affected by other people's teaching. We end this book with a resolution to be mindful about the influence of our practice on others. All animators have the power to influence others and affect their learning. They may effectively engage with learners' experience, they may earn their trust and they may lead them to confront some of the substantial barriers which constrain learning. But it is possible to end up doing quite the opposite. Which path animators take will be a function of the extent to which they can trust themselves, confront their barriers to learning and learn from their own experience.

REFERENCES

Boud, D., Cohen, R. and Walker, D. (1993) 'Understanding learning from experience', in D. Boud, R. Cohen and D. Walker (eds) *Using Experience for Learning*, Buckingham: SRHE and Open University Press, 1–17.

Boud, D. and Griffin, V. (eds) (1987) *Appreciating Adults Learning: From the Learner's Perspective*, London: Kogan Page.

Boud, D., Keogh, R. and Walker, D. (eds) (1985) *Reflection: Turning Experience into Learning*, London: Kogan Page.

Boud, D. and Walker, D. (1990) 'Making the most of experience', *Studies in Continuing Education*, 12, 2, 61–80.

—— (1993) 'Barriers to reflection on experience', in D. Boud, R. Cohen and D. Walker (eds) *Using Experience for Learning*, Buckingham: SRHE and Open University Press, 73–86.

Brookfield, S. (1990) *The Skillful Teacher*, San Francisco: Jossey Bass.

Hunt, D. E. (1987) *Beginning with Ourselves: In Practice, Theory and Human Affairs*, Toronto: OISE Press.

Miller, N. (1993a) *Personal Experience, Adult Learning and Social Research: Developing a Sociological Imagination in and Beyond the T-Group*, Adelaide: Centre for Research in Adult Education for Human Development, University of South Australia.

—— (1993b) 'How the T-group changed my life: sociological perspectives on experiential groupwork', in D. Boud, R. Cohen and D. Walker (eds) *Using Experience for Learning*, Buckingham: SRHE and Open University Press, 129–142.

—— (1993c) 'Doing adult education research through autobiography', in N. Miller and D. Jones (eds) *Research: Reflecting Practice*, Boston: SCUTREA, 88–92.

Mills, C. W. (1970) *The Sociological Imagination*, Harmondsworth: Penguin.

Stanley, L. (1992) *The Auto/biographical I: The Theory and Practice of Feminist Auto/biography*, Manchester: Manchester University Press.

Stanley, L. and Wise, S. (1993) *Breaking Out Again*, London: Routledge.

Usher, R. and Edwards, R. (1994) *Postmodernism and Education*, London: Routledge.

Index